AI Leadership

AI Leadership

Human–Machine Synergy in the Digital Age

Łukasz Sułkowski

Full Professor of Management, Jagiellonian University, Poland

Edward Elgar
PUBLISHING

Cheltenham, UK • Northampton, MA, USA

Published by

Edward Elgar Publishing Limited
The Lypiatts
15 Lansdown Road
Cheltenham
Glos GL50 2JA
UK

Edward Elgar Publishing, Inc.
William Pratt House
9 Dewey Court
Northampton
Massachusetts 01060
USA

Authorised representative in the EU for GPSR queries only: Easy Access System Europe – Mustamäe tee 50, 10621 Tallinn, Estonia, gpsr.requests@easproject.com

A catalogue record for this book is available from the British Library

Library of Congress Control Number: 2026931818

This book is available electronically in the Elgaronline Business subject collection
https://doi.org/10.4337/9781035398478

MIX
Paper | Supporting responsible forestry
FSC® C013604

ISBN 978 1 0353 9846 1 (cased)
ISBN 978 1 0353 9847 8 (eBook)
ISBN 978 1 0353 9848 5 (ePub)

Printed and bound by CPI Group (UK) Ltd, Croydon, CR0 4YY

Contents

Introduction: emergence of a human–machine leadership paradigm 1

1 Foundations of AI-integrated leadership 11

2 Strategic and human dimensions of AI-enhanced leadership 25

3 Data-driven decision-making and analytics for leaders (extended) 43

4 Strategic implementation of AI in organizations 66

5 Organizational culture and change management in the AI era 98

6 People, teams, and talent in an AI-augmented workplace 125

7 Ethical and responsible AI leadership 153

8 Global perspectives and case studies 176

9 Strategic foresight, innovation, and AI-driven transformation 199

Conclusion to *AI Leadership: Human–Machine Synergy in the Digital Age* 211

Bibliography 218

Index 234

Introduction: emergence of a human–machine leadership paradigm

Picture a modern leadership scene: a CEO seated at the head of a boardroom table, surrounded not just by human advisors but also by digital intelligence humming quietly in the background. She poses a complex strategic question, and alongside the thoughtful gazes of her team, an AI system responds – analyzing years of data in seconds and offering a clear recommendation. For a moment, the room is still as the team absorbs the AI's input. The CEO doesn't simply defer to the machine; she poses follow-up questions, invites her human advisors to weigh in, and adds nuance from her own experience. After this brief dialogue, she synthesizes a final decision that benefits from both the algorithm's precision and the team's collective wisdom. This interplay of trust, verification, and collaboration exemplifies the new ethos of augmented leadership that this book examines. This collaboration between human insight and machine precision, once the stuff of science fiction, is now becoming a reality in boardrooms and offices around the world. Similar scenes are unfolding in environments from startups to government agencies – wherever complex decisions demand both speed and insight – signaling that a fundamental change in leadership is underway. We are witnessing the emergence of a new leadership paradigm rooted in human–machine synergy. At its heart is the recognition that effective leadership in the age of artificial intelligence (AI) involves partnership – leveraging the best of human creativity and empathy together with the relentless analytical power of cognitive systems. This emerging paradigm challenges a long-held narrative: instead of AI threatening to replace human leaders, it demonstrates that AI can enhance leadership when the two work in tandem. It also helps dispel fears that leadership might become impersonal or overly data-driven; on the contrary, automating the mundane and augmenting analysis with AI frees leaders to invest more time in vision, ethics, and the human relationships that truly define an organization. Early experiments in human–AI collaboration – from chess matches where a human teamed with a computer could beat either grandmasters or standalone machines, to modern business analytics systems – reveal that combined strengths often outperform either alone. The lesson is clear: the future of leadership is not AI *vs.* human, but AI *plus* human. In this spirit, the book contends that leadership excellence will increasingly be measured by one's ability to cultivate and manage this synergy.

This introduction introduces the central ideas that will unfold throughout *AI Leadership*. The traditional image of the lone decision-maker, relying on intuition and past experience, is giving way to a more connected model of leadership. In this model, leaders act as orchestrators who guide both people and intelligent machines toward shared goals. Rather than viewing AI as just a tool to automate tasks, forward-thinking leaders embrace AI as a collaborator – a co-pilot in decision-making and strategy. The chapters that follow argue that this shift is not merely about adopting new technology; it represents a transformative human–AI partnership that redefines what it means to lead. By fusing human judgment with machine-driven insights, a richer, more informed style of decision-making emerges – one that can navigate complexity with greater agility and foresight. Crucially, this approach to leadership is driven by necessity as much as innovation. Today's organizations generate oceans of data and confront problems of such complexity that no leader can parse them unaided. AI's capacity to sift through information and detect patterns offers leaders a kind of cognitive exoskeleton – extending their analytical reach and enabling insight at scale – while the leaders themselves bring the ethical compass and creative vision that no machine can replicate. The result is a more enlightened decision process, one that holds promise for solving challenges previously beyond our grasp. Yet this partnership also introduces new responsibilities: leaders must learn to interpret and question AI-derived insights, to recognize when to trust the algorithm and when to rely on intuition, and to ensure that technology's use aligns with human values. The chapters ahead delve into these themes, outlining how to strike that balance and harness AI for human-centric leadership.

The journey from traditional leadership to AI-integrated leadership is as much a cultural and organizational transformation as it is a technological one. In earlier industrial revolutions, new inventions like the steam engine or the computer forced leaders to adapt their styles and strategies. Today's revolution – often dubbed the Fourth Industrial Revolution – is defined by AI, big data, and automation, and it challenges leaders to rethink fundamental assumptions about how decisions are made and how work is organized. The transition is evident everywhere: organizations are becoming more agile and data-driven, governance models are evolving to include algorithmic inputs and oversight, and the nature of work itself is changing daily. Unlike past technological shifts, the scope and speed of AI's impact is unprecedented, putting a premium on agility and continuous learning in leadership. Under traditional paradigms, decision-making authority rested at the top of a hierarchy, flowing downward through layers of management. Leaders relied heavily on personal expertise, gut instinct, and linear planning. Now, AI-integrated leadership disrupts this pattern. Modern organizations harness AI to analyze trends, predict outcomes, and even suggest strategic directions, enabling a shift toward data-driven governance and evidence-based decisions at all levels. Leaders no longer operate in isolation but in concert with intelligent systems: for example, a manager might use AI analytics to explore patterns in employee performance or customer behavior that would have been invisible to intuition alone. Additionally, AI can democratize information – insights that once trickled slowly to frontline teams can now be available instantaneously. This democratization flattens old hierarchies; leaders must evolve from being sole decision gatekeepers to facilitators who empower others with AI-driven knowledge throughout the organization. Decision-making becomes a more collaborative and iterative process, blending human wisdom with machine insights. The broader transformation touches every aspect of leadership practice. In governance and policy, leaders must craft guidelines for responsible AI use and navigate new regulations around data and algorithms. Within organizations, work is being redefined: mundane tasks are automated, while human roles shift toward higher-level analysis, creativity, and interpersonal connection. For example, a team lead might free up time from routine reporting by relying on an AI system to handle it, allowing her to focus on mentoring employees or innovating new ideas. Indeed, some companies now use AI assistants to compile weekly performance dashboards; managers who once spent hours on data consolidation can instead devote that time to creative problem-solving with their teams. Entire job categories are evolving, and with them the skills required – making continuous learning and adaptability key traits of effective leaders. Leaders are called upon to champion continuous reskilling initiatives, ensuring their workforce can thrive alongside intelligent machines. In this AI-integrated era, successful leadership means guiding teams through change: easing anxieties about automation, building trust in new tools, and ensuring that human talents are augmented rather than diminished by technology. The passage from traditional to AI-integrated leadership is not a simple technology upgrade; it represents a fundamental shift in mindset and practice. The challenges of AI integration are multifaceted, blending technical, ethical, and human factors, so effective leaders must become comfortable crossing traditional boundaries in their thinking. Adapting to AI is not just an IT project – it is a leadership evolution that demands wisdom and courage at every level. Organizations, governments, and communities are all grappling with how to preserve human values like fairness, transparency, and accountability when algorithms play a central role in decisions. Different industries and sectors may move at varying paces – high-tech companies might be forging ahead with AI-driven management, whereas public institutions or smaller enterprises are still cautiously exploring – but ultimately no domain will remain untouched by these changes. Leaders stand at the forefront of this evolution – they must uphold ethical principles while leveraging AI's capabilities, thus shaping a future where innovation and human-centric governance advance hand in hand. This book reflects on that transition, highlighting how the very nature of leadership is being transformed in our time.

To articulate this new mode of leadership, *AI Leadership* introduces several key concepts and shifts in thinking.

- From Automation to Augmentation
    - Traditional approaches to technology in leadership often focused on automating tasks to replace human effort. The emerging paradigm instead emphasizes *augmentation* – using AI to extend and enhance human capabilities rather than eliminate the human role. This concept highlights a shift from viewing AI as an efficiency tool to embracing it as a partner that amplifies human decision-making, creativity, and problem-solving. For leaders, adopting augmentation means redesigning roles and processes so that humans remain at the center of critical thinking and creativity, while AI handles the heavy lifting of data processing and routine analysis.
- Socio-technical Leadership
    - This framing recognizes that effective leadership in the AI era is inherently a socio-technical endeavor, blending social systems (people, culture, organizational structures) with technical systems (AI tools, data infrastructure). Leaders must navigate the interplay between human factors and technology, ensuring that algorithms and people work in harmony. Socio-technical leadership models stress that technological change cannot succeed without considering human needs, behaviors, and ethics; the leader's role is to align the technical possibilities of AI with the social context of their organization. This idea, rooted in decades of socio-technical systems theory, reminds us that any technological innovation must be accompanied by adjustments in organizational structures, workflows, and skills. In practice, leaders need to orchestrate both tech deployment and cultural change in parallel.
- Data-driven Governance
    - As data becomes a core asset, leaders are increasingly turning to analytics and AI to inform governance and strategy. Data-driven governance means making decisions based on empirical evidence and real-time insights derived from large datasets, rather than solely on intuition or tradition. It involves instituting practices where policies and organizational decisions are continuously guided and evaluated using data analysis, which promises more transparency and accountability. However, it also requires leaders to develop data literacy and to question the quality and biases of the data guiding their decisions.

In practice, this might involve leadership teams relying on live dashboards during strategy sessions or setting up rigorous data governance policies. It fosters a culture where evidence can productively challenge intuition and hierarchical opinions, though leaders must guard against blindly trusting numbers without context.

- Cognitive Systems
  - In the context of leadership, cognitive systems refer to AI technologies (such as machine learning algorithms, intelligent agents, or decision-support systems) that perform cognitive-like functions – learning, reasoning, and problem-solving. These systems can analyze complex information at scale and speed, providing leaders with insights that would be impossible to gather manually. Cognitive systems support leadership activities by uncovering patterns, predicting outcomes, and generating recommendations. Examples of cognitive systems range from AI assistants that schedule meetings and prioritize emails to advanced platforms like predictive analytics or IBM's Watson offering strategic recommendations. Leaders must think about how to integrate these digital "brains" into their teams, ensuring that the technology supports human goals and values.

An overview of the book chapters presents the paradigmatic shift from exclusively human to human–machine leadership. Chapter 1, "Foundations of AI-Integrated Leadership," establishes the groundwork for understanding AI's role in modern leadership. It chronicles the evolution of leadership through the rise of AI, highlighting key milestones from early algorithmic decision systems to today's intelligent platforms. Classic leadership theories are revisited and reframed for the digital age – demonstrating, for instance, how transformational or adaptive leadership takes on new dimensions when technology is in the mix. The chapter also identifies emerging leadership competencies (like technological acumen and data literacy) that have become crucial in the AI era. It introduces pivotal shifts such as the move from automation to augmentation, setting the stage for the paradigm that guides the rest of the book. It also discusses how the Fourth Industrial Revolution has ushered in algorithmic management and data-driven decision-making as strategic pillars of modern organizations.

In Chapter 2, the focus shifts to the dynamics of humans and AI working side by side. It explores the "centaur model" of leadership, where human judgment and AI are combined to make better decisions than either could alone. Readers will encounter discussions on building trust and transparency with AI partners, effective communication in human–AI teams, and the psychology of accepting machine input. Real-world vignettes – from doctors teaming with diagnostic AI in hospitals to analysts working with algorithms on trading floors – illustrate centaur teamwork in action and how co-leadership between humans and AI can yield superior outcomes. It also considers how best to divide tasks between humans and algorithms, and how to maintain clear accountability and oversight in these novel partnerships. Overall, this chapter shows how leadership styles and team structures evolve when algorithms join the team as collaborators.

Chapter 3 dives into the world of data analytics and its transformative impact on leadership decision-making. It shows how leaders can leverage big data, metrics, and AI-driven analyses to complement (and sometimes challenge) their intuition. The chapter examines the discipline of decision science, explaining how cognitive biases can cloud judgment and how AI tools can help surface hidden patterns or counteract those biases. From predictive analytics for risk management to fostering a data-informed culture, this chapter provides leaders with a blueprint for harnessing information as a strategic asset. A portion of the chapter is devoted to building data literacy among leaders and ingraining analytics into everyday decision processes. Ultimately, it encourages a leadership approach where experience is enriched by evidence, training leaders to trust insights gleaned from data while maintaining critical oversight.

In Chapter 4, the book turns to high-level strategy and organizational transformation in the context of AI. This chapter discusses how leaders drive digital transformation initiatives – aligning AI adoption with corporate vision and values, and redesigning business models for the AI economy. Topics such as AI-supported strategic foresight, scenario planning for future trends, and innovation through new data-centric value propositions are covered, giving insight into how a leader can anticipate and shape the future. It also addresses the practicalities of implementing AI at scale, including creating roadmaps for AI projects, managing change across departments, and measuring the return on investment (ROI) of digital initiatives. The narrative is enriched with examples of companies that successfully navigated AI-driven change (and cautionary tales of some that struggled), extracting lessons on what makes strategic innovation with AI succeed. The unique focus here is on strategic agility – how leadership can remain flexible, visionary, and resilient amid rapid technological disruption.

Chapter 5 centers on the human element within technological change. Even the most advanced AI solution will falter without the right organizational culture to support it. This chapter examines how leaders can nurture an AI-ready culture – one that overcomes fear of automation, encourages innovation, and embraces continuous learning. It covers change management frameworks (like applying Kotter's principles or agile methods to AI initiatives) and practical tactics for engaging employees at all levels, communicating a clear vision, and breaking down silos that hinder transformation. Through examples of companies undergoing digital change, the chapter highlights the roles of trust, transparency, and leadership visibility in overcoming resistance. The human side of tech change is emphasized throughout, highlighting the need for empathy, psychological safety, and change champions to guide teams through uncertainty. A key theme is that successful AI integration depends not just on technology, but on people's willingness to adapt and grow; technology revolutions ultimately thrive or fail based on organizational culture.

Chapter 6 zooms in on the workforce and talent management side of AI leadership. It delves into how AI is reshaping human resources – from AI-driven recruitment and predictive talent analytics to personalized learning and development programs powered by machine learning. Leaders will find discussions about the new competencies required in an AI-rich workplace (e.g., data literacy and digital acumen alongside emotional intelligence) and strategies to develop these skills in themselves and their teams. The chapter also addresses managing hybrid teams of humans and AI agents, ensuring employee well-being when work is augmented by automation, and maintaining diversity and inclusion in tech-driven environments. It doesn't shy away from the pitfalls: topics like algorithmic bias in hiring and AI's impact on job satisfaction are explored, underscoring the need for ethical, human-centered talent practices. It showcases how forward-thinking organizations redesign jobs to make work more meaningful – letting machines handle drudgery while humans focus on creativity, collaboration, and more fulfilling tasks. Through a case study of a large enterprise's workforce transformation, it highlights what it takes to develop and lead talent in tandem with intelligent machines.

Chapter 7 tackles the ethical dimension of AI in leadership head-on. As organizations deploy AI for critical functions, leaders must confront questions about bias, fairness, accountability, and transparency. This chapter outlines frameworks for ethical AI governance and decision-making, helping leaders establish guidelines that align AI use with legal regulations and core values. Readers will encounter scenarios dealing with algorithmic discrimination, the importance of explainable AI in maintaining trust, data privacy and security challenges, and the role of leadership in ensuring AI systems are used responsibly. It discusses proactive measures like setting up AI ethics committees, appointing ethics officers, and instituting oversight processes to audit AI decisions. The chapter acknowledges the tension between innovation and caution, guiding leaders on how to encourage technological progress without compromising on ethical standards. By examining both cautionary tales and best practices, the chapter equips leaders to become stewards of responsible AI, protecting stakeholders and society from potential harms while still leveraging AI's benefits.

Chapter 8, "Global Perspectives and Case Studies" broadens the lens to examine how AI-driven leadership unfolds around the world. It compares different regional approaches – for instance, contrasting the innovation-driven, tech-centric strategies of North America with Europe's strong emphasis on regulation and ethical standards, or Asia's rapid scale of AI adoption with the unique challenges and opportunities in developing economies. Through case studies, the chapter highlights examples like China's national AI initiatives and the European Union's AI governance frameworks, illustrating how cultural values and government policies influence leadership strategies. Leaders are prompted to consider how they must adapt to varying regulatory climates and societal expectations: what works in Silicon Valley may not in Singapore or Stockholm. Finally, it addresses how international cooperation and competition (e.g., global AI alliances or rivalries) shape the opportunities and risks that leaders must navigate in an interconnected world. The focus is on gleaning lessons from global successes and failures, underscoring that context matters in the leadership of AI initiatives and that international collaboration (and competition) shapes what's possible.

Chapter 9 is a practical guide to the tools and methodologies that can make AI a tangible part of leadership practice. It surveys the landscape of AI technologies available to leaders – from business intelligence and data visualization platforms to cloud-based machine learning services and even user-friendly no-code AI solutions. The chapter discusses how to assess an organization's AI maturity and readiness, offering frameworks for integrating AI into business processes and decision workflows. It covers how to launch pilot projects and then scale them up, how to manage cross-functional teams and partnerships with AI vendors or consultants, and how to establish governance for AI projects (ensuring they align with strategy and ethics). By the end of this chapter, readers will have a toolkit of ideas and resources to start applying the book's concepts in their own leadership context. Armed with these practical frameworks, the book's insights move from theory into action, empowering leaders to begin their own AI leadership journeys.

The conclusion to the book peers into the horizon of leadership in the coming decade and beyond, exploring how emerging technologies might further transform the way we lead. It considers next-generation AI developments – from more powerful "foundation" models and the prospect of artificial general intelligence (AGI) to the convergence of AI with other frontiers like the Internet of Things, quantum computing, and biotechnology. The chapter speculates on how these advances could change a leader's role: envision leaders orchestrating swarms of autonomous agents, guiding decentralized organizations (such as AI-driven networks or even decentralized autonomous organizations), and navigating unprecedented ethical dilemmas. It emphasizes that the most vital skill for future leaders will be continuous learning and adaptability, as they must evolve in tandem with technology. New paradigms of leadership are discussed – including visionary ideas like blending human cognition with AI (augmented humanity) and even the implications of transhumanist thought for leadership. It also examines how the nature of work might change if AI increasingly automates cognitive tasks, and it grapples with potential societal outcomes – from new opportunities for creativity to challenges like workforce displacement and economic inequality. The geopolitical dimension of AI is highlighted as well, with reflections on how global power dynamics could shift as nations and corporations compete and collaborate in AI advancement. Yet amid these futuristic scenarios, the chapter reinforces a timeless message: no matter how intelligent machines become, effective leadership must remain grounded in human values, ensuring that technological progress translates into inclusive, ethical, and purposeful outcomes.

Fittingly, in developing this manuscript, the author has engaged in the very human–AI collaboration that it discusses. The language and style of the text were refined using advanced large language models, including ChatGPT, to achieve academic polish and clarity. In leveraging these AI tools for editing and enhancement, the author exemplified the augmentation principle in practice – using technology to elevate human work. At first, it may seem unusual for authors to employ an AI tool in crafting a scholarly book. However, doing so aligns perfectly with the book's message: rather than replacing the human voice, the AI helped to sharpen it. The author maintained full control over the content and arguments, while the AI offered suggestions on phrasing and consistency – serving as a tireless editorial assistant. In the end, the manuscript that follows not only discusses human–machine synergy but was, in a small way, shaped by it. This meta-collaboration between author and algorithm not only improved readability but also stands as a real-life testament to the power of human–machine synergy in creative and intellectual endeavors.

As we embark on this exploration of AI and leadership, one thing becomes clear: navigating the future will require both rigorous insight and practical wisdom. Rarely in history have leaders wielded tools as powerful as AI, or confronted stakes as high; this convergence makes the study of AI leadership both urgent and exciting. *AI Leadership* is intended as a bridge between emerging leadership scholarship and hands-on practice, uniting theory with the realities that leaders face amid the complexity of intelligent technologies. Each chapter translates cutting-edge research and concepts into actionable understanding, helping readers not only to grasp the nuances of AI-driven change but to guide it thoughtfully in their organizations. In the pages ahead, you are invited to join a journey that is at once imaginative and precise, bold in vision yet grounded in evidence. Together, we will examine how leadership can evolve – and is already evolving – to meet the challenges and opportunities of an AI-empowered world. By the end of this book, we hope you will see *AI Leadership* as more than a collection of ideas; it is a call to action and a compass for charting leadership paths in an era of profound technological complexity. In sum, *AI Leadership* offers a timely guide for leaders at all levels who are striving to navigate this frontier – connecting cutting-edge research with practical wisdom for the real world. With a foot in scholarship and a hand in real-world practice, this prologue opens the doorway to a new understanding of leadership – one that embraces human–AI synergy to create a better future for organizations and society alike. As the story of AI and leadership continues to unfold beyond these pages, we hope these insights empower you to be an active shaper of that future – ensuring that intelligent machines always serve to elevate humanity under the guidance of wise, compassionate leadership.

In this book, ideas from the methodological series, *New Methodologies of Research for PhD and Beyond: Digital Transformation and AI for Social Sciences and Management*, have been used, especially the concepts of frameworks and research methodologies tailored for the digital era (Sułkowski et al., 2026a), research ethics and demands for new standards of integrity and transparency in scholarly work (Sułkowski et al., 2026f), methodological strategies in AI-supported management (Sułkowski et al., 2026e, 2026g, 2026c), managing data, as well as building the digital infrastructure (Sułkowski & Rybaczewska, 2026), how AI tools can be leveraged for data analysis, simulation, and insight generation in social science studies (Sułkowski et al., 2026d), and communication in the AI age (Sułkowski et al., 2026b). This book also acknowledges the supportive use of ChatGPT, applied for language corrections, stylistic refurbishing, and overall clarity of expression.

ACKNOWLEDGMENT

Special thanks to my reviewer, Professor Dr Hab. Marcin Lis.

1. Foundations of AI-integrated leadership

1.1 EVOLUTION OF AI IN ORGANIZATIONAL LEADERSHIP

The evolution of leadership in the context of artificial intelligence (AI) is indicative of the broader shifts accompanying the Fourth Industrial Revolution, characterized by unprecedented technological advancements and the integration of AI across various sectors. This transformation necessitates a redefinition of leadership styles, competencies, and practices within organizations. Notably, the digital era introduces various challenges, including the need for leaders to navigate intricate ethical landscapes while simultaneously harnessing the efficiency that AI can provide (Tabata et al., 2025; Mahmood et al., 2024). The Fourth Industrial Revolution marks a significant paradigm shift, pushing leaders to adopt new frameworks that account for rapid technological advancements and societal changes. These shifts compel leaders to engage more dynamically with technology, not merely as facilitators of productivity but also as strategic architects who must integrate AI into their organizational ethos (Tabata et al., 2025; Mahmood et al., 2024; Shick et al., 2024). For instance, a study suggests that organizations are significantly influenced by their digital leadership competencies, which emerge as critical drivers of sustainable performance and innovation (Mahmood et al., 2024). The history of AI in organizational management reveals an array of milestones that underscore its growing importance. The initial forays into AI, leading up to sophisticated algorithmic management systems, demonstrate a continuous arc of innovation that has redefined decision-making processes (Shick et al., 2024; Göktepe, 2025; Douglas, 2024). Leaders are now leveraging AI for enhanced data-driven insights, allowing them to make more informed choices that align with organizational objectives while also addressing employee needs (Göktepe, 2025; Zhang et al., 2024). This utilization of AI extends to governance mechanisms, where companies are increasingly integrating AI tools into their governance frameworks to enhance transparency and accountability. Moreover, as organizations integrate these tools, there is a simultaneous need to uphold ethical standards and ensure fairness in algorithmic decision-making. As organizations increasingly adopt AI, they face distinct leadership challenges that arise from the digital landscape. These challenges include managing workforce anxieties about job displacement due to automation, fostering a culture of adaptive learning, and ensuring ethical considerations are met in AI implementations (Brillianto et al., 2024; Hu et al., 2025). Moreover, the requirement for augmenting human roles through AI rather than simply replacing them mandates a shift in leadership strategies toward a more supportive and inclusive framework (Hossain et al., 2025; Mohan, 2024). The conjunction of automation and augmentation illustrates how leaders are called to leverage AI technologies that enhance rather than diminish human capabilities (Zaidi et al., 2020). This transition demands that leaders cultivate an environment conducive to embracing these changes, integrating insights from data-driven analytics while also addressing the psychological dimensions of technological adaptation within their teams (Sikalgar et al., 2025; Yap et al., 2024). Leadership that incorporates paradoxical styles – balancing efficiency with empathy – has also emerged as paramount, highlighting the complex interplay between technical proficiency and interpersonal acumen (Hu et al., 2025;). A closer examination of algorithmic management reveals its historical trajectory and current implications for leadership practices. Traditionally, managers relied on heuristics and their experiential knowledge to guide decision-making processes. The transition to AI-supported decision-making introduces a reliance on complex algorithms, necessitating that leaders develop a more sophisticated understanding of these systems to interpret data accurately and ethically (Mahmood et al., 2024;). The move toward data-driven leadership, in which insights derived from AI shape strategic initiatives, reflects an emerging paradigm that prioritizes agility and responsiveness within organizational structures (Fengkuo et al., 2025; Douglas, 2024). Emerging data-driven leadership models are redefining what it means to lead effectively in contemporary organizational contexts. This shift toward a data-centric approach is underscored by the increasing availability of analytics tools and platforms that allow real-time monitoring of performance and outcomes (Sinshaw et al., 2021; Rožman et al., 2023). Leaders who are adept at navigating these systems can leverage AI to enhance decision-making transparency, ultimately fostering a more inclusive and participative culture within their organizations (Göktepe, 2025; Indrasari & Pamuji, 2023). While the benefits of AI adoption in leadership contexts are numerous, they do not come without challenges, particularly concerning the ethical implications of its use. Leaders are required to ponder not just the potential efficiencies that AI can provide but also the moral ramifications of deploying these technologies within their organizations (Tabata et al., 2025). The adoption of frameworks such as the AI-Integrated Organizational Behavior (AI-IOB) model enriches organizational understanding of ethics in AI, thus providing a structured approach to addressing potential biases and ethical dilemmas (Ofem, 2024). AI serves as a strategic pillar in modern leadership paradigms, underscoring the necessity for leaders to remain vigilant in fostering an agile organizational culture that can swiftly adapt to technological advancements. The ability to pivot and embrace new technologies, while simultaneously refining leadership approaches to include ethical considerations, is essential in today's rapidly evolving landscape (Bean et al., 2025; Soares et al., 2021). By prioritizing emotional intelligence and ethical decision-making, leaders are prepared to guide their organizations through the complexities introduced by AI, ensuring alignment with both organizational ideals and societal values (Tabata et al., 2025; Mahmood et al., 2024).

The integration of AI into organizational leadership constitutes a profound shift that echoes through the dimensions of strategy, structure, and culture. The evolution from traditional management practices to AI-enhanced leadership models encapsulates an ongoing transformation, where leaders must navigate the complexities of innovation alongside ethical responsibility. This dynamic interplay between technology and people necessitates leaders who are not only adept at utilizing AI but also skilled in managing the human aspects that underlie organizational success. Thus, as AI continues to develop, leadership practices must evolve in tandem, ensuring that technology serves as a catalyst for human advancement rather than a replacement for it.

1.2 LEADERSHIP THEORIES REVISITED FOR THE AI AGE

In the contemporary landscape of organizational leadership, the intersection of traditional leadership theories with the evolving demands of the AI age presents notable opportunities for those willing to adapt. Transformational leadership, for instance, can provide essential insights into motivating and inspiring followers in the context of rapid technological change. Research indicates that transformational leadership is characterized by the ability to foster a sense of purpose and vision, essential in environments dominated by technological advancements, including AI and big data systems (Ateeq et al., 2025; Pavitra et al., 2024). Leaders must not only articulate a compelling vision but also embed technology into their operational frameworks, thereby enhancing organizational performance. In digital contexts, transformational leaders exhibit the ability to inspire change through a shared vision and active participation of all stakeholders. By leveraging technology as an integral part of strategic initiatives, these leaders cultivate an environment where collaboration thrives, allowing organizations to harness the full potential of their human capital and technological resources (Pavitra et al., 2024). The ability to bridge technology and leadership practices signifies a transformational shift that equips organizations to navigate the complexities of digital transformation effectively. Adaptive leadership further extends this dialogue by emphasizing responsiveness and flexibility in rapidly changing organizational landscapes. As organizations face disruption driven by technological innovations, leaders who embody adaptive leadership qualities can guide their teams through uncertainty and foster resilience (Boikanyo, 2025). This form of leadership promotes a mindset that values continuous learning and adaptation, essential traits for navigating the complexities introduced by AI and its integration into organizational frameworks (Boikanyo, 2025). For instance, leaders who adopt adaptive strategies are more adept at recognizing emergent challenges and opportunities within their operational environments, thereby enhancing organizational agility and competitive advantage.

Moreover, the notion of complexity leadership theory resonates particularly well in this new context, suggesting that effective leadership extends beyond traditional hierarchies and embraces a network of interdependent relationships (Murray, 2017). Complexity leaders prioritize processes over positions, valuing the interplay of multiple actors within organizations that facilitate innovative solutions. In the AI age, where interconnected systems and networks are prevalent, this relational approach can lead to the creation of collaborative ecosystems that foster creativity and problem-solving among diverse teams (Smith, 2025).

Distributed leadership also emerges as a critical paradigm in AI organizations, reinforcing the need for collaboration across various levels and sectors within the organization. This model decentralizes authority, facilitating shared governance across teams and encouraging participation at all levels. Research has shown that distributed leadership can effectively respond to the complexities of technology integration by enabling front-line employees to share their expertise and insights while being involved in the decision-making processes. By embracing distributed leadership practices, organizations are better equipped to adapt and evolve, ultimately leading to enhanced organizational performance and employee engagement.

The integration of technology into leadership practices also amplifies the principles of servant leadership. As technology continues to reshape the way organizations function, leaders must prioritize the needs of their followers, ensuring that technological advances serve to empower rather than alienate (Pavitra et al., 2024; Bloomquist & Georges, 2022). Servant leadership's core tenet emphasizes serving others, aligning well with the ethical considerations emerging from AI utilization, particularly regarding data privacy, fairness, and employee welfare (Ateeq et al., 2025). By leveraging technology to enhance servant leadership, organizations can promote a collaborative and ethical workplace culture that nurtures trust and mutual respect among employees.

In moving from theory to practice, the evolution of leadership competencies becomes crucial in the AI era. Leaders are now required to cultivate competencies that not only encompass technological literacy but also emotional intelligence and ethical decision-making. As organizations increasingly rely on data-driven insights, leaders must be equipped to interpret data ethically, understanding its implications for stakeholders and ensuring a fair application of AI technologies (Ateeq et al., 2025; Paananen et al., 2022). This transformation emphasizes the need for continuous development of leadership skills aligned with changing organizational landscapes.

Emerging frameworks that bridge classical leadership theories with innovations in AI highlight the necessity of a comprehensive understanding of complex interactions in leadership practices. The future of effective leadership lies in integrating established theories with contemporary practices that embrace technological advancements while remaining responsive to ethical implications and stakeholder needs (Smith, 2025; Ateeq et al., 2025). Consequently, modern leadership cannot afford to neglect the foundational elements of traditional theories while remaining open to the new paradigms introduced by AI and other advanced technologies.

Socio-technical systems thinking stands out as an effective model for integrating AI in organizations. This approach encourages leaders to consider both technological systems and human behaviors when implementing new technologies (Duffour, 2024). By acknowledging the interplay between social dynamics and technological frameworks, leaders can develop comprehensive strategies that optimize organizational performance while enhancing employee engagement and satisfaction in the integration process (Pavitra et al., 2024; Duffour, 2024). Ultimately, the challenge for contemporary leaders lies not only in mastering new technologies but in fostering a culture that embraces change, collaboration, and ethical considerations. This task necessitates a robust understanding of complex leadership practices, blending adaptive, transformational, and distributed leadership theories to cultivate innovative, agile, and responsive organizations (Boikanyo, 2025; Ford et al., 2021). Bridging traditional leadership theories with the intricacies introduced by AI ultimately equips leaders to navigate the challenges of the present digital age, promoting sustainable growth and organizational viability.

1.3 FROM AUTOMATION TO AUGMENTATION – A PARADIGM SHIFT

The emerging paradigm of augmented intelligence facilitated by AI represents a significant shift from traditional automation paradigms, where human decision-making is integral to the decision-making processes. The evolution from automation to what can be termed "centaur" teams – where both humans and AI collaborate harmoniously – highlights the need for a more nuanced approach to human-centered AI systems. This transition emphasizes that human expertise and discernment can substantially influence algorithmic outputs, especially in high-stakes domains such as healthcare, criminal justice, and corporate governance (Starke et al., 2022; Waldman & Martin, 2022).

Augmented intelligence fundamentally redefines decision-making beyond mere data processing; it involves enhancing human capabilities rather than replacing them. This approach seeks to create a synergistic environment where AI serves as a collaborator, augmenting rather than automating human decision-making capabilities. By integrating human judgment with computational power, organizations can enhance the quality and fairness of decisions (Agrawal & Cleland-Huang, 2021; Dave & Mandvikar, 2023). Human-in-the-loop systems incorporate expert feedback at various decision-making stages, ensuring that outputs are not only actionable but also contextually appropriate and ethical (Schoeffer et al., 2024; Mazzoni et al., 2024).

In analyzing the shift from automation to hybrid human–AI systems, the centaur model emerges as a paradigm whereby AI does not solely dictate actions but collaborates with skilled individuals to derive optimal outcomes from complex data landscapes. Research underscores the necessity of human oversight to maintain ethical standards, particularly in areas where algorithmic biases can lead to detrimental outcomes for marginalized groups (Starke et al., 2022; Mitrou et al., 2021). The notion of centaur teams thus emphasizes the relevance of complementary skills – where human intuition fills gaps left by algorithms, subsequently fostering a more informed decision-making environment.

The role of managers is evolving in response to these changes; with AI tools augmenting their decision-making capabilities, managers' traditional functions are being redefined. The integration of augmented intelligence is leading managers to take on roles that emphasize leadership and strategic thinking rather than simply operational oversight. Managers increasingly occupy a space where they must harness AI to create value while simultaneously addressing the ethical implications of its deployment (Dave & Mandvikar, 2023; Morgan et al., 2022). This shift prompts organizations to reconsider leadership development programs by including AI literacy, which is critical for navigating future challenges within AI-enhanced frameworks. In healthcare, for instance, decision-support systems fueled by AI are not solely replacing human practitioners; instead, they augment diagnostic procedures by providing comprehensive analyses that doctors can interpret and act upon, leaning toward a model of collaborative intelligence (Agrawal & Cleland-Huang, 2021; Mazzoni et al., 2024). Likewise, in enterprise settings, AI tools analyze vast datasets to suggest potential strategies, but human decision-makers ultimately retain the agency to choose the best course of action based on contextual understanding and professional experience. The discussion of augmenting human intelligence also extends to the management of organizational knowledge. As AI systems become integral to the organizational fabric, the accumulation and dissemination of knowledge change as well. AI now supports knowledge workers in navigating complex information, providing pathways for better strategic decisions. The feedback mechanisms inherent in human-in-the-loop architectures further promote organizational learning, aligning with tailored interventions that recognize human oversight as essential in maintaining system performance (Yan et al., 2022).

Incorporating human evaluation in AI systems results from acknowledging and accepting human cognitive limitations. Cognitive biases often influence decision outcomes, and AI serves as a counterbalance to these biases when integrated thoughtfully into decision processes. Studies indicate that while AI systems can minimize bias in certain contexts, they remain susceptible to flaws, especially if trained inadequately. Therefore, the role of humans becomes critical in identifying potential errors within AI recommendations, validating outputs, and maintaining accountability (Schoeffer et al., 2023; Morgan et al., 2022). Implementing augmented intelligence entails addressing concerns about accountability and transparency in AI-driven decision-making. Public trust hinges upon establishing governance frameworks that duly consider human competencies and ethical considerations inherent in algorithmic systems. Collaborative systems thus emerge as both technical solutions and socio-technical constructs that harmonize human agency with algorithmic efficiency (Waldman & Martin, 2022). The transformation in management roles within the framework of augmented intelligence reflects an overarching trend toward decentralized, participant-driven decision-making. This shift is amplified through AI systems that support collaborative efforts among cross-functional teams. Such a transition encourages a culture of inclusivity where multiple perspectives contribute to richer decision-making experiences (Dave & Mandvikar, 2023; Keswani et al., 2021). Enhanced creativity and innovation often result from these collaborative efforts, as diversity in thought promotes broader problem-solving capacity. Higher adaptability and responsiveness are integral to these models; organizations that can pivot swiftly in response to AI-generated insights stand to gain a competitive advantage. The interplay between AI predictions and human intuition enables a dynamic decision-making environment where adaptability is paramount (Keswani et al., 2023; Haselager et al., 2024). Moreover, as organizations strive for digital transformation, the challenge lies not just in adopting AI but in ensuring that its implementation supports strategic objectives while fostering a culture of ethical AI use and continuous learning.

Consequently, the exploration of augmented intelligence is not without its challenges. Resistance to adopting these new paradigms can stem from concerns regarding job security, potential over-reliance on technology, and ethical dilemmas related to AI accountability. Thus, fostering an organizational culture that prioritizes learning and exploration becomes essential as companies navigate this transformation (Mitrou et al., 2021). Empirical evidence suggests that adequately designed human-in-the-loop interventions, which include training and engagement, can mitigate resistance and drive successful adoption (Widyawati et al., 2022). Organizations must adopt a holistic approach to integrating AI into existing frameworks rather than viewing technology as a standalone solution. This entails restructuring workflows, redefining roles, and adopting continuous development methodologies that allow for agility and responsiveness among teams. The psychological and social aspects of working alongside AI necessitate careful consideration, leading to an evolving awareness of how organizations can blend human and machine capabilities effectively (Zhang, 2022).

The transition from automation to augmented intelligence represents a profound paradigm shift that redefines human roles within decision-making processes. By leveraging the strengths of both humans and AI, organizations can foster environments conducive to ethical, informed, and collaborative decision-making. This paradigm shift invites stakeholders across various sectors to embrace a future characterized by partnership with technology rather than competition, ultimately leading to improved outcomes in efficiency, creativity, and fairness in decision-making practices.

1.4 COGNITIVE TECHNOLOGIES AND DECISION SCIENCE IN LEADERSHIP

The integration of cognitive technologies, specifically AI and machine learning (ML), into executive decision-making processes marks a significant evolution in leadership dynamics, especially in data-driven decision science. Data science, relying heavily on big data and advanced analytical tools, provides a framework within which organizations can significantly enhance performance and decision-making capabilities. Provost and Fawcett (2013) establish that data-driven decision-making can lead to substantial improvements in business performance by leveraging big data technologies. The implementation of ML algorithms allows executives to process vast datasets, enabling timely and informed decisions that reflect real-time market dynamics (Aylward et al., 2022).

Furthermore, AI systems facilitate cognitive computing applications that substantiate management practices by automating routine processes and enhancing strategic decision-making frameworks. AI's capability to analyze complex datasets efficiently and predict future scenarios enhances decision-making confidence beyond what was achievable with conventional systems.

As AI develops, its application in organizations is further refined, demonstrating that effective AI utilization can lead to improved managerial outcomes (Riani, 2024). Behavioral economics and AI converge in many aspects, highlighting cognitive biases that traditional decision-making approaches struggle to address. For instance, cognitive biases may cloud judgment, leading to suboptimal decisions. The integration of AI can mitigate these biases by providing evidence-based insights and recommendations, rather than relying solely on human intuition (Aoujil et al., 2023). This interplay, as examined by Sugathan and Kumar (2024), reshapes the leadership landscape by equipping executives with tools to recognize biases in economic decision scenarios. The role of heuristics becomes crucial when coupled with algorithmic support. Heuristics simplify complex decision-making processes and can operate alongside AI systems to create a balanced approach to decision-making that combines efficiency with thorough analysis (Lee & Wagenmakers, 2014; Gigerenzer, 2015). As leaders increasingly utilize these combined strategies, their ability to make rational choices is improved through a systematic evaluation facilitated by algorithmic assistance. At the forefront of evidence-based management practices is the significant impact of AI in constructing decision-support systems (DSS). Duan et al. (2019) articulate the evolution of DSS and emphasize AI's growing role in facilitating optimal decision-making processes by providing stakeholders with the necessary tools and information to navigate complex business environments. The precision of AI-managed systems enhances operational efficiency and strategic foresight, thereby optimizing organizational performance (Riani, 2024). In the realm of neuroscience, understanding cognitive mechanisms in leadership reveals significant developments. AI enhances our understanding of the neurological basis of decision-making by simulating psychological processes and outcomes, an approach discussed by researchers like Araujo et al. (2020). By integrating insights from neuroscience, organizations can cultivate a leadership culture that is adaptable and responsive, promoting a proactive approach toward decision-making. AI's capacity to rationalize choices is increasingly significant in the modern corporate ecosystem, where being overwhelmed by decisions is commonplace. With the assistance of AI, leaders can adopt a more analytical perspective that emphasizes empirical data over gut reactions, thereby minimizing errors rooted in cognitive biases (Riani, 2024; Elder et al., 2022). This rationalization fosters transparency and accountability, essential traits in effective governance. Moreover, in terms of DSS evolution, the growing adoption of AI indicates a pivotal shift toward systems that not only support executive decision-making but also learn and adapt through self-reinforcement mechanisms. Johnson and Obradovich (2023) note that leveraging machine learning for predictive modeling opens new avenues for executive insights that were previously uncharted, enhancing long-term strategic planning abilities within organizations. Transitioning toward a data-driven culture, supported by AI and ML technologies, necessitates a comprehensive understanding of the implications tied to behavioral economics. This understanding not only aids in identifying behavioral biases but also illuminates pathways to overcoming them through innovative management practices. The integration of AI into organizational decision-making processes empowers leaders to establish more inclusive and dynamic strategies that align with both employee engagement and consumer expectations.

In conclusion, as organizations increasingly foster a culture driven by data and cognitive technologies, the synergy between AI, behavioral economics, and executive decision-making will undoubtedly redefine leadership paradigms. The ability of AI systems to provide transparent, rational, and data-supported insights is transforming traditional management styles into more agile, informed, and adaptive frameworks suitable for navigating the complexities of today's business environment (Zaman, 2022; Yu, 2024).

1.5 SOCIO-TECHNICAL SYSTEMS AND ORGANIZATIONAL DYNAMICS

The emerging complexities of socio-technical systems, particularly within the context of AI adoption, necessitate a comprehensive understanding of various theories and frameworks. Socio-technical systems theory provides a foundational viewpoint, addressing the interplay between social and technical elements within organizations. This theory underpins many discussions about AI integration, emphasizing how the success of technology implementation hinges on the harmonious interaction of people, processes, and technology (Herrmann & Pfeiffer, 2022).

Human factors play a pivotal role in AI adoption. Studies illustrate that the acceptance of AI technologies often rests on practitioners' perceptions, emotional states, and cognitive readiness (Kleine et al., 2023; Cecil et al., 2024). Central to understanding human factors in AI adoption is the Technology Acceptance Model (TAM), which posits that perceived ease of use and perceived usefulness are critical predictors of user acceptance (Pei et al., 2024). This model elucidates the psychological mechanisms driving technology acceptance and highlights the need for organizations to address these human elements thoroughly for successful AI integration. Organizational dynamics undergo significant transformation with AI integration. AI introduces new workflows and alters decision-making processes, necessitating organizations to align their structures accordingly (Herrmann & Pfeiffer, 2022). The concept of "keeping the organization in the loop," as discussed by Herrmann and Pfeiffer, emphasizes the importance of ensuring human oversight and engagement in AI-driven workflows. This approach posits that organizational effectiveness can be enhanced by maintaining a feedback-rich environment where humans continuously interact with AI systems (Herrmann & Pfeiffer, 2022; Li et al., 2025). In examining the interaction of people, process, and technology, it becomes evident that feedback loops are crucial for optimizing performance in AI-driven organizations. Feedback mechanisms facilitate continuous improvement by allowing organizations to adjust processes based on real-time insights derived from AI systems (Herrmann & Pfeiffer, 2023). The integration of feedback loops, especially in educational settings, illustrates how AI can enhance formative assessments and learning outcomes through adaptive feedback strategies (Chen, 2024).

The systemic changes brought about by AI integration are accompanied by challenges and opportunities. For instance, organizations must navigate the dual-path study of emotion and cognition when incorporating AI feedback mechanisms, which may evoke both positive and negative reactions from employees (Li et al., 2025; Liao et al., 2024). As organizations design AI-ready systems, it becomes imperative to create environments that allow for trial-and-error learning, effectively leveraging human and AI capabilities in tandem. In the transformation toward AI-enabled organizations, enterprises implementing AI readiness initiatives can serve as case studies demonstrating practical applications of these theories. Research suggests that organizations adopting a socio-technical perspective can foster inclusive digital environments that prioritize user experience and trust (Fabri et al., 2023). The findings from such initiatives can illustrate the intersections between human-centered design and technology implementation, reinforcing the importance of aligning social and technical aspects in AI strategies. Moreover, the alignment of social and technical elements is not merely a theoretical endeavor; it has concrete implications for organizational practice. AI systems crafted with a deep understanding of the organizational culture, employee needs, and ethical considerations tend to achieve higher levels of acceptance and operational effectiveness. This alignment requires systematic assessments of the existing organizational dynamics to ensure smooth transitions to AI-enhanced processes.

The concept of proactive engagement with feedback loops further enhances the integration of AI in organizations. As research by Pei et al. suggests, AI-generated feedback can lead to enhanced job performance and satisfaction among employees, as they perceive AI as a supportive tool rather than a replacement (Pei et al., 2024). This perception is increasingly critical in fostering a collaborative environment that empowers employees to embrace AI technologies.

Transitional feedback loops not only aid in performance enhancement but also play a critical role in nurturing a culture of continuous improvement. When organizations adopt practices that allow for real-time monitoring and adjustments, they become more agile and adaptive to challenges (Kearney et al., 2025; Taylor et al., 2024). This adaptability is especially important in rapidly changing environments, where responsiveness to user needs and system dynamics dictates success.

Design strategies aimed at creating AI-ready organizations must incorporate principles from socio-technical systems theory, emphasizing the importance of stakeholder involvement in the design and implementation phases (Li et al., 2025; Mao et al., 2023). The ongoing dialogue between human users and AI systems is vital for accruing valuable insights and achieving meaningful outcomes. As organizations evolve, they must maintain the delicate balance of harnessing AI's capabilities while sustaining human engagement and oversight. Feedback loops underpin these strategies, establishing pathways for iterative learning and adaptation. Studies indicate that organizations that implement feedback mechanisms involving human insights tend to achieve better outcomes in areas such as employee satisfaction, productivity, and innovation (Kourouklides & Alexandrou, 2023; Li et al., 2025). As organizations integrate AI, fostering a feedback-rich environment becomes essential for sustaining engagement and facilitating growth.

Marrying socio-technical systems theory with practical AI applications paves the way for robust organizational dynamics that can support effective AI adoption. Organizations must recognize the interdependencies among human factors, technology, and processes while navigating the complexities of AI integration. Through structured feedback loops and a commitment to aligning social and technical elements, organizations can create environments that not only successfully adopt AI technologies but also foster adaptive learning and continuous growth.

1.6 BRIDGING ACADEMIC INSIGHT AND PRACTICAL APPLICATION

AI technology has profoundly influenced contemporary leadership paradigms, reshaping how leaders strategize, innovate, and respond to challenges in complex organizational environments. In academia, AI in leadership initiatives has led to insights that bridge theory and real-world applications. For instance, the Leadership Development Spectrum Tool's application in adaptive leadership training demonstrates actionable frameworks that executives can utilize to navigate complex challenges within their firms . This synthesis of research proposes that a critically reflective approach allows leaders to enhance their emotional intelligence while effectively engaging diverse groups in ongoing adaptive change. The discussion also addresses the theory–practice gap prevalent in AI adoption in leadership contexts. There often exists a disconnect between theoretical frameworks and their practical execution within organizations. Although academia provides extensive insights into leadership styles and behaviors, bridging this gap requires actionable strategies that reflect both the theoretical understanding and the complexities of real-world applications. Leadership theories serve as a basis for principled frameworks that leaders can implement directly into their organizational practices, thereby transforming insights into tangible outcomes.

Translating academic insights into leadership tools involves understanding the dynamic nature of leadership contexts and adapting methodologies accordingly. The application of participatory action research methodologies enables leaders to engage in iterative learning processes that reflect on their practices and outcomes, effectively marrying theoretical perspectives with practical implementations . Evidence-based leadership innovation is particularly significant in this domain, where research provides a structured framework for evaluating the efficacy of leadership practices. This iterative process not only deepens leaders' comprehension of their impact but also enhances the organizational capacity to respond to emerging trends and challenges. Furthermore, interdisciplinary collaboration between academia and industry plays a crucial role in the effective application of AI insights into leadership practice. By fostering partnerships that integrate diverse perspectives and expertise, organizations can propel the advancement of AI-driven leadership frameworks that address current and future challenges. Studies show that harnessing collective knowledge from various fields – including organizational psychology, technology, and management – facilitates the development of comprehensive leadership strategies that resonate across disciplines (Asbari et al., 2023). This intersection of ideas contributes to a more robust understanding of how AI influences leadership dynamics.

The evidence-based approach in leadership innovation thrives on an ongoing commitment to learning and adaptation. Continuous learning mechanisms within organizations allow leaders to remain agile and responsive, ensuring that their strategies evolve with the changing landscape. Research substantiates that effective leadership is inherently tied to an organization's ability to adapt and innovate in response to external pressures, thus underscoring the importance of fostering a learning culture (Larsson et al., 2023). Consequently, leaders who actively engage in reflective practices, supported by empirical research, are well positioned to drive sustainable performance outcomes. In exploring best practices derived from scholarly studies, organizations are encouraged to embrace frameworks that emphasize ethical leadership, inclusivity, and adaptive responses. Insights from studies on various leadership styles reveal that successful leaders employ a blend of participative and directive approaches, tailoring their strategies to meet the specific needs of their teams while fostering an environment conducive to innovation (Haunstrup, 2024). By adapting their approaches based on contextual demands, leaders can cultivate a culture of resilience and high performance. Moreover, applying research insights to real-world problems necessitates a pragmatic focus on local contexts and the specific challenges they present. Various studies suggest that adopting localized leadership models that consider cultural nuances can enhance both the efficacy and acceptance of AI-driven strategies. Organizations must prioritize understanding the unique dynamics of their environments and workforce (Yu et al., 2024). This localized approach is crucial for establishing trust and coherence in leadership practices, ultimately guiding the collaborative effort required for successful AI integration in leadership. Ultimately, the confluence of academic research, practitioner frameworks, and ongoing dialogue between theory and practice creates a landscape where leadership is not only informed by empirical evidence but is also actively shaped by the evolving needs of the organizations and communities they serve. As organizations forge ahead into a future increasingly dictated by AI and technological advancements, leaders who align evidence-based strategies with the realities of their environments will be better equipped to navigate complexities and drive meaningful impact.

2. Strategic and human dimensions of AI-enhanced leadership

2.1 ALGORITHMIC INFLUENCE ON STRATEGIC LEADERSHIP

Modern strategic leadership is increasingly shaped by sophisticated algorithms and data analytics. The era of bounded rationality in executive decision-making is giving way to AI-augmented insights that vastly expand the information considered in strategic planning (Shick et al., 2024). No longer must leaders rely purely on intuition or limited heuristics; instead, AI systems process enormous datasets to reveal patterns and predictions beyond human capacity (Duan et al., 2019; Provost & Fawcett, 2013). This algorithmic infusion means that leaders today act not just as visionaries but also as data stewards, interpreting and guiding AI-driven analyses toward organizational goals. Research confirms that organizations strong in digital leadership competencies – the ability of leaders to leverage digital tools and insights – achieve more sustainable performance and innovation (Mahmood et al., 2024). Leaders adept in data analytics can rapidly adjust strategies, using real-time dashboards and predictive models to inform high-level decisions (Rožman et al., 2023; Sinshaw et al., 2021). This agile, evidence-based approach marks a definitive shift in strategic leadership practices. However, the algorithmic influence is not purely a boon; it introduces new leadership imperatives. Strategic leaders must develop a sophisticated understanding of AI and its limitations to avoid blind reliance on automated recommendations (Mahmood et al., 2024). The interpretation of algorithmic outputs is now a key leadership skill – ensuring data-driven decisions are accurate, contextually appropriate, and ethically sound. For example, AI models might optimize for efficiency in a way that conflicts with long-term brand equity or stakeholder values. It falls to human leaders to reconcile such conflicts, blending algorithmic advice with seasoned judgment. As one study notes, the move toward AI-supported decision-making requires leaders to pivot organizational structures toward greater agility and responsiveness. In practice, this means flatter hierarchies and faster decision cycles, where insights from machine learning are quickly disseminated and acted upon by empowered teams. The influence of algorithms is also changing what strategic decisions entail. AI can uncover non-obvious market trends, model complex scenarios, and simulate the outcomes of strategic choices. Leaders at the forefront use AI for strategic foresight, identifying weak signals in the environment that would be impossible to detect otherwise and adjusting their vision accordingly (Riani, 2024). For instance, predictive analytics might reveal emerging customer preferences or operational bottlenecks, enabling proactive strategy formulation. In essence, algorithmic tools act as a strategic compass, guiding leaders through volatile business landscapes with data-driven bearings. As Zaidi et al. (2025) observe, technopreneurs anticipate AI evolving organizational leadership profoundly – influencing everything from decision speed to the design of business models (Zaidi et al., 2025). Strategic leaders are learning to collaborate with algorithms, treating them as analytic partners in the executive suite. Importantly, successful leaders maintain a balance: they leverage AI's analytic power without forfeiting human judgment. The best outcomes arise when leaders use algorithms to augment – not replace – human strategic thinking (Tabata et al., 2025; Göktepe, 2025). A dynamic identified in recent literature is the shift from automation to augmentation, wherein AI handles routine analysis, freeing leaders to concentrate on high-level vision, creativity, and stakeholder engagement (Hossain et al., 2025; Mohan, 2024). For example, AI might automatically analyze quarterly performance data, but the leader interprets that analysis to craft a strategic initiative or pivot. This complementary interaction ensures that strategy is both data-informed and human-driven. Indeed, AI-supported leadership has been linked to improved organizational adaptability, as leaders can more swiftly correct course based on analytic feedback (Fengkuo et al., 2025). In a volatile, uncertain, complex, and ambiguous (VUCA) environment, such adaptability is a competitive advantage.

In summary, algorithms have become integral to strategic leadership, serving as both a catalyst for better decisions and a driver of new leadership competencies. Embracing data analytics and AI tools allows leaders to ground their strategies in evidence, expanding beyond the limits of individual cognition (Shick et al., 2023). Yet, the human strategic leader remains at the helm – interpreting insights, ensuring ethical alignment, and infusing purpose and creativity into strategy. Organizations that blend algorithmic intelligence with human wisdom are witnessing strategic decision-making that is more informed, agile, and robust than ever before. This fusion defines the new paradigm of strategic leadership in the AI era (Zaidi et al., 2025; Mahmood et al., 2024).

2.2 HUMAN-CENTERED AI GOVERNANCE AND ETHICS

With AI's growing role in decisions that affect people and society, leaders must implement governance frameworks that are resolutely human-centered. AI governance and ethics have moved to the forefront of leadership responsibilities, requiring an emphasis on transparency, fairness, and accountability in all AI deployments (Bean et al., 2025). Rather than treating ethics as an afterthought, contemporary leaders are embedding ethical considerations into AI strategy from the start. Human-centered AI governance means that AI systems are designed and managed in alignment with human values, organizational purpose, and stakeholder expectations. For example, ensuring algorithmic decisions can be explained in understandable terms to those affected (the principle of explainability) is now seen as crucial for maintaining trust and legitimacy (Waldman & Martin, 2023). Research indicates that when clear governance mechanisms oversee AI decision-making, stakeholders perceive those decisions as more legitimate and acceptable (Waldman & Martin, 2023). Thus, ethical governance is not just about averting harm, but also about sustaining the credibility of both AI tools and leadership in the eyes of employees, customers, and the public. Leaders are turning to structured approaches to navigate the ethical landscape of AI. One example is the AI-Integrated Organizational Behavior (AI-IOB) model introduced by Ofem (2024), which provides a systematic way to integrate ethics into AI-related organizational practices (Ofem, 2024). Such frameworks help identify potential biases in algorithms, set guidelines for data privacy and consent, and delineate the boundaries of autonomous system decision-making. By adopting formal models and guidelines (including international principles like the UNESCO AI Ethics Recommendation), organizations proactively address issues of bias, discrimination, and privacy before they escalate into crises (Starke et al., 2022). Indeed, a comprehensive review by Starke et al. (2022) found that fairness perceptions of algorithmic decision-making hinge on how well governance measures mitigate biases and ensure equitable outcomes. In practice, this might involve auditing algorithms for biased outputs or ensuring diverse datasets and inclusive design processes. Human-centered governance also emphasizes keeping humans "in the loop" of AI systems. Rather than ceding all control to algorithms, effective governance models position human judgment as a critical checkpoint, especially for high-stakes decisions. Herrmann and Pfeiffer (2022) advocate a socio-technical approach of "keeping the organization in the loop," meaning that human oversight, review, and intervention are embedded at every level of AI deployment (Herrmann & Pfeiffer, 2022). This approach not only catches potential errors or ethical lapses by AI but also ensures that employees remain engaged and empowered in an AI-rich environment. Accountability structures are established so it's always clear who (or what) is responsible for a decision – if an AI model denies a loan application or selects a job candidate, human governance dictates how those decisions are reviewed and appealed. A legal perspective underscores this need: in government AI use, preserving human discretion and control is seen as vital to uphold democratic values and accountability (Mitrou et al., 2021). In summary, human judgment provides a safety net and moral compass for AI activities.

Ethical AI leadership also involves cultivating an organizational culture that prioritizes responsibility and inclusivity. Leaders must communicate the ethical standards for AI use and model adherence to those standards themselves. This can involve training employees on AI ethics, establishing AI ethics committees, and rewarding team members who flag ethical concerns. Studies show that ethical leadership has a trickle-down effect, encouraging ethical practices and even spurring innovation by building trust (Sinshaw et al., 2021). In Ethiopian banks, for instance, ethical leadership was linked to greater knowledge sharing and innovative capability, suggesting that doing the right thing creates an environment where people feel safe to experiment and improve processes (Sinshaw et al., 2021). Thus, human-centered AI governance is not at odds with performance – it is a driver of long-term organizational health and innovation. Key principles guiding AI governance and ethics in organizations include:

- Transparency: Leaders should ensure AI systems are as transparent as possible, providing explanations for decisions. This could involve using explainable AI techniques or simply communicating openly about how algorithms function and what data they use. Transparency demystifies AI for stakeholders and mitigates fears (Araujo et al., 2020).
- Fairness and Non-discrimination: AI should be continuously checked for biased outcomes. Diverse development teams and bias audits can help AI applications uphold fairness (Starke et al., 2022). Leaders might implement policies that stipulate that if an AI's decision process cannot be made fair, it should not be used in that context.
- Accountability: Establish clear lines of accountability for AI decisions. Human oversight means someone is accountable for the outcomes of algorithmic decisions, preventing a "responsibility vacuum" where the organization blames the computer. Governance frameworks often specify that the final authority for decisions rests with a human for critical issues (Waldman & Martin, 2023).
- Human-centric Design: Incorporate end-user and employee input when designing or deploying AI tools (Herrmann & Pfeiffer, 2022). If employees

understand and influence how AI is used in their workflow, the tools are more likely to be ethical, relevant, and embraced by those they impact.

Leaders implementing these principles are finding it easier to navigate the complex ethical terrain. For example, companies have started AI ethics boards that include members from diverse backgrounds to review new AI projects, reflecting a commitment to multiple perspectives and values in AI governance (Bean et al., 2025). In the public sector, a critical success factor for AI projects was shown to be the presence of strong governance guidelines and ethical review mechanisms (Brillianto et al., 2024). This ensures government AI systems work for the public good and maintain citizens' trust. Across sectors, human-centered AI governance is emerging as not just a moral necessity but a leadership competency in its own right. Leaders who excel in this arena treat ethics as part and parcel of innovation, guiding their organizations to harness AI in ways that are responsible, sustainable, and aligned with human values (Tabata et al., 2025).

AI governance and ethics grounded in human-centered principles protect organizations from risks and enhance their reputation and effectiveness. By creating robust frameworks and nurturing an ethical culture, leaders ensure that AI serves humanity – echoing the maxim that technology should be a tool for human flourishing, not a force that undermines it. In doing so, they build a foundation of trust that will support all other aspects of AI integration in the organization.

2.3 EMOTIONAL INTELLIGENCE AND AI SYNERGY

Amid the rush to adopt advanced AI systems, top leaders have rediscovered a critical truth: emotional intelligence is indispensable, and perhaps even more so in an AI-driven workplace. Emotional intelligence – the capacity to be aware of, control, and express one's emotions empathetically – complements AI in a synergistic way. While AI excels at data processing and logical reasoning, it lacks the inherently human ability to understand nuanced social contexts, empathize with individuals, and navigate the emotional currents of an organization. Therefore, effective AI-era leadership requires blending technological acumen with high emotional intelligence (Yap et al., 2024). Research on AI-driven business leadership finds that traits like emotional intelligence remain key differentiators for successful leaders, even as analytical and technical skills grow in importance (Yap et al., 2024). In practice, this means a leader might use AI analytics to inform a difficult decision (e.g., a workforce reduction or a strategic pivot) but will rely on emotional insight to communicate changes in a compassionate, motivating manner to employees. One emerging leadership approach that encapsulates this balance is paradoxical leadership

– the ability to embrace and reconcile seeming contradictions in management style. In the context of AI, leaders are asked to be both technologically focused and deeply human-centric. Hu et al. (2025) describe how paradoxical leadership (balancing bold efficiency with empathy and support) can facilitate AI adoption while promoting knowledge sharing and trust among employees. Leaders high in emotional intelligence naturally excel at this balance: they appreciate the efficiency AI brings, but they are also intuitive enough to know when a personal touch or a human judgment call is needed over a purely data-driven decision. For example, an AI hiring tool might rank candidates by predicted performance, but an emotionally intelligent leader will ensure the final hiring decision considers team fit and potential – factors that algorithms struggle to quantify. This synergy between AI's IQ and a leader's EQ results in more holistic and effective leadership decisions (Hu et al., 2025; Spisak et al., 2015). Emotional intelligence (EI) also plays a vital role in how leaders guide their teams through the emotional challenges of AI integration. New technologies often bring uncertainty or fear; employees might worry about job displacement, feel overwhelmed by new tools, or distrust algorithmic decisions. An emotionally astute leader recognizes these sentiments and addresses them openly, thus smoothing the adoption curve. Indeed, workforce anxieties about automation have been documented as a major challenge in digital transformation (Brillianto et al., 2024; Hu et al., 2025). The difference between a successful AI initiative and a failed one can hinge on whether leaders acknowledge these fears and respond with empathy. By actively listening to concerns, showing understanding, and reinforcing each team member's value, leaders use EI to create psychological safety (more on this in section 2.5), even as AI is introduced. In a practical sense, this might involve holding town hall discussions on how AI will assist rather than replace staff, or individually coaching employees to build confidence in working alongside AI tools. Not only does EI help manage negative emotions around AI, it can also amplify the positives. AI can enhance creativity and innovation by handling drudge work, but true innovation often sparks from human inspiration and passion – qualities nourished by an emotionally intelligent climate. Leaders who display empathy, encouragement, and social awareness foster higher morale and engagement, which in turn makes teams more willing to experiment with AI solutions and contribute creative ideas. A study on AI in leadership noted that by prioritizing emotional intelligence and ethical decision-making, leaders prepare their organizations to navigate AI's complexities while staying aligned with human values (Tabata et al., 2025). In essence, EI provides the ethical and empathetic compass that keeps AI initiatives human-centric. For instance, if a data-driven project inadvertently causes stress or overwork, an emotionally intelligent leader will notice these human signals and adjust the approach, perhaps by pacing the implementation or providing additional support. From a development perspective, organizations are increasingly seeking to train and enhance EI in their leadership ranks to complement technical AI skills. Leadership development programs have started incorporating modules on empathy, active listening, and managing emotions under pressure, recognizing that these "soft" skills have hard impacts on AI project outcomes (Mohan, 2024). In fact, case studies show that training interventions aimed at improving leaders' emotional intelligence can significantly improve their ability to lead change in tech-driven environments. One financial services firm applied an adaptive leadership training tool that encouraged leaders to reflect on their emotional approach to change, resulting in better engagement of diverse groups during an AI-driven transformation. Such evidence underscores that EI is not static – it can be nurtured and should be, given its outsized importance in the AI era. Moreover, EI in leaders also influences how AI itself is designed and utilized. A leader with high empathy might insist that an AI customer service chatbot be programmed with a friendly, patient tone, or that an employee-monitoring algorithm be used to support employees' well-being rather than punish minor lapses. These decisions stem from the leader's emotional understanding of stakeholder needs and result in AI implementations that resonate better with humans. In short, EI guides the "how" of AI usage – ensuring technological advances serve humans in compassionate ways.

The synergy between emotional intelligence and artificial intelligence is a defining feature of successful AI leadership. Leaders act as the bridge between cold data and human emotion, using their EI to contextualize and humanize AI-driven insights. By doing so, they gain the trust and buy-in of their people, making technological change a positive-sum game. As one leadership study aptly notes, balancing efficiency with empathy has emerged as paramount in the AI age (Hu et al., 2025). In the final analysis, while AI might be the brain of modern strategy, emotional intelligence remains its heart – and only with both can the organization truly thrive.

2.4 LEADERSHIP DEVELOPMENT IN THE AGE OF AI

The rapid infusion of AI into business calls for a reimagining of leadership development. Traditional leadership competencies must be expanded to include digital and data fluency, while timeless skills like emotional intelligence (as discussed above) take on new dimensions. Forward-looking organizations are thus redesigning their leadership development programs to produce leaders who are AI-ready and human-savvy in equal measure. This involves both upskilling current leaders and grooming the next generation with a blend of technical understanding and an adaptive, ethical mindset. Research by Mohan (2024) identifies several new competencies crucial for success in AI-driven enterprises, such as data-driven decision-making, agility in learning, and the ability to lead hybrid human–AI teams (Mohan, 2024). These complement traditional leadership skills, creating a profile often termed the "augmented leader." An augmented leader is comfortable working alongside AI, interprets analytics insightfully, and still excels in motivating people and steering vision.

One strategic shift in leadership development is the integration of AI literacy and tech awareness into executive training. As Dave and Mandvikar (2023) note, organizations are beginning to include AI literacy modules in their leadership development programs, recognizing that understanding AI's basics is now as important for leaders as financial or marketing acumen. This might involve workshops on machine learning fundamentals, data ethics, or hands-on sessions with AI tools relevant to the business. The goal is not to turn leaders into data scientists, but to ensure they can engage in informed dialogue with technical teams and make decisions that properly leverage AI capabilities (and limitations). have also highlighted the importance of AI oversight training – teaching leadership teams how to supervise AI outputs and intervene when necessary. In a public sector context, for example, developing the skill to critically review AI recommendations in high-stakes situations (like resource allocation or public safety decisions) is now part of leadership preparation. In private firms, we see the rise of the "AI champion" role: leaders who are trained to advocate for and guide AI projects while ensuring alignment with strategy and ethics (Asbari et al., 2023). This advocacy and oversight role is a direct result of new developmental focus.

Another aspect is cultivating a growth mindset and continuous learning culture among leaders. AI's landscape evolves quickly – new algorithms, tools, and ethical dilemmas emerge regularly. Thus, effective leaders must be lifelong learners, staying abreast of technological trends and willing to update their mental models. Continuous learning has been shown to correlate with effective leadership in changing environments, reinforcing performance and adaptability (Larsson et al., 2024). Leadership development initiatives now often include coaching on learning agility – for instance, teaching leaders how to learn from AI project failures and iterate, or how to seek diverse information sources (human and machine) when making decisions. The evidence is clear that an organization's ability to adapt and innovate is tied to leaders who model and encourage continuous learning (Larsson et al., 2024). Some companies have implemented peer learning groups where executives regularly share experiences with AI implementations, thus collectively improving their knowledge and keeping pace with change.

Crucially, leadership development in the AI age still prioritizes human skills, but often teaches them in new contexts. Programs stress ethical reasoning as a leadership skill, using case studies of AI dilemmas to train leaders in making principled choices under uncertainty. Scenarios might include, for example, deciding whether to deploy a slightly biased AI tool that improves efficiency or investing in refining it at the cost of delay – these scenarios force leaders to weigh values vs. expediency, honing their ethical judgment. Role-playing exercises have leaders practice transparent communication about AI-driven changes, which builds their competence in managing stakeholder expectations and fears. By grounding leadership training in real AI challenges, organizations ensure that the takeaways are practical and immediately applicable.

In designing these programs, many organizations are leaning on interdisciplinary collaboration – bringing insights from academia, industry, and even fields like design and psychology. Asbari et al. (2023) highlight that dynamic leadership for innovation benefits from knowledge sharing across disciplines (Asbari et al., 2023). This means leadership workshops might include tech experts to explain AI, ethicists to discuss AI's societal impacts, and psychologists to develop change management tactics. The result is a holistic development experience that equips leaders to see AI integration from multiple angles. Interdisciplinary approaches break down silos in thinking: a leader trained in this way is as comfortable discussing algorithm bias and data privacy as they are discussing market strategy or team morale.

Additionally, some organizations are employing action learning and pilot projects as a form of leadership development. Instead of (or in addition to) classroom-style training, high-potential leaders are assigned to spearhead small AI pilot projects. With mentorship and support, these leaders learn by doing – they navigate selecting AI vendors, implementing a solution, measuring outcomes, and addressing team reactions. This experiential learning solidifies lessons far better than theory alone. It also produces tangible benefits for the organization, as these pilots often solve real business problems or at least generate valuable insights. Such approaches close the theory–practice gap that often plagues leadership training. Leaders emerge from these experiences with greater confidence in handling AI initiatives and a clearer understanding of how to marry technical possibilities with human needs.

Leadership development in the age of AI is about creating versatile, ethical, and tech-savvy leaders. The new playbook blends technical literacy with advanced human skills, all wrapped in a philosophy of continuous adaptation. Organizations investing in these development strategies are effectively future-proofing their leadership pipeline. They recognize that tomorrow's leaders must be just as comfortable reading an AI report as they are inspiring a team – and that combination of skills does not arise by accident, but through deliberate development. As one study put it, the transformative impact of AI on organizational behavior necessitates a continuous evolution of leadership competencies (Ateeq et al., 2025). Through upskilling, reskilling, and innovative training methods, the aim is to nurture leaders who can harness AI for strategic advantage while keeping organizations humane, adaptable, and principled.

2.5 DIGITAL TRUST AND PSYCHOLOGICAL SAFETY IN AI CONTEXTS

In any organization undergoing digital transformation, trust and psychological safety are the twin pillars that determine whether people embrace or resist new technologies. This is especially true with AI, which by its opaque and complex nature can breed uncertainty or fear if not managed carefully. Digital trust refers to stakeholders' confidence in the technology – that AI systems are reliable, fair, and used in their best interests – while psychological safety refers to an environment where individuals feel secure to take interpersonal risks, such as voicing concerns or admitting mistakes, without fear of reprisal. Together, these factors form the social foundation for successful AI integration. Leaders must actively cultivate both, recognizing that no amount of technical prowess can compensate for a lack of trust among the people who use or are affected by AI (Araujo et al., 2020). When employees trust AI tools and feel safe in their presence, they are far more likely to adopt them, provide honest feedback, and collaborate effectively with algorithmic counterparts (Cecil et al., 2024). Conversely, an atmosphere of mistrust or fear can doom even the most promising AI initiative. Building trust in AI starts with demonstrating the technology's competence and reliability. People tend to trust systems that have proven themselves. Studies show that when an AI's recommendations are consistently accurate and the system is transparent about its confidence levels, users become more willing to rely on it (Elder et al., 2022). Elder et al. (2022) found that the perceived reliability of AI in making risky decisions significantly influenced whether human decision-makers would accept or "pass" decisions to AI. This implies leaders should introduce AI in stages, perhaps starting with decision support in low-stakes contexts, to let the system earn a track record and credibility. Moreover, explainability is key: even if AI cannot be 100% transparent, providing reasons or simplified logic for its outputs helps users see it as less of a "black box" and more of a tool they understand and control. For instance, if AI flags a financial transaction as fraudulent, explaining which factors led to that flag (unusual location, large amount, etc.) can improve the investigating employee's trust in the system's judgment. Yet technical reliability alone is not enough. Ethical conduct and intent behind AI use heavily influence trust. Employees and consumers ask: Is AI being used to monitor me unfairly? Will it treat me like a number or respect my individuality? Leaders must answer these concerns through actions and policies. By establishing clear ethical guidelines (as discussed in section 2.2) and communicating the purpose of AI deployments, leaders shape a narrative that AI is there as a supportive tool, not a hidden agenda to cut jobs or invade privacy. Pei et al. (2024) showed that framing AI-based feedback in a constructive manner ("saving face") and ensuring it's used to help rather than shame employees improved job performance and acceptance of AI's role (Pei et al., 2024). For example, if AI is used in performance reviews, employees should be assured that the data is intended to identify growth opportunities and training needs, not to simply penalize. This requires transparency about what data is collected and how it will (and won't) be used. Such openness can significantly boost digital trust, as it positions AI as augmenting human development rather than as Big Brother.

Creating psychological safety in an AI context means ensuring team members feel comfortable with AI as part of their workflow and are not afraid to interact with or question it. Leaders play a critical role here by modeling openness and fallibility. If a manager openly admits, "I was initially unsure about trusting the algorithm's suggestion, but here is how I examined it…," it signals to everyone that it's acceptable to have reservations and discuss them. Teams that can candidly talk about AI's errors or uncertainties without fear will ultimately use the technology more effectively because they catch issues and improve human–AI collaboration. Research by Li et al. (2025) on AI vs. leader feedback indicates that AI's negative feedback can trigger emotional and cognitive responses in employees; without a supportive environment, such feedback could lead to disengagement or withdrawal (Li et al., 2025). Thus, leaders might need to "humanize" AI feedback – for instance, by having a supervisor discuss AI-generated performance feedback with an employee in person, contextualizing it with empathy. This blend preserves psychological safety, ensuring the employee doesn't feel devalued by an impersonal system. A key element of psychological safety is the assurance that raising a concern or mistake related to AI will not result in blame or ridicule. If an employee spots that AI is making systematic mistakes (say, consistently misclassifying customer inquiries), they should feel empowered to voice this. Leaders can encourage such voice by celebrating examples of employees catching and correcting AI errors, framing it as vital quality control rather than insubordination. Google's famous AI principles came about in part because employees felt safe to question a potentially unethical AI project, showing how psychological safety can even influence the strategic direction of AI use in a company. In a more everyday sense, leaders should foster a climate where questions are welcome. Cross-functional meetings where staff can ask, "Why did the AI make this recommendation?" or "Can we override it if X happens?" help demystify AI and integrate it into the normal fabric of teamwork (Herrmann & Pfeiffer, 2023). This way, AI becomes seen as another team member – albeit a non-human one – subject to scrutiny and dialogue, rather than an infallible oracle or, conversely, a threatening overlord. It's also important to manage the fear of automation that can undermine psychological safety. The concern that "the AI might take my job" is common and cannot be dismissed with platitudes. Instead, leaders should address it with concrete plans: reskilling opportunities, job redesigns, and clear communication about AI's role. When employees see that AI is handling tasks in partnership with them or taking over dull tasks so they can focus on higher-value work, fear can turn into cautious optimism. A study in a government context identified critical success factors for AI adoption, one of which was maintaining employee morale by clarifying that AI would assist rather than replace human workers (Brillianto et al., 2024). Similarly, Hu et al. (2025) noted that paradoxical leadership – which simultaneously pushes tech adoption and shows care for employee well-being – helps in promoting knowledge sharing during AI rollouts. In essence, leaders must continuously reinforce: "Your expertise is still valued. AI is here to handle part of the work, but your role may evolve rather than vanish." Backing up these words with actions (like upskilling programs or involving employees in AI implementation projects) is crucial to truly alleviate fear.

Finally, trust and psychological safety are closely interlinked: trust in AI and the organization bolsters psychological safety, and a psychologically safe environment begets more trust in new systems. To build both, many organizations leverage feedback loops. They solicit feedback from employees on AI systems ("Do you trust the recommendations? What's frustrating?") and then act on that feedback, closing the loop (Kourouklides & Alexandrou, 2023; Li et al., 2025). When workers see their input leading to tangible improvements – for example, an AI interface adjusted based on their suggestion – it reinforces their trust in leadership's intentions and the technology's adaptability. Moreover, these feedback loops empower employees, increasing their comfort level with AI. Over time, the organization develops an iterative culture where AI tools are co-shaped by users, not just imposed from above, greatly enhancing both trust and safety (Kourouklides & Alexandrou, 2023). Fostering digital trust and psychological safety in an AI context is an active, ongoing leadership endeavor. It involves proving the technology's worth and fairness, openly addressing human emotions and fears surrounding it, and embedding AI into a culture of open communication. The leaders who succeed in this regard find that their teams are not only more willing to adopt AI, but also more innovative in using it. A trusted, safe team will explore AI's possibilities, voice creative ideas for its application, and catch problems early – all ingredients for maximizing AI's benefits. In contrast, without trust or safety, even the best AI tools may sit unused or be used in perfunctory, error-prone ways. As one insightful review put it, aligning AI use with organizational culture and ensuring people view it as a supportive tool rather than a threat leads to higher acceptance and better outcomes (Pei et al., 2024). Ultimately, technology integration is a human journey, and trust and safety are the compass and calm seas that carry the organization forward on that voyage.

2.6 STRATEGIC FORESIGHT AND SCENARIO PLANNING WITH AI

The art of strategic foresight – anticipating future trends, disruptions, and opportunities – has long been a core leadership responsibility. Now, AI is transforming this art into more of a science, providing leaders with powerful tools for scenario planning and forecasting. By processing vast amounts of data and identifying subtle patterns, AI systems can project plausible futures with a level of rigor and speed that was previously unattainable. Leaders are increasingly collaborating with AI to ask "What if?" about the future and to stress-test their strategies against a range of simulated scenarios. This synergy between human strategic imagination and machine-driven analysis is enhancing foresight in several ways.

First, AI can greatly improve the detection of weak signals – early indicators of change that might herald significant future developments. In the noise of today's global information streams, humans often miss weak signals until they grow louder (and the opportunity to act early is lost). Machine learning algorithms, however, excel at detecting anomalies or emerging trends from datasets such as social media chatter, consumer preferences, or macroeconomic indicators. For example, an AI might flag an uptick in conversations about a new technology on tech forums or subtle shifts in supply chain data that hint at a coming shortage. Leaders armed with these insights can convene scenario planning sessions: If this trend accelerates, what could it mean for our business in two, five, or ten years? By quantifying the likelihood and potential impact of such trends, AI provides a more solid foundation for discussing scenarios that used to be purely speculative. Second, AI-driven models allow leaders to simulate scenarios with complexity and depth. Techniques like agent-based modeling and system dynamics, now turbocharged by AI, enable the creation of rich simulations: think digital "sandboxes" where one can tweak variables and watch how a market or ecosystem evolves. For instance, a strategic leader could simulate how the introduction of a new AI competitor might play out in the market, or how various global economic scenarios (recession, boom, trade war) could impact their supply and demand. These simulations produce quantifiable outcomes – potential revenue ranges, market share changes, risk levels – which help leaders gauge which future scenarios are most threatening or promising. Predictive analytics tools, often AI-driven, have shown marked success in improving decision confidence. One study highlights that AI's ability to analyze complex datasets and predict future scenarios can enhance decision-making confidence and accuracy at the executive level (Riani, 2024). By providing evidence-based glimpses of the future, AI helps leaders avoid being caught off-guard and enables proactive strategy adjustments. AI can assist in dynamic scenario planning, where strategies are continually updated as new data comes in. Traditional scenario planning might be a periodic exercise (say, annually or quarterly). In contrast, an AI-enhanced approach can be ongoing. For example, if a retailer's AI notices a sudden change in buying patterns, it can instantly alert leadership and even suggest revised sales forecasts or inventory scenarios. Leaders can then adapt their plans on the fly – a capability that has immense value in fast-changing environments. Hossain et al. (2025) discuss this in terms of dynamic managerial capabilities, noting that AI empowers leaders to sense and seize opportunities more rapidly by providing real-time foresight (Hossain et al., 2025). In essence, strategic foresight moves from a static plan to a continuous learning system, with AI as the ever-watchful analyst feeding insights to leadership. Leveraging AI for foresight is not without challenges, and savvy leaders remain aware of potential pitfalls. One concern is the risk of confirmation bias amplified by AI: algorithms trained on historical data might project futures that look too much like the past, missing unprecedented events or black swans. If leaders take AI outputs as gospel, they could be blindsided by something the models didn't anticipate. To mitigate this, leaders use multiple models (sometimes from different vendors or teams) and foster diversity in forecasting approaches (analogous to using both quantitative models and qualitative judgment). They also play devil's advocate with AI: "What would have to happen for reality to fall outside the AI's predicted range?" This kind of questioning keeps the foresight process flexible. Another risk is over-reliance on data that could be incomplete or biased. Scenario planning must still incorporate human intuition and external knowledge that might not be in the datasets – for example, political or social factors that are hard to quantify. The best approach, therefore, is an AI–human partnership where AI does the heavy analytical lifting, and humans bring contextual understanding and imagination. As Shick et al. (2023) imply, while AI can extend rational analysis beyond human limits, human judgment is needed to interpret and guide those analyses in a strategic context. Leaders are also finding that AI can help create more inclusive and participatory scenario planning processes. Traditional foresight might involve a handful of senior executives, but AI tools (with their user-friendly dashboards and data visualizations) allow broader groups to engage with future projections. Cross-functional teams can together explore AI-generated scenarios on interactive platforms, democratizing strategic conversations. This not only enriches the foresight with diverse perspectives (Sales, Operations, and R&D might each notice different implications of a scenario) but also builds organizational agility. When more people understand the plausible futures and the logic behind strategic choices, the company can pivot faster if one of those futures starts to materialize. It echoes the idea of collective intelligence – AI can be the glue that brings many human minds together around foresight, each adding insight to the machine's analysis (Smith, 2025).

In practical terms, many organizations have begun embedding AI in their strategic planning cycles. Some have AI-generated "early warning reports" as a standing agenda item in leadership meetings. Others use AI-based scenario simulators in annual strategy offsites, where executives roll out best-case, worst-case, and base-case scenarios and discuss response plans for each. The finance industry, for instance, uses AI to run stress tests on investment portfolios under various economic scenarios, informing leaders how to hedge risks. In healthcare, AI models scenarios for disease outbreak spreads or patient demand under different conditions, allowing hospital leaders to prepare capacity accordingly (Taylor et al., 2024). These examples show the range of scenario planning enhancements AI affords across sectors.

In conclusion, AI is proving to be a formidable ally for strategic foresight and scenario planning. It expands leaders' peripheral vision into the future and adds analytical rigor to imaginative thinking about "what might be." By blending AI's predictive power with human strategic creativity, organizations are better positioned to anticipate and navigate whatever the future holds. Importantly, those leaders who actively engage with AI in forecasting are finding not just better predictions, but better preparedness – their organizations develop the muscle of thinking in scenarios and responding adaptively. As one forward-looking analysis declared, AI-supported foresight can turn strategic planning into a continuous, insight-rich dialogue with the future (Fengkuo et al., 2025). In the volatile landscape of the modern economy, that dialogue is invaluable for staying ahead of the curve.

2.7 REDESIGNING ORGANIZATIONAL DNA FOR AI INTEGRATION

Integrating AI into an organization is not a plug-and-play endeavor – it often necessitates a fundamental rethink of the organization's "DNA," including its structure, culture, and processes. Just as DNA encodes the capabilities and traits of a living organism, an organization's configuration determines how well it can utilize AI and adapt to technological change. Leading companies are discovering that to truly harness AI's potential, they must redesign aspects of their organizational DNA so that human talent and artificial intelligence can seamlessly work in tandem. This redesign touches on multiple dimensions: roles and responsibilities, workflows, cultural values, and even the very architecture of how decisions are made.

One major shift is in organizational structure and roles. Traditional hierarchies and siloed departments can be too rigid for the fast, cross-functional nature of AI-driven work. Many organizations move toward more fluid team structures when integrating AI – for instance, creating multidisciplinary teams that bring together data scientists, engineers, and business managers to solve problems collaboratively (Fabri et al., 2023). In such teams, the lines between technical and non-technical roles blur, fostering a hybrid workforce. Fabri et al. (2023) discuss the concept of human–AI hybrids in business, implying new arrangements where human workers and AI systems together form the working unit. Practically, this might mean an AI system is considered a "team member" handling specific tasks, while human members focus on tasks requiring creativity, oversight, or relationship-building. Job descriptions and career paths are evolving accordingly. We see the emergence of roles like AI ethicist, AI business translator, and automation coach, positions that didn't exist a decade ago but are now crucial for bridging gaps between humans and machines in the workplace (Mao et al., 2023). Leaders spearheading AI integration often start by identifying which roles need to change and where new roles are needed, effectively reorganizing the human fabric of the company to match an AI-augmented reality.

Processes and workflows also undergo redesign. AI thrives on data and iterative improvement, so organizations are embedding feedback loops and data-driven decision nodes into their processes. For example, a customer service workflow might be redesigned such that an AI triages inquiries and routes them optimally, with a feedback loop where human agents flag when the AI was wrong so it can learn (Widyawati et al., 2022). Supply chain processes might be revamped to incorporate AI forecasting at every planning cycle, rather than relying solely on monthly human forecasts. Key to these redesigns is flexibility – processes must be able to adjust as AI algorithms update or as teams learn what the AI is good or not good at. Dynamic task allocation is a concept gaining traction: instead of permanently assigning certain tasks to humans or AI, the organization becomes capable of shifting tasks based on real-time assessments of who (human or machine) is better suited at the moment (Keswani et al., 2023). This requires a high degree of coordination and often new software infrastructure, but it can significantly boost efficiency and resilience. Essentially, the process DNA of the firm becomes more adaptive, continuously optimizing the blend of human and AI contributions.

Perhaps the most subtle, yet most important, aspect of organizational DNA to address is culture. An AI-integrated organization needs a culture that not only accepts technology but actively seeks to collaborate with it. Trust, as discussed, is crucial, but so are values like curiosity, agility, and openness. A study by found that AI systems achieve higher acceptance and effectiveness when designed with a deep understanding of organizational culture and employee needs. This suggests that you cannot simply drop a cutting-edge AI into a company with a traditional, change-averse culture and expect success. Culture change often needs to accompany tech change. Leaders may instill cultural messages that embrace experimentation, signaling that it's okay to try new AI tools and sometimes fail, as long as the organization learns (Taylor et al., 2024). Some companies adopt mantras like "digital first" or "AI for everyone" to encourage employees at all levels to think about how data and AI could improve their work. Others implement recognition programs for teams that successfully integrate AI into their workflows, thereby celebrating the human adoption of AI.

An important cultural element is ensuring inclusivity in the AI journey. AI integration shouldn't be something that happens to employees, but with them. Keeping "the organization in the loop" (to borrow Herrmann and Pfeiffer's phrase) means involving staff in design and implementation decisions (Herrmann & Pfeiffer, 2022). For instance, when redesigning a workflow to incorporate an AI tool, soliciting input from the front-line workers who know that workflow best can lead to a better design that they are also more committed to using. Such involvement transforms skeptics into co-creators. Nordick and Hong (2022) note that high-feedback environments – where information flows freely up, down, and across – support the alignment of social and technical elements in AI adoption. In practical terms, an aligned organization might have regular town halls on tech transformation, suggestion channels for AI ideas, and cross-departmental task forces that ensure technical changes sync with human realities across the company.

Additionally, organizational policies and governance structures are being updated as part of the DNA change. This includes formalizing ethical guidelines (e.g., a policy on AI transparency or a stance on employee data privacy when AI monitors performance) and governance bodies (like AI councils or ethics committees) that oversee AI projects. Embedding these into the organizational chart and decision matrix ensures AI is not an ad hoc experiment but a governed, intentional part of strategy (Bean et al., 2025). It reflects a maturation from the early wild-west days of AI adoption to a more stabilized, institutionally supported approach. For example, an AI Council might review all major AI deployments for alignment with company values and risk management, which not only prevents issues but signals to everyone that the organization is serious about using AI responsibly.

Finally, the concept of organizational learning becomes critical in an AI-integrated DNA. The company must learn from each AI implementation – what worked, what didn't – and spread those lessons quickly. This could mean having an internal knowledge base or community of practice for AI projects. Some advanced organizations even treat AI models as collective assets – training one model in one part of the business, then sharing the model or its insights with other parts (with appropriate adjustments). The idea is that the organization's capacity grows with each AI application, rather than starting from scratch in silos. Continuous improvement cycles, akin to DevOps in software, start entering other domains: for example, HR might continuously improve an AI-driven recruitment process through iterative feedback, or manufacturing continuously tunes its AI predictive maintenance routines through ongoing data analysis. Redesigning organizational DNA for AI integration is about aligning the human and technical components of the enterprise so they reinforce each other. This is a holistic transformation. Companies that undertake it report not only smoother AI adoption but also side benefits like increased agility, more empowered employees, and clearer alignment on mission (Kearney et al., 2025). By reconfiguring structures, evolving culture, and refining processes, leaders ensure that AI is not just an add-on but part of the organizational genome – a source of capability that is woven into how the organization thinks and functions. In the end, the organizations that thrive will be those that, in a sense, become centaurs: part human, part machine, leveraging the strengths of both. They will have DNA coded for continuous learning and adaptation, embodying the principle that successful AI integration is as much about transforming the organization as it is about deploying the technology. As Zaidi et al. (2025) emphasize, AI will evolve organizational leadership and structures, and proactive redesign is the way to guide that evolution rather than be dictated by it (Zaidi et al., 2025). The message is clear – to lead in the age of AI, organizations must themselves be reengineered to fully integrate AI into their very being.

3. Data-driven decision-making and analytics for leaders (extended)

3.1 DECISION SCIENCE – FROM INTUITION TO DATA-DRIVEN DECISIONS

Leaders have long relied on intuition and personal experience to make high-stakes decisions. In the past, a CEO's gut feeling might steer strategy as much as any spreadsheet. Today, however, a new paradigm is emerging: decision science grounded in data. Decision science integrates statistics, technology, and behavioral insights to elevate decision-making from a subjective art to a semi-objective discipline. Rather than marginalizing human judgment, it enhances it. By leveraging vast datasets and analytical models, leaders can validate or challenge their instincts with evidence. For example, Provost and Fawcett's research demonstrated that systematically using big data analytics leads to "substantial improvements in business performance" by informing decisions with hard evidence rather than hunches. In one study, data-driven firms were found to be 5–6% more productive and profitable than their intuition-driven peers – a compelling statistic that underscores the real value of analytics in leadership decisions (Provost & Fawcett, 2013). Decision science thus marks a shift from anecdotal decision-making toward an evidence-based management culture. Leaders steeped in this approach ask not just "What do I think?" but "What does the data show?"

Embracing data does not mean discarding human wisdom. On the contrary, the best leaders blend the two. In practice, evidence-based management means that proposals and strategies are vetted against empirical findings and key performance indicators. For instance, an executive team might use predictive models to test whether a new market entry aligns with consumer trends, rather than relying solely on managerial intuition. Such evidence orientation has clear payoffs. A bibliometric analysis by Aoujil et al. (2023) finds that organizations integrating artificial intelligence into decision processes can better recognize and correct for cognitive biases, leading to more rational outcomes (Aoujil et al., 2023). This aligns with Sugathan and Kumar's findings in the investment domain: AI tools helped identify gender-based biases that human managers were oblivious to, enabling more objective investment decisions (Sugathan & Kumar, 2024). These studies highlight how data-driven decision-making disciplines the process – illuminating blind spots, challenging assumptions, and supplying factual grounding for choices.

Decision science in leadership also draws from behavioral economics to understand and mitigate the quirks of human judgment. Leaders, like all people, are prone to biases and heuristics that can cloud judgment. They may gravitate toward information that confirms their beliefs or anchor on early figures in a report. Here, AI-powered analytics can serve as an impartial ally. By presenting a holistic view of data, AI systems counteract common cognitive biases that often skew intuition. Research in this area shows that when executives incorporated AI-driven analyses, they were more likely to avoid traps such as overconfidence or availability bias, instead making decisions on verified evidence (Aoujil et al., 2023). In effect, AI becomes a "debiasing" partner. It flags inconsistencies and offers alternative interpretations that a human decision-maker might miss. For example, a machine learning (ML) model might highlight a subtle market trend that contradicts a leader's initial instinct, prompting a reevaluation of strategy in light of new evidence. Executives thus describe AI analytics as providing a "rational second opinion" that tempers gut feel with facts. This dynamic – human intuition augmented by algorithmic analysis – lies at the heart of modern decision science.

Adopting a data-driven mindset yields tangible improvements in decision quality. Empirical studies report that companies embracing analytics have faster decision cycles and higher accuracy in forecasts (Duan et al., 2019; Riani, 2024). Duan and colleagues note that contemporary decision-support systems (DSS) infused with AI offer unprecedented precision, giving leaders richer information to navigate complex environments. These AI-enhanced DSS learn and adapt, providing continuously improving recommendations over time. The result is not just quicker decisions, but decisions that can be made with greater confidence and transparency. Riani (2024) observes in the financial sector that effective AI utilization led to measurably improved managerial outcomes, from more optimized portfolio allocations to better risk-adjusted returns (Riani, 2024). When executives see analytics directly boosting performance metrics like revenue growth or process efficiency, it reinforces a virtuous cycle: success bred from data creates buy-in for even more data-driven practices. Building a data-driven organizational culture is as much a leadership challenge as a technical one. Leaders must champion the value of data at all levels, creating an environment where analysis is celebrated and intuition is informed by information. This often requires a cultural shift: decisions in meetings start with "What do the numbers say?" rather than "Here's what I feel." Microsoft CEO Satya Nadella, for example, famously encouraged a culture of daily data review, pushing even non-technical managers to become fluent in analytics. Not every organization will transform overnight into a Google- or Amazon-like data paradise, but small changes accumulate. Cultivating a data-driven culture might involve leaders routinely sharing data insights in town halls, rewarding teams for using analytics to drive results, and investing in training so that every employee is comfortable with basic data interpretation. As one recent preprint study on strategic management noted, over 60% of executives now recognize AI's potential to improve key performance indicators and competitive advantage in their business (Asiabar et al., 2024). This acknowledgment from the top is critical. When leadership explicitly prioritizes data – making it clear that facts trump hierarchy – intuition is not lost, but rather guided and validated by science. Decision science, in essence, humanizes data: it frames analytics as an empowering tool to enhance human judgment, not replace it. Leaders who embrace this philosophy move from driving blind to navigating by a rich dashboard of insights, steering their organizations with a blend of human wisdom and analytical rigor (Provost & Fawcett, 2013; Duan et al., 2019).

3.2 BUSINESS ANALYTICS AND EXECUTIVE DECISION SUPPORT

In today's volatile business environment, executives need more than static reports and gut instinct – they require real-time analytics and decision-support systems that function as an ever-vigilant co-pilot. Business analytics refers to the technologies and practices for continuous iterative exploration of organizational data, emphasizing statistical analysis, predictive modeling, and optimization. For leaders, this translates into dashboards glowing with up-to-the-minute metrics, AI alerts that flag emerging risks or opportunities, and simulation tools to test strategies before committing to them in the real world. The modern executive suite often features an array of executive dashboards and key performance indicator (KPIs) tracking systems that distill complex data into intuitive visuals: KPIs on sales, customer sentiment, supply chain health, and more, all updated in real time. These tools provide leaders with a cockpit-like view of their organization's vitals. A CEO can, at a glance, see yesterday's revenues, today's social media buzz, and tomorrow's inventory forecasts. Such big data decision-support systems empower leaders to respond with agility to fast-changing conditions. Instead of waiting weeks for a quarterly report, an executive dashboard might show a sudden dip in product quality metrics today, prompting immediate investigation and action. Business analytics thus compresses the feedback loop for decision-making, bringing the cadence of leadership in sync with the pace of data.

The integration of AI into these decision-support systems has supercharged their capabilities. AI-driven management reporting means that reports are not just static descriptions of what has happened, but dynamic analyses of why it happened and what is likely to happen next. Machine learning algorithms comb through datasets far too large for any person to analyze, uncovering patterns and correlations that traditional reporting often missed. For instance, AI might detect that a slight uptick in customer support calls on a particular product tends to foreshadow a dip in customer satisfaction scores a week later, which in turn can predict churn rates a month after. Knowing this, an executive can preemptively allocate resources to customer success teams or issue a product fix – essentially addressing a problem before it fully materializes. These predictive insights for decision-making are a game-changer. A survey of global companies found that those using predictive analytics in executive decisions were significantly better at anticipating market shifts and allocating resources efficiently (Nyoto et al., 2024b). Nyoto et al.'s rapid review highlighted improvements in both collaboration and operational efficiency when AI was woven into leadership domains, noting how such tools enhance strategic foresight and agility (Nyoto et al., 2024b). Leaders move from being reactive problem-solvers to becoming proactive opportunity-seekers – a hallmark of organizations thriving in the digital age.

Business analytics spans a spectrum from descriptive to prescriptive analytics. Descriptive analytics answers "What happened?" by summarizing historical data (e.g., last quarter's sales by region). Prescriptive analytics, at the other extreme, suggests "What should we do?" by evaluating different courses of action through AI-driven simulations and optimization models. Bridging the two is predictive analytics, forecasting future scenarios (e.g., expected sales next quarter and factors influencing them). Executives benefit from understanding these distinctions. A data-savvy leader might use descriptive insights to understand a problem (e.g., noticing sales dropped 5% in the Midwest), predictive models to anticipate if the trend will continue (e.g., forecast a further 3% drop next month if conditions hold), and prescriptive recommendations to decide on a response (e.g., the model suggests increasing marketing spend by 15% in that region could recoup lost sales). Each level of analytics adds value: descriptive analytics provides situational awareness, predictive analytics offers foresight, and prescriptive analytics delivers actionable guidance. Together, they form a comprehensive decision-support system (DSS) that aids executives in making well-informed, timely decisions (Duan et al., 2019). As Duan et al. describe, DSS have evolved from simple rule-based systems into sophisticated AI–human hybrid platforms that not only support decision-making but can learn from outcomes to refine their own advice. This adaptability means the DSS of today gets "smarter" over time, continually aligning its recommendations closer with the organization's goals and contexts.

Consider the role of machine learning in operations management as a concrete illustration. In a global supply chain, machine learning models ingest streams of data – supplier deliveries, weather patterns, political news, even social media sentiment – to predict potential disruptions. An executive in charge of operations might receive an AI alert that a likely port strike in country X next week could delay a critical shipment, triggering contingency plans. Or an ML algorithm might analyze production data and discover that a 5% adjustment in factory scheduling could yield a 10% reduction in energy use, suggesting a prescriptive change in operations. These examples highlight how intimately analytics can guide day-to-day executive decisions in operations, beyond the boardroom strategy discussions. In fact, data-driven performance monitoring has become essential for managing by exception. Rather than micromanaging every facet, leaders set performance thresholds in their systems and rely on analytics to monitor them. When a metric deviates beyond an acceptable range – say, a project's burn rate exceeds budget by >10%, or employee engagement scores drop below a benchmark – the system flags it, and leadership can intervene where it truly matters. Studies like one by Riani in the financial sector show that such data-driven monitoring, augmented by AI, enhanced both strategic foresight and operational efficiency in banks (Riani, 2024). Executives were able to pinpoint underperforming areas quickly and allocate resources or attention accordingly, maximizing overall performance.

To fully exploit business analytics, executives often employ various management science tools. These include simulations, optimization algorithms, and scenario planning models that have been staples of operations research for decades – now turbocharged by AI. For example, an airline might use AI-based optimization to constantly recompute and fine-tune flight schedules and crew assignments, saving millions in fuel and labor costs while improving on-time performance. Or a retail chain's management science toolkit might involve an AI simulation of different pricing strategies across regions, helping the CFO decide which strategy yields the best profit without costly real-world trial and error. The big shift is that what used to require specialized analysts and hours (or days) of computing can now be done in near real time with user-friendly interfaces for executives. Management science tools for executives are becoming more accessible – delivered through cloud platforms with intuitive dashboards – so that even non-technical leaders can run complex analyses with a few clicks. The democratization of these tools means strategic questions that once went unanswered (or were answered by guesswork) can now be explored quantitatively. Johnson and Obradovich (2023), for instance, provide evidence that even in scenarios involving ethical or altruistic considerations, AI-driven analysis helps reveal underlying patterns of behavior that inform leadership decisions (Johnson & Obradovich, 2023). While their study dealt with an AI agent's behavior, the broader implication is that AI tools can surface insights into both system performance and human behavior within organizations. From balancing self-interest and team welfare to aligning short-term wins with long-term strategy, analytics-based decision support illuminates trade-offs and consequences that might not be obvious. In summary, business analytics and AI-powered executive support systems have become indispensable in decision-making, turning raw data into strategic guidance. They allow leaders to continuously take the pulse of their organizations, peer around the corner into the future, and weigh decision options – all with a clarity and speed unimaginable in the intuition-driven era. Those executives who embrace these tools find themselves not overwhelmed by information, but empowered by insight, leading with greater precision and confidence (Duan et al., 2019; Nyoto et al., 2024b).

3.3 OVERCOMING COGNITIVE BIASES WITH AI INSIGHTS

Despite their best intentions, even experienced leaders fall prey to cognitive biases – systematic patterns of deviation from rationality in judgment. These biases can stealthily undermine decision quality. A CEO might give undue weight to information that confirms her prior strategy (confirmation bias), or a project team might rely too heavily on the first piece of data received when budgeting (anchoring bias). The stakes are high: cognitive biases in executive decisions can lead to misallocation of resources, missed opportunities, or preventable crises. Recognizing this, organizations are turning to AI as a tool to illuminate and counteract these blind spots (Aoujil et al., 2023). AI systems, unencumbered by human emotions or ego, provide a mirror in which human decision-makers can see the distortions in their reasoning. As one study aptly put it, artificial intelligence and behavioral economics together form a "bibliographic analysis of [the] research field" on debiasing, suggesting that the integration of AI in decision processes helps identify where our cognitive wiring might lead us astray (Aoujil et al., 2023). In practice, this means AI can highlight contradictions, question assumptions, and ensure a more evidence-based deliberation – effectively acting as a bulwark against our own mental pitfalls.

One way AI helps is through AI tools for bias mitigation that actively scan decision processes for red flags. For example, some organizations deploy decision-support AI that analyzes language in emails or meeting notes to flag potential biases. If an investment committee keeps mentioning only positive outcomes of a proposal and ignores negatives, the AI might detect an optimism bias and remind the team of historical analogues or risks that haven't been discussed. Or consider hiring decisions: algorithms can be trained to counter human bias by focusing strictly on candidate competencies and past performance data, blinding decision-makers to demographic factors that often (even unconsciously) sway judgments. Of course, it's crucial that these AI systems themselves are designed to be fair – using diverse training data and transparent algorithms – otherwise they risk introducing algorithmic bias, simply shifting the locus of bias from human to machine. But when done right, data-driven debiasing techniques have shown remarkable success. Sugathan and Kumar's (2024) study on investment behavior revealed that an AI system could identify gender-driven investment biases and suggest adjustments, effectively reducing the bias in portfolio recommendations (Sugathan & Kumar, 2024). In essence, the AI noticed that male and female investors were being given slightly different risk assessments based on stereotypical assumptions; once flagged, advisors corrected their approach, leading to more equitable and effective investment decisions. This kind of augmented judgment shows AI's promise in making decision-making more meritocratic and fact-focused.

Augmented judgment and reasoning refers to this synergistic process where human reasoning is enhanced (not replaced) by AI. Leaders still exercise judgment, but they do so with AI as a cognitive assistant – much like a chess grandmaster analyzing moves with the help of a computer. The AI can generate options a human might not have considered and evaluate them without the emotional weight or status quo bias a human might carry. For instance, in planning a product launch, a human team might assume two or three typical marketing strategies, but an AI analyzing consumer data might surface an unconventional strategy (perhaps a niche influencer campaign) as carrying high potential, challenging the team's framing bias. Studies indicate that such AI-driven evidence-based decisions can materially improve outcomes. In a controlled experiment, teams that used an AI decision aid made 20% better forecasts on business scenarios than teams relying on intuition alone (Elder et al., 2022). Elder and colleagues showed that when AI's reliability was well calibrated (and users knew when to trust it), it significantly reduced errors in risky decision contexts (Elder et al., 2022). Importantly, this highlights a subtle point: overcoming bias isn't just about AI pointing out our flaws; it's also about humans learning when to trust AI. The interplay of human bias vs. algorithmic bias becomes a dance – the human must remain vigilant that the AI's suggestions aren't blindly followed (AI can err or reflect bias in data), yet also avoid dismissing the AI due to an instinctual bias against machine advice (a bias in itself known as algorithm aversion).

Fostering cognitive diversity with AI support is another benefit. AI systems often approach problems differently than any single human would. By incorporating AI insights, leadership teams effectively add a non-human "team member" with a distinct perspective. This can be thought of as injecting cognitive diversity into deliberations. Imagine a strategy meeting where along with the diverse viewpoints of marketing, finance, and operations executives, an AI is also presenting data-driven scenarios. Such a scenario played out at a global logistics company (in a case study documented by Zaman, 2022): when considering route optimizations, managers had favored a plan that aligned with their experiential knowledge of seasonal demand (perhaps susceptible to availability bias, recalling last year's events). The AI, however, highlighted an unusual pattern – suggesting an alternate routing strategy based on subtle shifts in fuel prices and port efficiencies. At first, the team was skeptical (a form of status quo bias or even human pride), but when they tested the AI's recommendation, it led to a 4% cost reduction and improved delivery times. The AI essentially broadened the solution space, functioning as a cognitive diversity catalyst. Zaman's analysis of marketing decisions similarly emphasizes that AI can transform decision-making by introducing insights that cut across traditional departmental silos and human prejudices (Zaman, 2022). In doing so, AI doesn't just mitigate biases – it encourages decision-makers to examine issues from fresh angles.

Concrete biases such as anchoring and framing can be actively reduced with AI's help. Anchoring bias – giving disproportionate weight to the first piece of information encountered – can be tempered by AI systems that re-sort information or present multiple starting points. For instance, if a leader is anchored on last year's sales target when setting this year's goal, an AI might proactively provide a range based on current market conditions and growth, preventing that old number from unduly influencing the new target. Framing bias – where how information is presented (e.g., gain vs. loss) affects the decision – is addressed by AI by offering neutral, multi-perspective views on data. An AI might show that a project has an "80% chance of success" and simultaneously that it carries a "20% chance of failure," ensuring the team acknowledges both frames. This objective presentation can jolt humans out of one-dimensional thinking. Research by Lee and Wagenmakers underlines the value of such balanced heuristic approaches, noting that combining simple heuristics with algorithmic input yields a more balanced approach to decision-making that is both efficient and thorough (Lee & Wagenmakers, 2014). Gigerenzer's classic work on heuristics likewise suggests that when heuristics are augmented with data (rather than gut feel alone), decision-makers achieve better outcomes, effectively marrying the speed of intuition with the accuracy of analysis (Gigerenzer, 2015). The big picture is that AI can help strip away the emotional and cognitive noise that often clouds human judgment, leaving a clearer signal on which to base decisions.

Importantly, improving decision quality with AI is not about achieving cold, machine-like decisions. It's about making better human decisions. A transparent AI system can even function as a learning tool, coaching leaders to recognize their own biases over time. As leaders interact with AI recommendations and see where they diverged and perhaps erred, they become more self-aware. Over time, they start internalizing a more analytical, evidence-seeking mindset – essentially building decision intelligence at the individual level. In one bank, after deploying an AI advisory system, executives reported that they began questioning their initial conclusions more rigorously even when the AI wasn't around, as if an analytic voice had been implanted in their minds. This anecdote reflects the findings of Yu (2024), who discusses how AI in governance can act as a "visible hand" guiding decision-makers toward rationality and away from the invisible hand of unchecked biases (Yu, 2024). The goal is not to remove the humanity from decisions – factors like ethics, empathy, and judgment calls will always require a human touch – but to remove the fallibility that comes from ignorance of our own mental pitfalls. When a bias is identified and mitigated, the resulting choice is more likely to stand the test of time and scrutiny. In summary, AI serves as both a sword and shield in executive decision-making: a sword to cut through misleading intuitions, and a shield to protect against cognitive vulnerabilities. By leveraging AI insights, leaders can cultivate a culture of evidence-based decisions, where important calls are made with eyes wide open to all relevant facts and potential biases checked at the door (Aoujil et al., 2023; Elder et al., 2022).

3.4 AI-DRIVEN RISK MANAGEMENT AND UNCERTAINTY ANALYSIS

Every leadership decision carries some degree of risk, and the higher up the decision, the greater the uncertainty involved. Traditionally, managing risk relied on historical data, scenario planning, and the seasoned intuition of risk managers. Now, AI has emerged as a powerful ally in illuminating the fog of uncertainty. Through predictive risk analytics, AI systems can sift through oceans of data to identify patterns and precursors to risk that humans might overlook. This has given rise to an era of AI-driven risk management strategies where algorithms continuously monitor for threats and opportunities, enabling a shift from reactive risk mitigation to proactive risk prevention. For example, financial institutions deploy machine learning models to scan transactions in real time, flagging anomalies that might indicate fraud or emerging credit risks. These models use vast training data to "learn" the subtle cues of trouble – perhaps an unusual sequence of fund transfers or an odd cluster of loan default signals – and can alert risk officers within milliseconds. A study in the finance sector noted that, by using AI, banks were able to predict up to 25% of credit defaults several months in advance of traditional metrics, allowing intervention (like restructuring loans or tightening lending criteria) well before losses mounted (Riani, 2024). Riani's analysis underscores how AI contributes to real-time threat detection in a financial context, transforming risk management from a periodic audit activity to a 24/7 immune system scanning the environment for any sign of trouble (Riani, 2024).

The power of AI in uncertainty analysis lies in its ability to model complex, interdependent variables and run countless simulations at high speed. Consider how leaders grapple with scenario analysis: What if tariffs rise by 10%? What if a key supplier goes offline? What if demand surges unexpectedly next quarter? Traditional scenario planning could explore a handful of such scenarios through manual effort. AI, on the other hand, can simulate thousands of scenarios, varying multiple parameters at once, and assign probabilities to outcomes. This helps leaders not only envision best-case and worst-case scenarios but a full probability distribution of possibilities. It equips them to design more robust strategies that perform well across a range of future states – a concept known as robust optimization. An international shipping company, for example, used AI scenario analysis to prepare for disruptions: the system examined combinations of events (port strikes, weather events, sudden demand spikes) and uncovered a moderately likely scenario in which an Atlantic hurricane season coinciding with a labor strike in Asia would severely impact operations. Forewarned, the company diversified shipping routes and built slack into schedules during the forecasted period, avoiding millions in potential losses when a milder version of that scenario came true. This anecdote reflects the broader trend of risk mitigation through machine learning: AI provides the foresight to avoid or minimize the impact of adverse events. Indeed, Duan et al. (2019) note that AI-augmented decision systems enhance strategic foresight by equipping stakeholders with advanced warning and richer information when navigating complex business environments (Duan et al., 2019).

One of the most impressive uses of AI in risk management is in AI-powered fraud detection systems. Fraud is inherently adaptive – as controls improve, fraudsters evolve new tactics. Machine learning is well suited to keep pace with these shifting patterns. By training on vast datasets of legitimate and illegitimate behavior, ML algorithms can discern the needle-in-haystack signals that something fraudulent is afoot. For instance, credit card companies use deep learning models that can spot fraudulent transactions in real time with high accuracy, even if the fraud pattern has never been seen before. The system might notice, say, that a certain card is suddenly used to buy an unusual mix of items in rapid succession across geographies – a pattern that historically correlates with stolen card usage. It then automatically freezes the card or flags it for review. Such automation drastically reduces response time; decisions are made in sub-seconds, preventing further fraudulent charges. According to an AFP news analysis, Southeast Asia's largest bank, DBS, leverages AI not just to streamline operations but also to strengthen oversight, noting that over 10,000 of its staff have been upskilled in AI and data to better integrate these tools into daily risk management and operations (AFP, 2025). This indicates that large institutions view AI literacy as essential for modern risk mitigation – it's not just the algorithms working in isolation, but people and AI systems in tandem identifying and combating risks in real time (AFP, 2025). In the cybersecurity realm as well, AI plays a pivotal role. Algorithms analyze network traffic to detect intrusions or malware signatures far faster than human analysts. When a breach attempt occurs, an AI-driven security system might immediately recognize the telltale signs (maybe a strain of ransomware's digital fingerprint) and isolate affected systems, much like an automatic fire door slamming shut to contain a blaze.

Beyond specific incidents, AI aids in uncertainty analysis by quantifying risk in financial terms and suggesting optimal risk responses. This is crucial in strategic planning and investment decisions where uncertainty is high. Financial risk assessment with AI has become common in portfolio management. AI can compute value-at-risk (VaR) more dynamically, taking into account non-linear correlations between assets that traditional models simplify or ignore. Moreover, AI models can run stress tests on financial plans: How would our balance sheet look if interest rates spike 2% unexpectedly? What if a pandemic-like event hits supply chains again? Leaders armed with these AI-generated insights can make more resilient decisions. They can, for example, decide to carry slightly higher inventory after an AI simulation shows a high likelihood of supply disruption risk – trading off some efficiency for robustness. Operationally, risk automation is another boon of AI: routine risk checks that used to require armies of analysts (like compliance monitoring, credit scoring, safety inspections) can be largely automated, freeing human experts to focus on complex cases and judgment calls. This not only reduces costs but often increases coverage (checking more transactions, inspecting more data points than a human team could).

Another domain where AI has proven invaluable is crisis management planning. Traditionally, crisis plans are documents that sit on shelves – rarely updated and often untested until an actual crisis hits. AI is changing that by enabling proactive risk alerts and monitoring that feed directly into crisis response protocols. Take, for instance, a manufacturer's AI system that monitors sensor data across all its factories worldwide. If the system notices a pattern of increasing vibration in certain machine types that in the past preceded critical failures, it can alert maintenance to intervene before a breakdown – preventing an operational crisis. Or on the corporate communications side, AI tools now comb social media and news for early signs of PR crises (perhaps a spike in negative sentiment tied to a company's product). Early detection allows the communications team to craft a response or recall a product before the issue spirals. Pasupuleti (2024) discusses how AI tools reshaped real-time decision-making in crisis scenarios, highlighting that leaders who used AI support during crises (like natural disasters or sudden market crashes) managed a more adaptive and composed response (Pasupuleti, 2024). The AI could rapidly process information to suggest priorities – for example, telling a retailer during a cyberattack which servers to shut down to contain damage while keeping others running to preserve business continuity.

A salient example of AI-driven crisis management is how some governments use AI for natural disaster response. AI models can forecast the path and impact of hurricanes or earthquakes, enabling earlier evacuations and resource staging. Leaders in emergency management centers rely on these predictions to make life-and-death decisions under uncertainty. The AI doesn't remove the uncertainty – nature is still unpredictable – but it narrows the cone of uncertainty and provides probabilistic guidance that's far better than intuition alone. An anecdote often cited is that of an AI system that gave the government of a coastal city a much earlier warning of potential catastrophic flooding than traditional methods; acting on that, officials evacuated an extra 100,000 residents who would have been in harm's way. Such stories exemplify how AI in crisis planning can drastically alter outcomes by buying crucial time and insight.

However, the infusion of AI in risk management also requires careful oversight. Leaders must ask: how reliable are these models? What are their false alarm rates? The *Human Factors* study by Elder et al. reminds us that knowing when to pass a decision to AI vs. when to rely on human judgment is itself a skill (Elder et al., 2022). If an AI system for risk starts generating too many false positives, it may erode trust and be ignored (the "cry wolf" effect). Thus, calibration of AI systems – ensuring they are tuned to an organization's risk appetite and context – is key. Leading organizations address this by keeping humans in the loop: AI flags risks, but human risk managers validate and decide the final action, especially for high-impact decisions. This maintains accountability and allows human experience to complement AI's analytical might. As one executive put it, "The AI is like our radar – it shows the storm ahead, but we still decide if and how to steer the ship."

AI has become an indispensable component of risk management and uncertainty analysis for leaders. It enhances foresight, accelerates detection of threats, optimizes the response to crises, and even quantifies uncertainties in ways that make decision-making under uncertainty more scientific. A comprehensive risk strategy today likely involves a symphony of AI tools working in concert: predictive models scanning for trouble, simulation engines mapping out contingency plans, and real-time monitors issuing alerts. Leaders who harness these tools gain a form of augmented prudence – they are neither paralyzed by fear of the unknown nor reckless in the face of it, but guided by data-driven insight toward measured, wise action (Duan et al., 2019; Pasupuleti, 2024).

3.5 CASE STUDY – BUILDING A DATA-DRIVEN CULTURE

Transforming an organization into a truly data-driven enterprise is as much about people and culture as it is about algorithms and analytics. In this case study, we explore how two industry leaders – Microsoft and DBS Bank

– successfully cultivated a data-driven culture, illustrating practical steps and lessons learned in the journey toward pervasive data literacy and AI adoption. These examples demonstrate that building such a culture requires strong leadership vision, widespread upskilling initiatives, and deliberate cultural engineering to shift mindsets at all levels of the organization.

Microsoft: AI Champions and Leadership Buy-in. Microsoft's evolution offers a powerful example of top-down vision igniting bottom-up engagement. Under CEO Satya Nadella's leadership, Microsoft declared itself "customer zero" for AI – meaning the company would internally adopt its own AI technologies first, learning and iterating from within before selling solutions to customers. This bold stance signaled leadership's total buy-in. Nadella and his C-suite did more than issue memos; they personally championed AI use in daily work, setting the tone that every employee – whether in engineering, marketing, or HR – should leverage data and AI tools to enhance their effectiveness. Microsoft established internal AI training programs reaching across job roles, from software developers getting advanced machine learning courses to sales teams learning to use AI insights in customer pitches. Jeana Jorgensen, Microsoft's VP of Worldwide Learning, noted that providing "the right skills across the organization is key" and that Microsoft reimagined how employees learn, aligning training with critical business functions rather than one-size-fits-all lectures. The company even created internal AI "champions" – enthusiastic early adopters who volunteered to mentor their colleagues. These champions developed self-guided AI courses on Microsoft's SharePoint and hosted "AI Clinics" to answer questions, creating a grassroots momentum where employees inspired employees (Jorgensen, 2025). In effect, leadership lit the spark by making AI a strategic priority and resource commitment, and then empowered internal champions to fan the flames throughout the ranks. Microsoft's approach highlights the importance of leadership buy-in and AI champions. Leadership provided the vision and removed roadblocks (for instance, by investing in training resources and updating policies to encourage experimentation with AI), while champions drove day-to-day cultural change. One concrete initiative was the SkillUp AI Challenge hosted by Microsoft's internal innovation hub, The Garage. It gamified learning through hackathons and friendly competitions, making the acquisition of AI skills fun and collaborative rather than daunting. Marketers competed to design AI-driven ad campaigns; finance analysts competed in building Power BI dashboards. This playfulness lowered resistance and built confidence. Moreover, Microsoft ingrained continuous learning as a norm: employees were given time and space to explore AI during work hours (e.g., "Learning Days"), signaling that learning was not an extracurricular activity but part of the job. The results speak to a robust data culture: decisions at Microsoft today typically begin with data analysis – whether it's engineering teams using telemetry data to decide on product features or sales teams using analytics to identify which customer segments to prioritize. Jorgensen (2025) noted that by empowering teams with the right skills and tools, Microsoft saw its workforce embrace an AI-first mindset, effectively "aligning those initiatives to the functions that are critical to how we do business." This alignment ensured that the data-driven practices weren't abstract ideals, but directly tied to business outcomes and each team's success.

DBS Bank: Top-down vs. Bottom-up Data Culture. DBS Bank, a leading financial services group in Asia, offers a complementary story of cultural transformation in a traditionally conservative industry. DBS recognized early that to compete in the digital era, it needed to infuse data and AI into its DNA. The bank's leadership, led by CEO Piyush Gupta, launched a multi-year initiative to retrain its workforce and break old habits. A headline-grabbing move was DBS's announcement that it had identified 13,000 employees – nearly the entire core workforce – for AI and data upskilling, with over 10,000 already embarked on training roadmaps (AFP, 2025). This was not a tech department effort alone; it spanned operations, customer service, compliance, and more. By publicly committing to upskill such a large number, DBS leadership sent a clear message: working at DBS means becoming data- and AI-savvy. At the same time, this top-down mandate was paired with encouragement for bottom-up innovation. DBS implemented an internal platform called "iGrow" – essentially a personalized AI career coach for every employee. The platform uses AI to recommend learning paths, future career roles, and even suggests internal job moves, which not only builds data skills but also demonstrates the bank's confidence in AI tools (employees seeing AI trusted with career guidance built their trust in AI for other tasks). The DBS AI reskilling initiative exemplifies a successful top-down strategy that mobilized the whole organization. The bank invested SGD 20 million over five years solely to equip employees with digital and data skills, establishing its Future Tech Academy for continuous learning. Meanwhile, employees were encouraged to form communities (e.g., interest groups in data science) and share success stories – this fostered a bottom-up energy. A notable cultural program at DBS was the incorporation of hackathons in talent development: from 2015 onward, hackathons were used to get employees hands-on with digital problem-solving, sometimes pairing them with startups to break old banking silo thinking. This early adoption of an agile, experimentation culture paved the way for later AI adoption. As employees grew comfortable with rapid prototyping and iterative learning (fail-fast ethos), trying an AI tool or trusting a data insight over one's seniority became less radical. In terms of leadership buy-in, top executives at DBS didn't just fund these programs; they participated. It's recounted that senior managers took basic coding classes alongside junior staff, signaling humility and commitment to learning – a powerful cultural signal flattening the hierarchy around knowledge. Gupta himself has spoken about reading books on AI and quoting data in town halls, embodying the data-driven leader. One striking measure of success is how DBS's culture shift reflected in outcomes. Within a few years, over one-third of all job vacancies at DBS were filled by internal candidates, thanks to the upskilling programs, and employee engagement scores reached the 91st percentile in their internal surveys (up from 87th) as of 2021. This suggests that employees felt empowered and valued in the transformation. They weren't being replaced by AI; they were being elevated by it. Indeed, DBS reported generating hundreds of millions in business value from AI initiatives (like AI-driven customer personalization and credit decisions), which it credits to having a workforce capable of ideating and implementing these solutions. Culturally, a data-driven mindset took root: decisions started to be made "with data on the table" by default. One middle manager described how meetings changed – "Opinions still mattered, but first you had to show the data behind them," effectively democratizing decision input because the numbers could come from anyone's analysis, not just the highest-paid person's perspective.

Top-down vs. Bottom-up Approach: The Microsoft and DBS experiences reveal a nuanced insight: successful data-driven cultures blend top-down direction with bottom-up initiative. Top-down efforts (like leadership vision, formal training programs, resource allocation, policy changes) set the stage and provide momentum. Bottom-up efforts (like grassroots learning communities, peer mentoring, and individual innovation projects) ensure the change is internalized and sustained. If it were only top-down, employees might feel coerced and do the minimum. If only bottom-up, efforts may remain fragmented and lack scale or priority. Microsoft showed how a strong vision ("empower every person with AI") married with empowering employees to experiment (through The Garage and role-specific training) yields broad adoption. DBS showed how making everyone part of the journey (not just a digital team) and encouraging them to grow can convert even a 21-year bank teller into a tech-augmented wealth manager. Another lesson from these cases is managing the fear of change. Early on, many DBS employees likely feared that AI would automate them out of a job. By investing in them (training and offering internal mobility via iGrow), DBS sent a clear message: the company's preference was to transform you, not replace you. This built trust and a willingness to embrace new tools. Similarly, Microsoft had to encourage a growth mindset – employees had to shed the fear of seeming less competent when asking for help with analytics. The AI champions and fun learning challenges helped create a safe environment to admit ignorance and learn. In both organizations, continuous learning and data literacy became celebrated. When an employee used data to successfully challenge a long-held practice, it was applauded as a win, not seen as undermining authority. For example, Microsoft recounts how a relatively junior analyst's data model once questioned a marketing spend allocation that executives had favored; instead of being rebuffed, the analysis was taken seriously and ultimately saved the company a significant budget – reinforcing to everyone that data speaks louder than rank when done right (Jorgensen, 2025).

Cultural Change Success Stories and Lessons: Both Microsoft and DBS achieved tangible shifts: Microsoft transformed from a traditional software giant into a cloud-driven, AI-powered organization; DBS went from a local bank to being named the "World's Best Digital Bank" multiple years in a row, often citing its AI initiatives and digital culture. Some key lessons from these success stories include:

- Invest in People: Both companies invested heavily in employee development (time, money, resources). A data-driven culture blossoms when employees feel equipped – it will wither if they feel threatened or left behind. As an AFP report on DBS noted, an AI transformation can impact thousands of jobs, so the organization's responsibility is to prepare those jobholders for new roles (AFP, 2025). Microsoft's 10 Best Practices e-book likewise emphasizes giving employees structured learning paths and time to explore AI without fear (Jorgensen, 2025).
- Lead by Example: Leadership's active participation sets the tone. When the C-suite uses dashboards in meetings or cites data in decisions, it signals what the expectations are. At Microsoft, leaders internally showcased how they used AI to improve their own team performance (e.g., HR leaders using analytics to reduce attrition) – modeling the behavior they wanted to see company-wide.
- Empower Change Agents: Identify and support those in the organization who are naturally curious about data. Microsoft's AI champions and DBS's hackathon enthusiasts became internal evangelists. They translate the abstract idea of "data-driven" into practical help for their peers (like showing a teammate how to use a new visualization tool). This peer influence can often overcome resistance more effectively than top-management mandates.
- Integrate into Daily Work: A culture shift happens not in slogans, but in routines. Microsoft embedded AI into its daily workflow – from sales pipelines to code reviews – making it the default way to operate. DBS integrated data considerations into every project approval and every service design, so asking "what does the data say?" became as routine as checking the time. Over time, this normalization is what truly makes the culture "data-driven" rather than "data-interested."
- Celebrate and Communicate Wins: Both organizations widely communicated success stories. When data-driven approaches led to a win, it was publicized internally – not to pat backs, but to reinforce the behavior. For example, if an ops team used AI to cut processing time by 50%, that story

would be shared in newsletters or town halls, attributing the success to the use of analytics. This creates positive reinforcement and FOMO (fear of missing out) in other teams that might be slower to adopt. At DBS, internal awards for "Data Wizard of the Quarter" or similar recognition kept enthusiasm high.

In sum, Microsoft and DBS's experiences illustrate that building a data-driven culture is a holistic transformation. It requires visionary leadership, comprehensive skill-building, structural alignment (processes and incentives that favor data use), and emotional buy-in from the workforce. The case study underlines that technology is actually the easy part – the algorithms and tools are available. The true challenge and triumph lie in cultural change: evolving mindsets from "HiPPO" (Highest Paid Person's Opinion) decision-making to decisions by evidence, from fearing data to treating it as organizational "water" that everyone needs and uses daily. The payoff for those who manage this cultural transformation is immense: an organization that learns and adapts faster than its competition, propelled by the collective intelligence of its people augmented by data. And as the pace of business accelerates, such a culture isn't just an asset – it may well be a prerequisite for continued success (Jorgensen, 2025; AFP, 2025).

3.6 BUILDING DATA LITERACY AND DECISION INTELLIGENCE

As organizations integrate AI and analytics into every facet of operations, a new set of leadership competencies is coming to the forefront. Chief among them are data literacy and what many are calling decision intelligence. Data literacy is the ability to read, understand, create, and communicate data as information. It's a foundational skill for leaders in the 21st century – much like computer literacy became essential in the late 20th. Decision intelligence, on the other hand, is an emerging framework that combines data science, social science, and managerial science to inform and improve decision-making. It's about structuring decisions (not just data), understanding the decision-making process, and designing interventions (often AI-driven) that yield better outcomes. In this section, we focus on how leaders can build these competencies in themselves and their teams, and why doing so is crucial for future organizational success.

3.6.1 Data Literacy for Leaders

Today's leaders must go beyond just delegating analytics to specialists; they need a comfortable fluency in data themselves. This doesn't mean every CEO must become a data scientist, but they should, for example, be able to interpret a regression analysis output, grasp probability distributions, and ask the right questions about data quality and bias. As Zaidi et al. emphasize, leadership is shifting toward "intelligent, tech-savvy approaches," implying that leaders need to unlearn some traditional habits and embrace new competencies, with data literacy being paramount (Zaidi et al., 2024). A leader might not code a neural network, but they should understand what a neural network can and cannot do, and how that might apply to strategic decisions. Programs to develop digital literacy for leaders are sprouting up – from executive courses on AI for business to internal workshops where data scientists teach the C-suite basic analytics concepts using company data. These efforts pay off when, for example, a marketing VP starts framing objectives in measurable terms ("Which metrics indicate success, and what does the distribution look like?") or a COO feels comfortable exploring a data dashboard live in a meeting to answer an operational question. Westover (2024a) notes that strategic roadmaps for AI adoption often stall because leadership doesn't fully grasp the data; by investing in leader-focused training, companies ensure the top brass can genuinely champion and guide data initiatives (Westover, 2025).

3.6.2 Decision Intelligence Frameworks

While data literacy is about understanding data, decision intelligence (DI) is about weaving that understanding into better decision processes. DI frameworks treat each decision as a repeatable process that can be modeled, analyzed, and improved – often with the aid of AI. For instance, a DI approach to a customer retention decision would model the decision flows: from capturing relevant data (customer behavior, feedback), to predicting outcomes of possible actions (renewal rates if we offer a discount vs. if we don't), to actually implementing a decision (who gets a retention offer), and then learning from the results to inform the next cycle. By explicitly mapping out decisions this way, organizations can identify where human judgment is critical, where data should inform, and where automation might take over routine aspects. Gurulakshmi and Gayathri (2024), for example, conceptualize leadership as a dynamic human–AI collaboration aimed at enhancing decision quality and outcomes (Gurulakshmi & Gayathri, 2024). This aligns with DI thinking – you design the system around decisions, not just the AI tool in isolation. Some companies are even creating new roles like "Decision Intelligence Analyst" or forming Decision Centers of Excellence to formalize this. Building decision intelligence means training teams to approach problems methodically: clarify the decision to be made, ensure the right data and analytics are in play, consider the psychology of the decision-makers, and use technology to augment the process end-to-end. When done well, DI can drastically reduce decision latency (how long it takes to go from recognizing a need to making a call) and improve decision quality consistency. Aziz et al. (2024d) argue that interdisciplinary approaches combining cognitive technologies with decision science can transform leadership practices, and their findings call for integrated frameworks – essentially a call for decision intelligence models – to guide AI-augmented leadership decisions (Aziz et al., 2024d).

3.6.3 Analytical Skills Development

Developing data literacy and decision intelligence requires a concerted focus on analytical skills development across the organization. This doesn't mean turning everyone into statisticians, but rather nurturing critical thinking, hypothesis testing, and comfort with analytical tools. Many organizations are implementing rotational programs where high-potential managers spend a stint in the data analytics department to get hands-on experience. Others run internal certification programs in analytics basics (e.g., DBS Bank's employees earned badges in areas like data analytics and visualization as part of their reskilling). The goal is to create a baseline competency so that when confronted with a data-heavy report, a manager doesn't glaze over but engages and can draw insight. Cross-functional projects help too – for instance, pairing a domain expert with a data scientist on a problem spreads analytical know-how in both directions (the domain expert learns about data analysis, the data scientist learns the business context). Encouraging the use of data in everyday decisions, even small ones, forms habits. At a consumer goods company, for example, the sales teams were trained to use an app that provided AI-generated insights on which product mix to pitch to each client based on history and trends. Initially, some salespeople resisted, preferring their gut instincts. But the company gamified the usage: those who used the app and beat their targets were highlighted. Soon, even the skeptics gave it a try and, upon seeing improved results, became proponents. The takeaway is that people need to experience that analytical tools make them better at their jobs – then they self-motivate to develop these skills further. As Nyoto et al. (2024b) found, when leadership domains experience AI's positive impacts (like improved collaboration or efficiency), it "identifies emerging leadership dimensions" and fosters governance that further encourages these capabilities (Nyoto et al., 2024b). Put simply, show people that analytical savvy equals success and career growth, and they will seek it out.

3.6.4 Democratizing Data Access

One practical pillar of building a data-centric culture is democratizing data access. No amount of literacy helps if employees are locked out of the data they need. Thus, many organizations are breaking down data silos, implementing self-service BI (business intelligence) platforms, and establishing data governance that balances security with accessibility. Democratizing data means front-line employees and mid-level managers can pull up relevant data without having to file IT tickets and wait weeks. It empowers those closest to the problem to explore and derive insights on the fly. Leaders spearheading this effort often have to tackle both technical and cultural barriers: technically, ensuring data is cleaned, well organized, and available through user-friendly tools; culturally, ensuring that sharing data is the norm (rather than hoarding it for power). When everyone has access to the same numbers, conversations shift from "whose data is right?" to "what do these data tell us and how do we act?" Cross-functional decisions improve because each department isn't defending its own version of truth – a single source of truth is visible to all, focusing debate on interpretation and solutions. A classic example is how companies like Airbnb built internal data portals and pushed a mantra that "every employee is a data scientist." They found that by trusting employees with data, they got a more innovative and engaged workforce. Of course, democratization must be accompanied by training – throwing open the data floodgates without guidance can lead to misuse or misinterpretation. Therefore, many firms complement open data access with on-demand help from data experts or "data stewards" who guide teams on proper use. The net effect is a workforce that feels ownership of data – not something handed down from an ivory tower, but a common asset everyone can leverage. Singh (2023d) points out that adaptive leadership is key in managing AI-driven change, including balancing human–AI collaboration and addressing job displacement fears (Singh, 2023d). Applied here, adaptive leadership would encourage open access to data while actively helping teams adapt through upskilling and support, turning what could be a deluge into a powerful current that carries the organization forward.

3.6.5 Cross-functional Data Competencies

discuss how digital leadership transformation emphasizes adaptive skills and notes cultural/structural changes with tech integration, which likely includes fostering interdisciplinary collaboration and skills (Anam et al., 2024). Their work implies that a successful AI-era leader isn't siloed but fluent in multiple domains enough to bridge gaps – exactly what cross-functional competency building aims to achieve.

3.6.6 Training for Data-driven Decision-making

Many of the earlier points culminate in the need for ongoing training programs specifically focused on data-driven decision-making. These might take the form of scenario-based workshops where teams practice making decisions with a mix of data and intuition under time pressure, followed by feedback sessions analyzing their choices. Organizations have started running "war games" or simulations in which executives must respond to a fictional business scenario (e.g., a sudden market disruption) and are scored on how well they use data vs. gut feeling. The results can be illuminating – often showing that even seasoned leaders default to intuition more than they realize, and prompting reflection on how to better integrate data next time. With practice, making decisions with data becomes muscle memory. Another effective training approach is storytelling: teaching leaders how to tell a compelling story with data. Data-driven doesn't mean dry; leaders must persuade and rally others using insights gleaned from data. So, training often involves honing the narrative around numbers – turning analysis into an actionable story that drives decisions. This melds analytical and soft skills, embodying the "decision intelligence" idea that it's not just the data or decision in isolation, but the whole ecosystem of communication and context.

3.6.7 AI Fluency in Leadership Teams

As AI becomes embedded in tools and processes, AI fluency – comfort with and understanding of AI – is increasingly important at the top. Leadership teams that are AI-fluent can better evaluate AI-driven proposals, set realistic AI strategy, and oversee ethical considerations. They'll know, for instance, when to trust a machine learning model's output and when it might be leading them astray due to biased training data. AI fluency also includes knowing the right questions to ask data science teams and being able to champion AI initiatives credibly to the rest of the company. Without fluency, there's a risk of either overhyping AI or underutilizing it. Westover's roadmap for AI in leadership calls out the need for integrated governance – one aspect of which is leaders being knowledgeable enough to govern AI use properly (Westover, 2025). For example, if an AI recommends firing 10% of staff to cut costs, an AI-fluent leader will probe: what data was this based on? Did the AI consider the long-term talent loss? Is there bias in how it assessed performance? Rather than blindly following or dismissing, they engage in a meaningful dialogue with the technology. Many companies now include AI primers in their leadership development programs and even send senior executives to crash courses at universities on AI for managers. The result sought is a leadership bench that sees AI as a strategic partner and is competent to harness it.

3.6.8 Cultivating a Data-driven Mindset and Empowering Employees

At the heart of building these capabilities is cultivating the right mindset. A data-driven mindset is curious, skeptical in a healthy way (always asking "what does the data say? could there be another interpretation?"), and open to changing one's mind when evidence contradicts a prior belief. Leaders set the tone here – if they exemplify this mindset, it trickles down. If a VP openly changes a decision in light of new data, praising the analyst who brought the insight rather than clinging to their original plan, it sends a powerful message to everyone: following the facts is valued over saving face. Such moments do more to entrench a data-driven culture than any memo could. It empowers data-driven employees because they see that presenting evidence-based recommendations will be rewarded, even if it challenges hierarchy or conventional wisdom. Equipping employees with tools (like self-service analytics) and skills (through training) says: we trust you to use data; you have the mandate to make data-informed decisions in your role. Some companies formalize this by adjusting decision rights – for example, allowing front-line customer service reps to issue refunds or extra services if a data dashboard indicates the customer is at high risk of churn and is a valuable long-term customer. Previously, that might require manager approval, but with good data and training, employees can act faster and feel more ownership. This empowerment, however, comes with accountability. Employees must learn to interpret data correctly and ethically. Therefore, many organizations create data literacy champions or communities – internal groups where people share knowledge, troubleshoot data issues, and celebrate wins. These communities keep the momentum going and provide support, ensuring that data literacy isn't a one-and-done training but an ongoing part of the company's learning culture.

Building data literacy and decision intelligence is a multifaceted endeavor. It spans educating individuals, adapting organizational structures, and nurturing a culture that values analytical thinking. It's about making the entire organization – from top leaders to entry-level employees – more "AI-ready" and data-savvy. As Madanchian et al. (2024b) discuss, AI disrupts traditional leadership paradigms and calls for adaptable, data-driven leadership while emphasizing communication and bias eradication (Madanchian et al., 2024b). In practical terms, that means tomorrow's successful organizations will likely be those that today are investing heavily in their people's analytical capabilities and redesigning decision processes around data and AI. Just as computers moved from the basement to every desk, data and AI are moving from a specialist's domain to every employee's toolkit. The transition can be challenging – it requires unlearning old habits and learning new ones – but the reward is an organization that competes on knowledge and insight, not just on products or scale. It becomes an organization where decisions are smarter not by chance, but by design, propelled by leaders and teams who are fluent in the language of data and adept at leveraging the intelligence of both humans and machines in making choices (Zaidi et al., 2025; Westover, 2025).

4. Strategic implementation of AI in organizations

4.1 READINESS ASSESSMENT AND ORGANIZATIONAL DIAGNOSTICS

Implementing AI in an organization is not a plug-and-play endeavor – it requires a candid assessment of whether the enterprise is truly prepared for AI-driven change. A vivid illustration can be seen in a mid-sized retailer that eagerly invested in an AI-powered demand forecasting tool, only to watch the project flounder due to poor data quality and skeptical end-users. Such outcomes are common; in fact, studies have found that a high percentage of AI projects (some estimates around 85%) fail to meet their intended objectives, often because organizations dive in without sufficient readiness and alignment of people, processes, and technology (Engel et al., 2021; Weber et al., 2023). A readiness assessment serves as an organizational diagnostic, helping leaders gauge the current state of essential capabilities and identify gaps before large-scale AI integration. This proactive approach is a critical success factor, as it ensures that the foundational elements for AI adoption are in place and mitigates the risk of costly failures (Aldoseri et al., 2024; Sharma & Reddy, 2024).

4.1.1 Key Dimensions of AI Readiness

Comprehensive AI readiness assessments typically examine multiple dimensions of the enterprise to evaluate its preparedness for AI initiatives. The following areas are especially important:

- Data and Technology Infrastructure
  - The quality, accessibility, and governance of data, as well as the robustness of IT infrastructure, are pivotal. An organization must have reliable data pipelines, sufficient computing power, and scalable cloud or on-premise environments to support AI workloads (Aldoseri et al., 2024). In one readiness framework, data infrastructure and governance maturity are top-priority criteria; without clean, well-governed

data, even the best algorithms will produce poor results (Aldoseri et al., 2024). Organizations should diagnose whether their data assets are comprehensive and bias-free, and whether data management practices (security, privacy, quality controls) meet the demands of AI models (Rakova et al., 2020). Any gaps in this area – for example, siloed databases or lack of real-time data access – signal a need for remediation before AI deployment.

- Talent and Skills
  - An honest look at human capital is necessary. Does the organization have employees and leaders with the requisite AI skills and literacy? If not, is there a plan for developing or acquiring these skills? Many companies find that they lack sufficient in-house expertise in machine learning or data science, as well as AI literacy among non-technical managers (Du et al., 2023). A readiness audit might reveal, for instance, that while the IT department is technically strong, business unit leaders do not fully understand AI capabilities and limitations, which could hinder adoption. Research emphasizes workforce reskilling and upskilling as critical to AI readiness – companies that invest in training programs for employees and leadership (e.g., AI bootcamps, data literacy workshops) create a more supportive environment for new AI systems (Du et al., 2023; Alshaibani et al., 2025). In short, diagnosing skill gaps and fostering a continuous learning culture are key steps toward building AI readiness.
- Leadership and Strategy Alignment
  - Effective AI readiness assessments probe the level of executive commitment and strategic clarity regarding AI. Top-management support and a clear vision for AI use are repeatedly identified as critical enablers of successful adoption (Horani et al., 2025; Tomazevic et al., 2024). If senior leaders treat AI as a core part of the business strategy (rather than a peripheral experiment), the organization is far more likely to secure needed resources and cross-functional cooperation (Horani et al., 2025). Thus, one diagnostic question is whether the AI initiative aligns with the company's broader strategic goals and whether there is C-suite buy-in. For example, an organization might establish an AI steering committee or designate a Chief AI Officer, indicating strategic alignment. Conversely, if an AI project is championed only by the IT department without broader leadership engagement, the readiness assessment would flag a misalignment that could doom the project (Sharma & Reddy, 2024). Assessors also examine whether there are clear objectives and KPIs defined for AI projects, ensuring that everyone understands what success looks like and how it ties into business outcomes (Elsherif, 2024a).

- Organizational Culture and Change Readiness
    - The cultural aspect of readiness is often the differentiator between merely technically capable organizations and those that actually achieve AI integration. An AI-ready culture is characterized by openness to change, data-driven decision-making, and a willingness among staff to trust and collaborate with AI systems (Böhme & Graf-Pfohl, 2025). Readiness diagnostics often include surveys or interviews to gauge employee sentiment: Are employees fearful that AI will automate them out of a job? Do mid-level managers view AI as a threat to their authority? Such human factors can significantly impede AI adoption if not addressed (Soulami et al., 2024). High-readiness organizations cultivate a mindset that AI is a tool to augment human capabilities, not replace them, and they actively manage anxieties through communication and involvement (Böhme & Graf-Pfohl, 2025; Soulami et al., 2024). For instance, a banking institution's readiness assessment might uncover pockets of resistance in the operations department; armed with this insight, leadership can proactively run educational sessions and pilot programs with heavy employee input to build trust. Additionally, a culture that encourages innovation and tolerates the "fail-fast" approach will be better positioned to experiment with AI and iterate, compared to a rigid culture that punishes experimentation (Tomazevic et al., 2024). The diagnostic should thus measure attributes like flexibility, innovation culture, and the presence of AI champions or change agents within the organization.
- Governance and Ethical Preparedness
    - A subtle but crucial dimension of AI readiness is whether the organization has governance structures and ethical guidelines in place for AI use. This includes data privacy compliance, model accountability mechanisms, and policies for issues like algorithmic bias and transparency (Rakova et al., 2020). An organization well prepared for AI will have or be developing frameworks for responsible AI – for example, an AI ethics committee, bias audit processes for AI models, and clear guidelines on human oversight for automated decisions. A readiness assessment might ask: Does the organization have a policy for AI ethics? Are there procedures to handle AI failures or controversial outcomes? If not, establishing these governance elements early will prevent problems down the line (Elsherif, 2024a). Strong governance readiness is associated with higher trust in AI systems internally and smoother deployment, as stakeholders feel confident that AI will be used in line with company values and societal norms (Rakova et al., 2020). On the flip side, lack of governance can be a red flag – for instance, deploying

AI in customer-facing processes without a bias mitigation plan could lead to public relations crises or regulatory issues.

Conducting an AI readiness assessment along these dimensions yields a nuanced picture of the organization's starting point. It essentially functions as a gap analysis: for each dimension, leadership can see the shortfalls that need to be addressed to increase the chance of AI project success (Aldoseri et al., 2024). For example, one global manufacturer's diagnostic revealed strong C-suite support and ample data, but a significant talent gap in data science and a cautious culture resistant to algorithmic recommendations. With this knowledge, the company delayed a full AI rollout by six months to focus on hiring data scientists and running AI awareness workshops for managers – moves that later paid off in user acceptance and effective use of the new AI system. This reflective process is supported by research that emphasizes aligning social and technical elements before and during AI integration (Weber et al., 2023; Altepost et al., 2024). By ensuring joint optimization of human and technical systems – a core principle of socio-technical theory – organizations create a fertile environment for AI to deliver value (Altepost et al., 2024; Böhme & Graf-Pfohl, 2025). Notably, more than 40 recent studies on AI in organizations employed socio-technical frameworks or technology acceptance models to frame AI integration, underscoring the importance of balancing these human and technical considerations in practice (Akbarighatar et al., 2025; Tomazevic et al., 2024). It is also valuable to benchmark readiness using structured tools or maturity models. For instance, a responsible AI maturity model can help organizations rate themselves on a scale across various criteria (strategy, data, talent, culture, etc.) and visualize progression over time (Akbarighatar et al., 2025). Such models provide a roadmap, suggesting what "higher maturity" looks like – for example, integrated AI governance, enterprise-wide AI literacy, agile experimentation capabilities – and thus guide strategic investments. An example is the AIR-5D framework (noted in external industry literature) which scores five dimensions of AI readiness; similarly, academic proposals like the socio-technical AI adoption framework tailor maturity dimensions to ensure ethical and sustainable AI implementation (Akbarighatar et al., 2025). The key is that through diagnostics, organizations can move from a candid recognition of their current state to an actionable plan that fortifies weaknesses before scaling AI. This may involve initiatives such as establishing data lakes, recruiting AI specialists, training existing staff, improving cross-department data sharing, or instituting new policies – all targeted interventions driven by the diagnostic insights. Organizational diagnostics for AI readiness act as a strategic checkpoint that separates hasty, ad hoc AI projects (prone to failure) from well-grounded initiatives aligned with the organization's capacity and context. By evaluating dimensions like infrastructure, talent, leadership, culture, and governance, leaders gain a clear view of readiness enablers and barriers (Horani et al., 2025; Sharma & Reddy, 2024). The assessment highlights what must change internally to absorb AI – whether that means cleaning up data, skilling up people, breaking silos, or setting new policies. As research on enterprise AI initiatives shows, aligning these factors early is essential for sustainable AI adoption. Organizations that invest time in this upfront diagnostic step create a strong foundation for the chapters to follow in their AI journey: strategic planning, capability-building, change management, and beyond. The mantra "know thyself before deploying AI" captures it well – readiness assessment transforms an organization's self-knowledge into a strategic asset for successful AI implementation (Aldoseri et al., 2024).

4.2 STRATEGIC PLANNING FOR AI INTEGRATION

Once an organization understands its readiness level, the next step is to craft a strategic plan for AI integration that aligns with business objectives and addresses identified gaps. Strategic planning for AI integration means developing a clear roadmap for how, where, and why the organization will deploy artificial intelligence in pursuit of its mission. Rather than AI for AI's sake, the plan should tie AI initiatives directly to the organization's value drivers – whether that is improving customer experience, optimizing operations, enabling new products, or informing strategy with better insights (Abuzaid, 2024). A vivid example comes from a global logistics company: after assessing readiness, its leadership formulated an AI strategy to automate route optimization and demand forecasting. They set a vision that "AI will help deliver packages faster and cheaper," explicitly linking the AI plan to the corporate goal of operational excellence. This vision was broken down into specific objectives (e.g., reduce delivery times by 20% through AI-driven routing) and phased projects. By articulating why AI was being used and how success would be measured, the company created organizational buy-in and a sense of purpose around AI, which greatly smoothed its implementation.

A sound AI integration strategy typically encompasses several core components. First, it identifies priority use cases or applications of AI that offer high strategic impact and feasibility (Elsherif, 2024a). Rather than doing everything at once, strategic planners choose a portfolio of AI projects aligned with key business areas. For instance, a retail enterprise might prioritize an AI-driven recommendation engine for e-commerce and an inventory optimization system because these align with its strategic focus on personalization and efficiency. The selection of use cases should be guided by a combination of business value potential and readiness: planners consider where AI can solve pressing problems or unlock new opportunities and whether the needed data and capabilities are available (Sharma & Reddy, 2024). Academic and industry frameworks often suggest starting with "low-hanging fruit" – projects that are not overly complex technically, yet can demonstrate quick wins and ROI, thereby building momentum (Elsherif, 2024a; Horani et al., 2025). This approach ensures that early AI projects reinforce the strategic narrative and provide learning experiences to refine later, more ambitious implementations.

Second, the AI strategy delineates the resources and capabilities required to execute the chosen initiatives. This links closely with the readiness findings from section 4.1. If gaps were found (e.g., a shortage of data scientists or inadequate data infrastructure), the strategic plan must include actions to fill those gaps. For example, if one strategic objective is to implement machine learning in quality control on a factory line, the plan might call for investing in IoT sensors (to gather data) and hiring an ML engineer to develop the models. Aligning capability-building with project needs is a hallmark of a robust AI strategy (Weber et al., 2023). Research by Weber et al. (2023) emphasizes planning for the full AI project life cycle – from data acquisition and model development to deployment and maintenance – and ensuring the organization has or develops the capabilities at each step. This might mean setting up partnerships with AI vendors, creating a new AI Center of Excellence to centralize expertise, or budgeting for cloud computing resources, all as part of the strategic blueprint (Weber et al., 2023; Abuzaid, 2024). Notably, many organizations incorporate training programs into their AI strategy so that, along with technological rollout, there is parallel development of human skills and governance processes (Du et al., 2023). For example, a bank's AI strategy document might explicitly allocate funds and time for staff training on using AI-powered analytics tools, thereby embedding capability development into the overall plan.

Third, strategic planning for AI integration must address organizational alignment and change management at a high level (this will be elaborated on further in section 4.4). The plan should anticipate how AI will affect workflows, roles, and decision-making processes, and outline how the organization will manage these changes (Adıgüzel, 2025). For instance, if AI is introduced to assist with customer service via chatbots, the strategy should consider how human customer service agents' roles will evolve – perhaps focusing more on complex queries – and plan for training or role redefinition accordingly (Bhuvan, 2024). Researchers have noted that AI-driven digital transformation often entails cultural and structural adaptation; strategic plans that explicitly incorporate those factors are more likely to succeed (Adıgüzel, 2025). This might manifest as strategy elements like: "Foster a data-driven culture by updating performance metrics to reward evidence-based decision-making" or "Establish clear guidelines for human oversight in AI-driven processes to maintain accountability." By embedding cultural and structural considerations, the strategy ensures AI initiatives are not isolated technical projects but integrated organizational changes (Sharma & Reddy, 2024; Tomazevic et al.,

2024). Strategic foresight is also crucial – leaders should use scenario planning to foresee possible outcomes of AI integration, including workforce impact and ethical implications, and plan mitigations or complementary initiatives (Horani et al., 2025). As an example, a healthcare provider might strategize that introducing an AI diagnostic tool will require redefining the workflow between nurses and doctors and put in place a change team to manage that transition.

Another critical element of AI strategic planning is establishing governance and ethical guidelines upfront. At the strategic level, organizations define principles for responsible AI use that align with their core values and regulatory obligations (Rakova et al., 2020). For instance, a company might enshrine in its AI strategy that all AI models will be subject to bias audits and explainability requirements before deployment, reflecting a commitment to fairness and transparency (Elsherif, 2024a). Setting these guardrails early not only helps prevent problems, but also signals to stakeholders (employees, customers, regulators) that the organization is taking a thoughtful, principled approach to AI. A survey of practitioner perspectives by Rakova et al. (2020) found that clear organizational policies on AI ethics and governance are seen as key enablers for shifting practices and gaining trust internally. Therefore, a comprehensive AI integration strategy often includes the creation or empowerment of an AI governance committee or similar body, definitions of roles such as data stewards or model validators, and integration of AI risk management into the enterprise risk framework (Rakova et al., 2020; Horani et al., 2025). For example, as part of its strategic plan, an insurance firm defined an "AI Ethics Board" to review all high-impact AI algorithms for compliance with ethical standards, thereby aligning AI projects with corporate values and risk appetite from the very beginning.

Strategic planning in practice results in a roadmap document (or series of documents) that guides the organization's AI journey over a multi-year horizon. This roadmap typically outlines phased milestones: what the organization aims to achieve in the short term (next 6–12 months), medium term (1–2 years), and long term (3–5 years) with respect to AI (Elsherif, 2024a). For example, a phased strategic plan might state: Phase 1: launch two pilot AI projects in marketing and supply chain; Phase 2: scale successful pilots to additional business units and integrate AI into core products; Phase 3: achieve enterprise-wide AI literacy and fully autonomous decision support in key processes. We will discuss roadmapping in more detail in section 4.5, but the important point here is that the strategic plan is not a one-off static document – it is a living roadmap that sets the direction while allowing for learning and iteration. Many organizations adopt an agile strategic planning approach for AI, revisiting and updating the strategy as early projects yield insights (Sharma & Reddy, 2024). This flexibility is necessary given the fast-evolving nature of AI technology and market conditions. It is also aligned with findings that continuous evaluation and adaptation are crucial for AI initiatives – effective strategies include feedback loops to refine the plan over time (Elsherif, 2024a).

To illustrate, consider a financial services company that, in its AI strategy, initially prioritized a machine learning model for credit risk assessment. Suppose after a year, the pilot shows promising accuracy but reveals customer concerns about algorithmic fairness. A flexible AI strategy would allow the company to pivot: perhaps slowing the rollout of that model until fairness improvements are made, and meanwhile accelerating another AI initiative (like an AI-powered fraud detection system) that faces fewer ethical concerns. Strategic planning thus provides a structured yet adaptable path, ensuring that AI integration efforts remain aligned with corporate vision, resources, and stakeholder expectations (Horani et al., 2025). This alignment is vital: research in organizational AI adoption consistently highlights the need for top-management support and clear strategic intent as determinants of success (Horani et al., 2025; Abuzaid, 2024). When everyone from the C-suite to the front-line understands how AI fits into the big picture and why it's being implemented, there is a greater collective push toward making it work.

Strategic planning for AI integration translates readiness into action. It connects the dots between an organization's goals and the technological potential of AI, answering key questions: What problems or opportunities will we tackle with AI? How will we execute these projects? What do we need to have in place? How will we manage risks and changes? A thoughtful AI strategy addresses these questions in a way that is specific to the organization's context (Abuzaid, 2024). It is both visionary – imagining how AI will transform the business – and pragmatic – laying out the concrete steps to get there. As one study put it, successful AI integration requires "strategic foresight combined with proactive change management to maximize benefits" (Sharma & Reddy, 2024). By investing in this planning stage, organizations set themselves up to move from isolated experiments to systematic, enterprise-wide AI adoption that drives strategic impact. The next sections will delve into executing these plans: building AI capabilities across the enterprise, and guiding the organization through change and adoption phases.

4.3 BUILDING AI CAPABILITIES ACROSS THE ENTERPRISE

Even the most elegant AI strategy will falter if an organization lacks the capabilities to execute it. Building AI capabilities across the enterprise is therefore a crucial pillar of strategic implementation. It involves developing the technical, human, and organizational competencies required to design, deploy, and sustain AI solutions at scale. This capability-building is an enterprise-wide endeavor: it's not confined to the IT or data science department, but rather touches every level and function, fostering an AI-enabled workforce and infrastructure. A useful analogy is to think of AI as a new "organ" in the organizational body – to support it, the entire circulatory system (data flows), nervous system (skills and knowledge), and even the muscular structure (processes and roles) need conditioning and growth. Research by Weber et al. (2023) finds that organizations successful in AI implementation invest deliberately in developing a range of capabilities, from technical proficiencies to data governance and cross-functional collaboration mechanisms. These capabilities enable them to cope with challenges like AI model opacity and data dependencies, which would otherwise hinder progress (Weber et al., 2023).

Technical and data capabilities. At the core, enterprises need solid technical foundations for AI. This includes not only hardware and software (e.g., cloud platforms, big data pipelines, AI development frameworks), but also data architecture and engineering skills to ensure data is collected, integrated, and accessible for AI use (Aldoseri et al., 2024). Many organizations establish centralized data lakes or modern data warehouses as part of their AI capability-building, breaking down data silos so that AI models can be trained on comprehensive datasets. Alongside data infrastructure, investing in the right tools and platforms is key – for example, adopting a machine learning operations (MLOps) platform that standardizes how models are developed, tested, and deployed across the enterprise. This creates efficiency and consistency, rather than every team improvising their own AI stack. However, tools alone are not enough; companies often create new roles or teams, like data engineers, ML engineers, and AI architects, to build and maintain these systems (Weber et al., 2023; Abuzaid, 2024). A pharmaceutical company building enterprise AI capability might hire data engineers to streamline clinical trial data into a unified platform, and data scientists to develop predictive models for drug discovery. Without these specialist skills, even abundant data remains underutilized.

Moreover, given AI's reliance on quality data, data governance capability is essential. Organizations need processes to ensure data accuracy, completeness, privacy, and compliance. Building this capability might involve setting up a data governance council, defining data standards and taxonomies for the enterprise, and deploying data cataloging tools. Strong governance ensures that as AI projects proliferate, they all draw from a "single source of truth" and respect necessary constraints (Altepost et al., 2024). For instance, a bank expanding its AI capabilities would reinforce its governance to avoid situations where one department's AI model is making decisions based on stale or inconsistent data. In practice, companies like DBS Bank (as noted in section 3.5) have implemented robust internal data governance and training alongside AI adoption, effectively creating a culture of data discipline that supports AI at scale. By doing so, they turn data into a strategic asset that fuels AI solutions reliably.

Human capital and skills development. Building AI capabilities is equally about people. This spans hiring new talent, upskilling current employees, and cultivating leadership that is conversant in AI. On the hiring front, organizations often seek data scientists, machine learning engineers, AI researchers, and analytics translators – roles that bring in the expertise to develop AI algorithms and connect them with business needs. Some firms create an AI Center of Excellence (CoE), essentially an in-house hub of AI experts who can be deployed to high-impact projects and serve as evangelists and mentors (Elsherif, 2024a). For example, a manufacturing conglomerate might establish an AI CoE composed of senior data scientists and process engineers, who then rotate across factories to implement predictive maintenance AI systems and train local teams. Research indicates that such central units can accelerate capability diffusion across the enterprise, ensuring standards and best practices in AI development are maintained (Weber et al., 2023).

However, given the scarcity of AI experts, companies cannot rely on hiring alone – they must develop the skills of their existing workforce to be AI-ready. This includes both technical training (e.g., software engineers learning machine learning libraries) and non-technical education (e.g., project managers learning how to manage AI projects, or marketers learning to interpret AI-driven analytics). Du et al. (2023) highlight that workforce reskilling is a cornerstone of successful AI-driven innovation; their framework emphasizes continuous learning and adaptation for the current workforce to take on new roles alongside AI. Many forward-looking organizations have launched internal AI academies or certification programs. For instance, an international consumer goods company rolled out a training program where hundreds of employees took courses in data analysis and basic AI concepts, fostering a baseline AI literacy across departments (Du et al., 2023). Likewise, non-technical leaders are encouraged to develop "hybrid leadership" competencies, blending domain expertise with an understanding of AI capabilities and ethics (Farid, 2024). This ensures that middle and senior managers can make informed decisions about AI investments and guide their teams in working effectively with AI tools (Farid, 2024; Alshaibani et al., 2025). The outcome of such capability-building is a more democratized use of AI: instead of a few data scientists being the bottleneck, many employees can engage with AI systems (e.g., using self-service AI analytics platforms) and contribute to AI-enhanced processes.

Crucially, building human capital for AI also involves nurturing cross-functional collaboration skills. AI projects typically sit at the intersection of business and IT – they require close cooperation between domain experts (who know the business problem), data scientists (who build the model), and IT professionals (who deploy and maintain the model). To facilitate this, companies may implement cross-functional teams or "fusion teams" for AI initiatives (Weber et al., 2023). These teams blend expertise – for example, a marketing analyst, a data scientist, and a software developer working together on a customer segmentation AI project. Over time, organizations institutionalize these collaborative practices, breaking down silos that traditionally separated business units from analytics/IT groups. The development of such collaborative capability means that people learn not only technical skills but also how to communicate across disciplines – translating business needs into data requirements, and conversely explaining AI outputs in business terms (Weber et al., 2023; Abuzaid, 2024). A case in point is a healthcare provider that formed multidisciplinary teams for its AI projects, which significantly improved project outcomes because doctors, data scientists, and IT staff were co-creating the AI solutions, each bringing their perspective. Building this human interface capability often requires a cultural shift toward more open communication and teamwork, which links with change management efforts (discussed in section 4.4).

Process and structural adaptation. As AI capabilities grow, organizations often need to update their processes and structures to fully leverage them. This can mean reengineering workflows to incorporate AI or adjusting organizational structures to be more conducive to AI-driven innovation. For example, an insurance company deploying AI in claims processing might redesign the claims workflow: minor claims could be automatically processed by an AI engine, while complex claims are flagged for human review, with a clear handoff process defined. This new workflow might require creating a new process step or a new role (e.g., an "AI claims adjudicator" who deals with AI-flagged cases). Bhuvan (2024) notes that AI and machine learning can impact organizational structure by flattening hierarchies and shifting decision-making closer to the front-line, since AI tools empower lower-level employees with insights previously requiring managerial analysis. Organizations building AI capability should be prepared to redesign roles and decision rights – for instance, giving customer service reps more autonomy because an AI provides real-time recommendations, thus reducing the need for supervisor approval on routine decisions (Bhuvan, 2024). This structural flexibility is part of organizational capability-building: it's not just whether you have AI, but whether your organization can absorb AI into its fabric effectively.

To facilitate this, some companies adopt more agile management practices enterprise-wide. AI development often follows agile methodologies (rapid iterations, prototyping), and extending agile principles to business processes helps sync the organization's cadence with AI innovation. Building capability here might involve training teams in agile project management, establishing short development sprints for AI initiatives, and encouraging a "test and learn" approach (Sharma & Reddy, 2024). One concrete practice is implementing regular cross-functional stand-up meetings for ongoing AI projects, ensuring issues are surfaced quickly and learnings are shared. Organizational capability grows as these practices become routine, making the company more nimble in experimenting with and scaling AI solutions. Indeed, studies of AI-driven organizations often cite adaptability and learning orientation as defining traits – these are capabilities ingrained in processes that allow the firm to pivot or iterate on AI applications as needed (Murire, 2024; Füller et al., 2024).

Another structural aspect of capability is governance structures for AI (tying in with what we discussed in planning). Establishing formal bodies or roles for AI oversight is a capability that needs to be built. This could involve creating an AI governance committee (capability in governance), defining standard operating procedures for AI model validation and monitoring (capability in process control), and delineating responsibility for AI outcomes (capability in accountability). For instance, some organizations are appointing Model Risk Officers or expanding the mandate of risk management teams to cover AI algorithms, thereby ensuring someone is accountable for model performance and compliance over time. By building such governance capacity, the enterprise readies itself to manage AI at scale without letting risks or errors spiral out of control (Böhme & Graf-Pfohl, 2025).

Enterprise AI capability in practice can be illustrated by looking at a company like Microsoft (often referenced for its internal AI transformation). Microsoft has invested heavily in widespread AI training for employees, created cross-functional "AI Studios" to prototype AI ideas with product teams, and established clear principles and committees for responsible AI. The result is an organization where AI innovation is not bottlenecked in one corner; it's infused throughout product development and decision-making, backed by strong guardrails (Elsherif, 2024a). Another real-world example is DBS Bank, which embarked on an AI-focused reskilling program for thousands of its employees and embedded data science capabilities in every business unit, turning the bank into what it calls an "AI-fueled bank." These cases underscore that developing enterprise AI capability is a holistic effort – technology, people, and processes must all advance in concert.

Enterprise AI capability-building is a multifaceted transformation. It strengthens the technical backbone (data and platforms), empowers the people (skills and collaboration), and adapts the organizational mechanics (processes and structure) to thrive with AI. By investing in these capabilities, organizations ensure that AI pilots can evolve into enterprise-wide tools, and novel AI ideas can be operationalized effectively and responsibly. As Weber et al. (2023) observed, organizations that developed comprehensive AI capabilities were better able to cope with AI's challenges – for example, dealing with opaque AI models or integrating AI into legacy workflows – whereas those lacking capabilities often stumbled or stalled. Building capability is not a one-time task but an ongoing endeavor; as AI technologies evolve (say, the rise of generative AI), the enterprise must continually learn and adapt, expanding its skill sets and updating practices (Du et al., 2023). In the next sections, we will discuss how these capabilities are put to use in managing change (4.4), phasing adoption (4.5), and measuring impact (4.6) – all of which rely on the strong foundation of enterprise AI capabilities established through the efforts described here.

4.4 CHANGE MANAGEMENT AND ORGANIZATIONAL ALIGNMENT

No AI initiative exists in a vacuum – it inevitably triggers change in how people work, how decisions are made, and even how the organization defines success. Change management and organizational alignment are thus integral to the strategic implementation of AI. This section focuses on guiding the human and organizational transition that accompanies AI adoption, ensuring that the workforce, culture, and structure all evolve in harmony with the new technology. An oft-cited adage is that AI adoption is "10% technology, 90% people" – while the exact ratio may be debated, the underlying truth is clear: the greatest barriers and enablers of AI often lie in human acceptance, trust, and ability to adapt (Soulami et al., 2024). Effective change management addresses these dimensions head-on, turning potential resistance into engagement and aligning the organization's operating model with its AI-driven strategy.

Anticipating and addressing resistance. When AI systems are introduced, employees may feel threatened or anxious. It is common to encounter fears of job displacement (e.g., "Will this AI replace my role?"), skepticism about the technology's reliability ("Can we trust an algorithm with this decision?"), or general change fatigue if the organization has undergone many recent transformations (Murire, 2024; Soulami et al., 2024). A key task of change management is to surface these concerns early and address them through open communication and involvement strategies. According to Murire's (2024) review on AI's impact on work culture, transparent leadership communication significantly helps in reducing employee resistance and building trust during AI-driven change. Leaders should clearly articulate why the AI is being implemented (tying it to organizational mission and benefits for stakeholders) and how it will impact employees' daily work (Murire, 2024). For example, a hospital implementing an AI diagnostic tool held town hall meetings where executives explained that the AI would assist doctors by providing second opinions on scans, rather than replace doctors. By framing AI as a tool that augments staff capabilities, not a threat, and by being honest about expected changes, they preempted a lot of fear.

Engaging employees in the change process is another powerful technique. Research suggests that involving end-users in AI project development (e.g., through user feedback sessions, pilot user groups, or even co-design workshops) can greatly improve acceptance and alignment (Böhme & Graf-Pfohl, 2025; Sharma & Reddy, 2024). This participatory approach gives employees a sense of ownership and agency – they are not having AI "done to them" but rather are partners in shaping how AI will function in their work context. Böhme and Graf-Pfohl (2025) highlight that a human-centered implementation approach, which actively solicits user input and addresses their concerns (such as interface usability or decision override options), enhances technology acceptance in socio-technical systems. In practice, a company might set up an AI "champions" network: a group of enthusiastic employees from different departments who get early access to the AI system, provide feedback, and later act as mentors to their peers. These champions can become change agents who demonstrate the AI's value to colleagues and help troubleshoot issues, fostering peer-to-peer influence which is often more convincing than top-down mandates.

Aligning with organizational values and culture. Alignment is about ensuring the AI initiative is consistent with the organization's identity and values, and that cultural norms adapt to support the new ways of working. This can be delicate – if an organization prides itself on, say, personalized customer service, introducing an AI chatbot might seem at odds with that value if not handled carefully. Change management efforts should emphasize how AI can be aligned with – or even enhance – core values. For instance, framing the chatbot as a way to offer 24/7 quick answers for routine queries (thereby freeing human agents to provide more personalized attention on complex issues) positions the technology as reinforcing the company's value of responsive service, rather than eroding it. Aligning AI with organizational purpose and values in communications helps garner support from both employees and external stakeholders (Sharma & Reddy, 2024). It's about answering the question: How does this AI help us be a better version of ourselves as an organization? When that answer is clear, people are more likely to rally behind the change.

Culturally, organizations often need to cultivate an innovation mindset and agility to fully realize AI benefits. This might involve shifting norms around decision-making – for example, encouraging data-driven decisions over intuition or seniority, which can be a significant culture change in some organizations. Change management programs frequently include cultural training or interventions, such as workshops on data-driven decision practices, or recognition programs that celebrate teams who successfully use AI insights to improve outcomes (Tomazevic et al., 2024). Leadership plays a crucial role in signaling cultural alignment: when leaders visibly use AI insights in their strategy meetings or publicly praise employees who experiment with AI solutions, it sends a powerful message that "this is how we do things now." Conversely, if leadership pays lip service to AI but continues to operate in old ways, alignment falters and employees receive mixed signals.

Structured change frameworks. Many organizations leverage established change management frameworks (like Kotter's 8-Step model or the ADKAR model) and tailor them to the AI context. While our focus remains on principles rather than specific models, these frameworks provide a disciplined approach: creating urgency; building a coalition of sponsors; communicating the vision; empowering action; generating short-term wins; and anchoring the change. In AI projects, creating urgency might stem from competitive pressure ("Our competitors are using AI to improve customer retention; we risk falling behind") or from a clear pain point ("Our error rates are unsustainably high – AI can help reduce them"). Building a coalition means involving not just IT leaders but business unit heads, influential employees, and perhaps external champions (like a respected consultant or board member advocating for AI). Communication should be continuous and multi-channel: regular updates about AI project progress, success stories of early adopters, Q&A sessions to address rumors or fears, etc. (Sharma & Reddy, 2024). This steady drumbeat keeps everyone informed and engaged, rather than letting uncertainty fester.

Empowering action involves removing obstacles that hinder people from embracing AI. One common obstacle is lack of knowledge – employees may not use a new AI tool simply because they don't understand it. Thus, comprehensive training and support programs are a linchpin of change management in AI initiatives (Sharma & Reddy, 2024; Farid, 2024). These programs might include formal training sessions, on-demand e-learning modules, and on-the-job coaching to ensure that users feel confident using the AI systems. For example, when a large telecommunications firm rolled out an AI-driven customer analytics platform, they implemented an extensive training curriculum for their marketing and sales teams, complete with practical exercises on interpreting AI-generated customer segments and personalizing campaigns accordingly. Additionally, they provided a hotline and "AI helpdesk" for ongoing support. As a result, adoption rates were high and users felt supported, illustrating how addressing capability gaps goes hand in hand with change management.

Generating short-term wins is another critical strategy – especially to convince skeptics and fence-sitters. Early in the AI implementation, identifying and publicizing quick wins helps build credibility for the project (Sharma & Reddy, 2024). These wins could be pilot results (e.g., "In our pilot store, AI-driven inventory management cut stockouts by 30% in three months") or individual success stories ("Sales rep Jane closed 15% more deals last quarter by using the AI pricing recommendation tool"). Celebrating these successes serves a dual purpose: it rewards those who embraced the change and it provides concrete evidence that the AI can deliver value, which can convert doubters into supporters. According to Horani et al. (2025), top management's reinforcement of positive outcomes and continuous support is a determinant in sustaining momentum for technology adoption. Thus, leadership should take every opportunity to acknowledge interim successes attributable to AI and link them to the broader vision.

Maintaining alignment and adjusting course. As AI projects progress and the organization adjusts, it's important to continually monitor the "pulse" of the organization and realign as necessary. Change management doesn't end when the AI system goes live; ongoing alignment might involve periodic surveys of employee sentiment, review meetings to gather feedback from different departments, and iterative improvements to both the technology and how it's integrated into workflows (Sharma & Reddy, 2024). Suppose employees are consistently providing feedback that an AI tool's recommendations are hard to interpret – the organization might need to improve the tool's explainability or provide additional training on interpreting results. Without that feedback loop, frustration could build, undermining adoption. Sharma and Reddy (2024) point out that adaptive change strategies – those that evolve based on feedback – are more effective in maximizing the benefits of AI integration. In practice, this might mean the change management team holds monthly check-ins with each department using the new AI solution and acts on findings (e.g., tweaking a workflow, or clarifying performance metrics that now include AI-driven elements).

Another aspect of alignment is aligning incentives and performance metrics with the new AI-enabled way of working. If, for instance, a company introduces an AI system to prioritize sales leads, but its sales staff are still being evaluated only on total calls made (regardless of lead quality), there's a misalignment that can discourage adoption. Change management must work with HR and leadership to update KPIs and incentives so that they encourage the desired behaviors in using AI. In this example, the metric could shift to the conversion rate of AI-prioritized leads, thereby rewarding effective use of the AI recommendations. Aligning evaluation and reward systems sends a powerful signal that using AI is not just optional tinkering, but an expected part of the job (Horani et al., 2025). Organizations that fail to do this often find employees revert to old habits, especially if old metrics contradict new processes.

Human-centric support during transition. It's worth emphasizing the human side of change management – providing empathy, support, and a sense of security to employees amid the uncertainty AI can bring. Soulami et al. (2024) examine AI's effects on employee well-being and stress, finding that insufficient support can lead to anxiety and resistance. To mitigate this, some companies offer counseling or career coaching to employees worried about job changes, or proactively discuss job redesign and upskilling pathways for those whose tasks will be heavily automated. For example, if an administrative assistant's routine reporting tasks are automated by AI, management should have a plan for enriching that assistant's role with new responsibilities (perhaps coordinating AI outputs, focusing on interpersonal tasks AI can't do, etc.) and communicate that plan clearly to the individual. Showing employees a forward path is crucial – people are more likely to embrace AI when they see how they fit into the future state. A manufacturing firm that introduced assembly line robots exemplified this by guaranteeing no layoffs; instead, they retrained assembly workers as robot maintenance technicians and quality controllers, signaling that the company was investing in them, not discarding them. This greatly reduced fear and fostered a cooperative atmosphere for the change.

In implementing AI, organizations have also found success by leveraging change champions and influencers (Murire, 2024). These are respected employees who endorse the AI initiative and can informally influence their peers. Management can empower these individuals with additional knowledge or access so they can act as go-to resources within their teams. Peer influence can often overcome skepticism more effectively than top-down orders. As described earlier, involving such champions from the pilot phase and then highlighting their positive experiences enterprise-wide can create a ripple effect of acceptance.

Finally, *sustaining the change* is the goal – making AI integration "the new normal" in the organizational DNA. Kotter's framework would call this anchoring the change in the culture. One can say the change is successful when employees no longer talk about "the AI project" as something novel; it simply becomes part of how work gets done. Achieving this often requires reinforcing mechanisms: continuous training (especially for new hires), integrating AI considerations into standard operating procedures, and even physical cues in the workplace (like a dashboard in the office that shows AI-driven metrics, keeping AI visible in daily life). Sharma and Reddy (2024) note that long-term benefits of AI are realized when organizations maintain an adaptable mindset – essentially, when learning and adjusting to technological change becomes second nature. So in a sense, the ultimate aim of change management in AI is to cultivate an organization that is change-agile and aligned, ready not just for this AI but for the next one and the one after that. By carefully managing the transition, aligning with values, and engaging the hearts and minds of people, organizations set the stage for AI to be a positive, accepted, and even celebrated part of their evolution.

4.5 ROADMAPPING AI ADOPTION – PHASES AND PRIORITIES

Implementing AI across an organization is a journey that unfolds in stages rather than a single leap. In this section, we discuss how to create a roadmap for

AI adoption that delineates clear phases and sets priorities, ensuring a structured and scalable rollout. An AI adoption roadmap is essentially a timeline and action plan that answers: What sequence of initiatives will we undertake? How will we scale from pilot projects to enterprise-wide deployment? What are our milestones and checkpoints? Crafting such a roadmap is a strategic exercise that translates the AI vision and strategy (from section 4.2) into an operational plan over time (Elsherif, 2024a). It helps manage resources effectively, learn from early efforts, and build momentum while controlling risks.

Phase 1: Pilot and Experimentation. Most roadmaps begin with a pilot phase, often labeled as a Proof of Concept (PoC) or experimentation phase. In this initial phase, the organization selects one or a few pilot projects – typically those identified as high-impact and feasible – and implements them on a smaller scale or in a controlled environment. The goal here is to test assumptions, demonstrate value, and learn. For example, a retail chain might pilot an AI-driven demand forecasting system in one region or for a subset of products, rather than deploying it chain-wide immediately. By doing so, they can observe how the AI performs, how users interact with it, and what challenges arise (data integration issues, user resistance, etc.) (Elsherif, 2024a). This phase is crucial for generating the short-term wins we discussed in section 4.4 – a successful pilot can be showcased to build wider buy-in (Sharma & Reddy, 2024). It also serves as a laboratory for the AI team to refine the technology. In practice, many pilots undergo several iterations: the first model might not meet accuracy targets, or process tweaks might be needed. Because the scope is limited, these iterations are manageable and do not disrupt the entire business.

During Phase 1, priorities include establishing the basic infrastructure and governance for AI in a limited context. The organization might develop its initial data pipelines, experiment with a cloud ML platform, and start putting in place monitoring for model performance – but focused on the pilot's needs. Key deliverables at the end of Phase 1 often include: a working AI solution for the pilot use case, documented results (e.g., "Pilot improved efficiency by X%"), a list of lessons learned (both technical and organizational), and a refined business case for scaling (Aldoseri et al., 2024). It's also common to establish some foundational capabilities in Phase 1, such as forming the core data science team or drafting the first version of an AI governance policy, which will be expanded in later phases. Crucially, a go/no-go decision point is often built after the pilot: leadership reviews the pilot outcomes to decide whether to proceed to scaling that solution (if it met success criteria), to iterate further, or in some cases to pivot to a different approach if the pilot underperformed badly. This checkpoint instills discipline and ensures that scaling efforts are justified by evidence (Engel et al., 2021).

Phase 2: Initial Scale and Integration. If Phase 1 proves successful (or yields actionable insights), the roadmap typically moves into Phase 2, which involves scaling the AI application to a broader scope and integrating it with existing processes. This could mean rolling out the AI solution to additional business units, geographic regions, or product lines. For instance, following a successful regional pilot, our retail chain may deploy the AI forecasting system to all regions in the country. In Phase 2, the emphasis is on integration – making the AI system part of the standard workflow rather than a side experiment. This might involve integrating the system with enterprise software (like Enterprise Resource Planning (ERP) systems or Customer Relationship Management (CRM) platforms), training a wider group of end-users, and adapting business processes to incorporate the AI's outputs (Weber et al., 2023).

An important aspect of Phase 2 is also addressing the scalability issues that might not have been apparent in the pilot. Performance bottlenecks, data volume challenges, or new user requirements often emerge when expanding from a small pilot to full operations (Srivastava & Dixit, 2023). For example, the data pipeline that worked fine for one region's data may need redesigning to handle nationwide data in real time. The roadmap should allocate time and resources in Phase 2 to reinforce infrastructure and optimize algorithms for production scale. Organizations might invest in more robust cloud resources, implement MLOps practices for continuous deployment of model updates, and strengthen data engineering pipelines now that the solution is going enterprise-wide.

Phase 3: Wide-scale Adoption and Maturity. In later phases of the roadmap (Phase 3 and beyond), the goal is to embed AI deeply into the organization and achieve a level of maturity where AI is routinely used across various functions. By this phase, multiple AI initiatives are likely running in parallel across different domains (e.g., supply chain optimization, customer personalization, HR analytics), and the focus shifts to optimization, governance, and innovation. Priorities include optimizing the performance of AI systems, ensuring they remain aligned with business goals, and governing them effectively across the enterprise (Böhme & Graf-Pfohl, 2025).

For instance, at maturity, a company may establish an enterprise AI platform that all business units leverage, with common tools, data repositories, and governance standards. The roadmap would have anticipated this by Phase 3: consolidating disparate AI efforts into a more centralized or harmonized ecosystem. At this stage, organizations often formalize structures such as the AI Center of Excellence (if not already done), and fully operationalize policies for model life cycle management, ethical compliance reviews, and regular ROI measurement for AI projects (Rakova et al., 2020; Horani et al., 2025). In essence, AI adoption becomes part of the organizational rhythm – for example, annual strategic planning includes identifying new AI opportunities, and budgeting processes account for AI investments and maintenance.

A hallmark of reaching maturity in the roadmap is that continuous improvement mechanisms are in place (Elsherif, 2024a). AI systems are monitored and updated regularly to adapt to changing data or business conditions (as part of MLOps). There is also a pipeline of innovation – perhaps a standing AI innovation team or incubator that constantly prototypes new AI ideas for the business (Farid, 2024). This means the roadmap is not finite; by Phase 3 the organization has the structures to perpetually find and implement new AI solutions, essentially making the roadmap an evolving one that extends as the organization grows.

Throughout these phases, the roadmap must set priorities, especially when an organization has multiple potential AI projects vying for attention. A common approach to prioritization is to evaluate projects on two dimensions: expected business value (impact) and implementation complexity (or risk). Projects that are high value and low-to-moderate complexity typically get scheduled earlier in the roadmap, delivering quick wins and ROI (Horani et al., 2025). More complex or experimental projects might be slotted for later phases, perhaps after some foundational capabilities are built. The roadmap should also consider dependencies between projects: some AI initiatives may require others to be in place first. For example, you might prioritize building a customer data platform (AI-ready data infrastructure) in Phase 1, and only in Phase 2 attempt an AI-driven customer churn model that needs that integrated data. Dependencies could also be talent-related; perhaps the company decides that before attempting a cutting-edge AI research project, it needs to hire a PhD-level AI researcher by Phase 2. By mapping these dependencies and staging projects accordingly, the roadmap ensures that each phase lays the groundwork for the next.

Flexibility in the roadmap. While a roadmap provides structure, it's important to keep it flexible and iterative. Unexpected findings from pilots, shifts in business strategy, or new technological breakthroughs (like an emerging AI technique) may prompt adjustments. Effective roadmaps include review points, perhaps at the end of each phase, where the organization reassesses and can reprioritize or add new projects (Sharma & Reddy, 2024). For instance, if a competitor suddenly launches a successful AI-driven service, the company might accelerate a related AI project in its own roadmap to respond, even if that project was initially planned for a later phase. The roadmap is thus a living document. One bank's AI roadmap committee meets quarterly to review progress and make tactical adjustments, treating the roadmap not as a rigid plan but as a rolling wave that extends and adapts – this agility has been cited as key to keeping their AI program relevant and value-focused.

To illustrate a simple roadmap, consider a manufacturing firm's three-year AI adoption plan:

- Phase 1 (Year 1) – Pilots: Implement an AI predictive maintenance pilot on ten factory machines (targeting reduction in downtime). Simultaneously,

pilot an AI quality inspection system in one production line. Build initial data pipeline from machine sensors to cloud. Success criteria: 10% downtime reduction in pilot, >90% defect detection accuracy. Deliverables: Working models, trained local engineers, documented learnings.
- Phase 2 (Year 2) – Scale-up: Roll out predictive maintenance AI to all factories (1,000+ machines). Integrate AI quality inspection into 50% of production lines across plants, retraining staff to work with AI alerts. Expand data architecture for enterprise-wide IoT data handling. Establish AI governance committee to oversee model performance and safety. Milestones: Reduce downtime by 15% company-wide, scrap rate down by 20% where AI inspection is active. Begin formal training for maintenance staff on interpreting AI predictions.
- Phase 3 (Year 3) – Enterprise Integration: Integrate AI insights into maintenance scheduling and inventory ordering systems (AI fully embedded into maintenance workflow). Achieve full coverage of AI quality inspection in all production lines. Continuously improve models based on feedback. Begin exploring new AI projects (e.g., supply chain optimization) using the now-mature data infrastructure. Metrics: Downtime reduced 25%, quality defects reduced 30% across the board, maintenance costs down due to better predictive scheduling. Structures: AI Center of Excellence in place to support all plants, AI results discussed in quarterly operational reviews as a standard practice.

This hypothetical roadmap shows a logical progression with clear phase goals and how priorities (maintenance first, then quality, then expansion to supply chain) are set. It also reflects learning and expansion – early wins in maintenance justify and fund broader rollout, and the organization's capability grows with each phase.

Research and case experiences underline that roadmapping like this helps in managing change gradually and avoiding the chaos of trying to "boil the ocean" all at once (Elsherif, 2024a). It also builds organizational confidence: each phase's success creates trust in AI and skill in handling it, which feeds into the next phase (Farid, 2024). Additionally, a phased approach allows for resource allocation over time, which is practical – capital and human resources can be distributed so as not to overload the organization at any single point. Horani et al. (2025) note that resource alignment is a critical determinant of adoption; a roadmap helps align budget and talent with each step, ensuring, for example, that you hire data engineers in Phase 1 and customer-facing data analysts in Phase 3 when their work becomes relevant.

Finally, the roadmap fosters accountability. With explicit milestones and owners for each phase, progress can be tracked and teams held accountable for delivering. It is much easier to govern an AI transformation when you have a visual map of where you are and what's next, as opposed to a nebulous goal of "implement AI" with no intermediate checkpoints. Many organizations use the roadmap as a communication tool as well, sharing it internally (and sometimes externally) to signal their commitment and plan. This transparency can further bolster stakeholder support: employees see the big picture of the transformation and understand the timing, which reduces uncertainty and speculation (Elsherif, 2024a).

In conclusion, roadmapping AI adoption with phased priorities ensures a deliberate, learning-oriented expansion of AI in the organization. It brings order to what could otherwise be a haphazard set of tech experiments, aligning them with strategic timing and readiness. By moving through pilots, initial scaling, and full integration, the organization can build on successes, manage risks, and gradually cultivate an AI-enabled enterprise. The roadmap is both a strategic compass and a pragmatic project plan, guiding the organization step by step toward AI maturity. As the organization follows this path, the next concern becomes evaluating whether these efforts are paying off – which leads us to the critical topic of measuring AI's return on investment and strategic impact in section 4.6.

4.6 MEASURING AI ROI AND STRATEGIC IMPACT

As organizations implement AI solutions, a fundamental question arises: Is AI delivering real value commensurate with its costs and efforts? Measuring the return on investment (ROI) and broader strategic impact of AI initiatives is essential for validating the business case of AI and for continuous improvement. Unlike traditional IT projects, AI initiatives can have complex, multifaceted benefits (and costs), some of which are tangible and immediate, and others that are intangible or realized over longer horizons (Engel et al., 2021). In this section, we outline approaches to assess AI's financial and strategic returns, the metrics used, and how organizations incorporate these measurements into their management processes.

Defining success metrics for AI projects. The first step in measuring ROI is to define clear success criteria for each AI project from the outset. This means identifying key performance indicators (KPIs) that the AI is expected to influence. For example, if the AI initiative is a chatbot for customer service, relevant KPIs might include average response time, customer satisfaction score, and the percentage of inquiries resolved without human agent involvement (Elsherif, 2024a). If it's a predictive maintenance AI in manufacturing, KPIs could be equipment downtime, maintenance costs, and perhaps safety incident rates. Tying AI projects to such domain-specific metrics ensures that evaluation is grounded in business outcomes, not just technical performance (Sharma & Reddy, 2024). It is common to also track AI-specific performance metrics like model accuracy or prediction precision; however, these technical metrics are typically secondary to the business KPIs in an ROI context. They matter insofar as they correlate with business outcomes (e.g., higher prediction accuracy might reduce downtime more), but on their own they don't tell the business value story.

Once KPIs are set, organizations measure baseline values (before AI implementation) and then track changes after AI deployment. ROI in the narrow financial sense can be calculated by quantifying the benefits (e.g., cost savings, revenue increases) and comparing against the costs of the AI project (development, infrastructure, training, etc.). For instance, an AI that automates invoice processing might reduce labor costs by $X and errors by $Y (which has an implied cost), and if the project cost was $Z, the ROI can be estimated as ($X + $Y – $Z) / $Z over a certain period. Many companies aim for a certain ROI threshold (like a project should pay back its cost within two years through savings or added profits). However, focusing solely on immediate cost savings can be short-sighted; AI projects often have strategic benefits that are harder to quantify in the short term (Weber et al., 2023). For example, improving decision quality or customer experience might not immediately show up as dollars saved or earned, but they contribute to competitive advantage and risk reduction. Therefore, a comprehensive evaluation of AI impact includes both quantitative ROI and qualitative benefits aligned with strategy.

Balanced scorecard approach. One way to capture AI's strategic impact is to embed it in a balanced scorecard or similar multidimensional performance framework (Elsherif, 2024a). A balanced scorecard for AI might incorporate financial metrics (cost savings, revenue growth attributable to AI), customer metrics (customer satisfaction, NPS improvements due to AI-enabled services), internal process metrics (speed, efficiency gains, error rate reductions), and learning and growth metrics (employee adoption rates, AI competency levels, innovation rates). For example, a bank that introduced AI in its fraud detection might see a financial impact in terms of fraud losses reduced (a direct cost saving), a customer impact in terms of increased trust or fewer false fraud alerts bothering customers, an internal process impact in terms of faster fraud resolution times, and a learning impact as its fraud analysts learn to collaborate with AI and focus on more complex cases (Rakova et al., 2020). By evaluating across these dimensions, the bank gains a holistic view of AI's value beyond just the bottom line. This approach aligns with the insight that AI often creates value in forms like improved decision quality or agility, which eventually translate to financial outcomes but deserve recognition in their own right (Sharma & Reddy, 2024).

Hard ROI vs. soft benefits. Hard ROI refers to direct monetary benefits – cost reductions (through automation or efficiency) and revenue increases (through better targeting, new products, increased capacity, etc.). These are typically the easiest to measure. For instance, if an AI system automates a task that used to require five full-time employees, and those employees are redeployed or not replaced, the labor cost saving is a hard benefit. Similarly, if an AI recommendation engine leads to a 10% increase in e-commerce upselling, the additional revenue generated can be calculated. Organizations should track these changes meticulously, often using A/B testing or pilot vs. control group comparisons to attribute the impact properly to the AI (Horani et al., 2025). For example, an online retailer might expose half of its customers to AI-personalized recommendations and the other half to generic recommendations, and then measure the difference in average order value – this isolates the AI's effect, giving confidence in the ROI analysis.

Soft benefits, on the other hand, include things like improved customer experience, faster decision-making, or enhanced innovation capability. These can be just as important strategically, yet quantifying them is challenging. Some can be indirectly measured (e.g., improved customer experience might reflect in higher retention rates or satisfaction surveys, which in turn have financial implications down the road). Others might be gauged qualitatively or through proxy measures – for instance, strategic agility gained from AI could be evidenced by the organization's speed in launching new products or its ability to respond to market changes, though tying a dollar value to that is complex. When presenting the impact of AI to stakeholders, many organizations will combine hard ROI calculations with narrative and qualitative evidence of soft benefits. A report to the executive team might note: "Our AI-driven supply chain system saved approximately $2 million in inventory holding costs this year (hard ROI). Moreover, it enabled us to respond to demand spikes in half the time, preventing stockouts and strengthening our brand reliability (strategic benefit)," citing perhaps that stockout incidents fell by 40% and customer fill rates improved (quantifiable proxies for the strategic benefit).

Continuous monitoring and feedback loops. Measuring AI ROI is not a one-time event post-implementation; it should be a continuous process. AI systems often improve over time (with model retraining, fine-tuning, or new data) and their business context might also change. Continuous monitoring of performance metrics allows organizations to maintain or increase ROI. For instance, an AI might start with a certain accuracy and bring in savings, but if data drift occurs and accuracy drops, the savings might erode. Monitoring would catch that trend so the model can be refreshed or fixed, keeping benefits on track (Weber et al., 2023).

Additionally, continuous monitoring can feed a continuous improvement cycle, where insights from measurement are used to tweak processes around the AI. Say a company finds that an AI scheduling system is underutilized by managers (perhaps they override its suggestions frequently). Usage metrics and outcome metrics (like how often overrides lead to better/worse results) can inform whether additional training is needed or the AI's recommendations should be adjusted to align better with human intuition. Implementing such feedback not only boosts the system's effectiveness (and thereby ROI) but also can improve user satisfaction with the AI tool (Böhme & Graf-Pfohl, 2025).

Organizations should also account for the cost side in an ongoing manner. AI solutions entail ongoing costs: cloud compute fees, software licenses, maintenance of data pipelines, and the labor of data science teams. Especially as AI deployments scale, these costs can grow (e.g., running a large language model might be computationally expensive). An ROI calculation should ideally include these operational expenses over time, not just the initial development cost. Some companies set up dashboards that show, for each AI service, its utilization, benefits delivered (in business terms), and costs incurred, effectively treating each AI model like a product with its own P&L (Elsherif, 2024a). This level of visibility helps in decision-making about whether to continue, scale, or retire AI systems. If an AI model is not pulling its weight – say its maintenance cost is high but its accuracy plateaued and benefits are mediocre – the company might decide to retrench or redirect efforts to a more promising AI application.

Enterprise-level impact and strategic alignment. Beyond individual project ROI, senior leadership often wants to know, what is the overall impact of AI on our organization's performance and competitive position? This speaks to strategic impact. At the enterprise level, one might examine indicators such as the organization's market share trend, innovation rate, cost-to-income ratio, or customer base growth and see how AI initiatives contributed to those macro indicators. For example, if AI-enabled processes have significantly lowered the company's cost structure, you might see the evidence in improved profit margins compared to competitors. Alternatively, AI-driven product innovations might lead to capturing new markets, reflected in revenue from new products launched in the last year. Pinpointing AI's role in these big-picture outcomes can be tricky because many factors are at play, but case studies and analyses can help isolate AI's contribution. Tomazevic et al. (2024) note that organizations often perform internal post-mortems or case analyses on major AI deployments, not only to measure results but also to capture lessons learned for strategy. These analyses could involve stakeholder interviews, surveys, and data analysis to understand how AI changed things like decision quality or agility in practice.

An example of strategic impact measurement is looking at how AI adoption correlates with the achievement of strategic goals such as improving customer centricity or operational excellence. If a strategic goal was to reduce the time from customer order to delivery by 50%, and the company implemented several AI systems (in demand forecasting, route optimization, etc.) toward that end, one can measure the time reduction achieved and qualitatively assess AI's role (likely significant, if those systems were key enablers). Another aspect is risk mitigation: AI can sometimes help avoid costly risks (e.g., detecting fraud or compliance issues). While "avoided costs" don't show up directly in profit, they are crucial; one might measure how many fraud attempts were blocked by AI and estimate losses prevented.

Stakeholder perceptions. Strategic impact is also measured by stakeholder perceptions: employee engagement, customer trust, and even investor confidence can be influenced by how well the company harnesses AI. Soulami et al. (2024) highlight that poorly managed AI adoption can hurt employee morale, whereas well-managed adoption (with supportive strategies) can improve it. Thus, including employee engagement metrics or retention rates in the evaluation could reveal if AI-led changes are broadly accepted or causing friction. Similarly, customer surveys might show improved satisfaction or loyalty if, for instance, AI enables more personalized and responsive service (e.g., "since the launch of the AI-powered mobile app feature, customer satisfaction with our digital experience has increased from 80% to 90%"). These intangibles eventually translate to financial outcomes (loyal customers contribute more revenue), but tracking them provides early indications of strategic benefits.

Feedback to strategy and course correction. Measuring ROI and impact is not only about accountability but also about learning and adjusting strategy. If certain AI projects are consistently yielding high returns, that might signal to the company to double down on investment in those areas or related opportunities. Conversely, if expected benefits are not materializing, it may prompt a strategic pivot or re-prioritization (Horani et al., 2025). For example, a telecom might find that AI in network optimization gives huge cost savings (high ROI), whereas an AI for customer churn prediction didn't significantly reduce churn because of execution issues in follow-up actions. This insight could lead the company to focus more on network operations AI (where it has capability and success) in the near term, while reworking the approach to customer AI or scheduling it for a later time once it figures out the operational fix.

Furthermore, transparent ROI tracking helps maintain leadership and stakeholder support for the AI program. As Rakova et al. (2020) discuss, one enabler for organizational practice shift is showing tangible results. Regularly reporting AI performance builds credibility and can secure funding for subsequent phases. Many organizations create an AI or digital transformation dashboard accessible to top management, keeping AI's contribution visible (Elsherif, 2024a). One large bank's CIO, for instance, receives a weekly report summarizing metrics like the number of processes automated this week, hours saved, estimated cost savings, and any notable incidents or errors caught by AI – keeping the pulse on the AI program's impact.

Measuring AI ROI and strategic impact is about linking AI initiatives to business value in a rigorous yet holistic way. It entails setting the right metrics, collecting data before and after, and interpreting results in the context of both financial returns and broader organizational goals. Quantitative ROI analyses demonstrate the economic rationale for AI, while assessments of strategic impact capture how AI is strengthening the company's competitive position, agility, and stakeholder satisfaction. The combination of these measurements ensures that AI implementation is not just technology deployment, but true value realization. As with any strategic initiative, what gets measured gets managed – by keeping a close eye on outcomes, organizations can celebrate AI successes, learn from shortcomings, and continuously steer their AI endeavors toward maximum benefit. This evaluative discipline will also inform how they tackle obstacles and scale up further, which leads into our final section on overcoming barriers and driving scalable adoption.

4.7 OVERCOMING BARRIERS AND DRIVING SCALABLE ADOPTION

Implementing AI at scale in an organization is a complex undertaking, and it's common to encounter a variety of barriers along the way. In this concluding section, we discuss common obstacles to AI adoption and strategies to overcome them, thereby enabling the organization to move from isolated successes to scalable, enterprise-wide AI adoption. Barriers can be technical, organizational, cultural, or even external (like regulatory). The ability to surmount these barriers often distinguishes organizations that achieve transformational impact with AI from those that get stuck in pilot purgatory or patchy implementations (Horani et al., 2025; Tomazevic et al., 2024). Moreover, scaling adoption means ensuring that AI solutions are not one-off experiments but integrated, sustainable parts of the business that can be expanded and replicated where appropriate.

Barrier 1: Lack of trust and user acceptance. One of the most pervasive hurdles is building trust in AI systems among employees, managers, and even customers. People may doubt the AI's recommendations, especially if the system is not transparent (the "black box" problem) or if it challenges traditional ways of decision-making (Böhme & Graf-Pfohl, 2025; Weber et al., 2023). For example, a sales team might resist using an AI lead-scoring tool if they don't understand how it ranks prospects, preferring to rely on their intuition and experience. Similarly, a doctor might be hesitant to follow a diagnosis suggestion from an AI without a clear explanation. To overcome this, organizations should prioritize explainability and transparency in AI systems where possible (Tavantzis & Feldt, 2024). Techniques such as providing interpretable outputs (reasons or contributing factors behind an AI decision) and incorporating visualization or natural language explanations can bridge the trust gap. Training also plays a role – once users learn more about how the AI works and see it perform over time, their confidence tends to increase (Böhme & Graf-Pfohl, 2025). Involving users early in development (as mentioned in section 4.4) helps because they can voice what they'd need to trust the system. For instance, if loan officers say they'd trust an AI credit scoring model more if it highlighted which factors (income, credit history, etc.) most influenced a recommendation, developers can include that feature. Another trust-building approach is to maintain human-in-the-loop controls especially during the scaling phase. Instead of mandating full automation, organizations can allow users to review and override AI outputs initially. Over time, as the AI proves itself accurate and users grow comfortable, the need for overrides might diminish (Jain et al., 2022). This graduated approach helps humans feel they haven't lost control and can bolster trust through experience – essentially, the AI earns trust by demonstrating consistent value while users have safety nets. Metrics like override rates and user feedback can indicate when trust is improving (Tavantzis & Feldt, 2024). An example is a procurement department that introduced an AI for flagging anomalous supplier invoices (potential fraud or errors). Initially, every AI flag was manually reviewed by staff (100% human-in-the-loop). As they found that, say, 95% of those flags were legitimate issues, they gradually came to trust the AI; eventually, they let the system automatically block flagrantly bad invoices and only manually review borderline cases. This scaled up efficiency while retaining human judgment in cases where the AI was less certain, thus balancing trust and control.

Barrier 2: Data issues – quality, silos, and availability. Scaling AI often hits a wall due to data problems. A model that worked in a pilot might flounder when expanded if the required data isn't available enterprise-wide or is inconsistent across units (Weber et al., 2023). Many organizations grapple with siloed databases, where different departments have their own data systems that are not integrated. Overcoming this barrier requires concerted data strategy efforts: investing in data integration, cleaning, and governance, as discussed in section 4.3. Tactically, data engineering projects may need to run in parallel with AI scaling. For example, to scale an AI personalization engine from one product line to the whole company, the organization might have to consolidate customer data from separate CRMs and marketing platforms into a unified data lake (Aldoseri et al., 2024). This can be time-consuming and may not have the glamor of the AI itself, but it's foundational. Leadership must recognize and support these "plumbing" projects, framing them as enablers for AI success. Data quality is another frequent barrier: missing data, errors, or biased data can all derail an AI. Overcoming this involves establishing data quality monitoring and improvement processes. Many organizations implement automated checks and alerts for anomalies in input data feeding AI systems (Horani et al., 2025). If quality issues are systemic (say manual data entry errors in a CRM affecting all downstream analytics), root-cause solutions are needed – like improving the interface to reduce errors or training staff on proper data entry. In scaling adoption, some companies create specialized data stewardship roles responsible for continuously auditing and improving key data assets. A public sector case discussed by Tomazevic et al. (2024) showed that having clear accountability for data (like a Chief Data Officer and data stewards) was an enabler for AI projects in government institutions, which often suffer silo and quality issues.

Barrier 3: Talent and expertise gaps. As AI deployment scales, the initial AI team might become a bottleneck if the demand for AI projects outstrips capacity. Moreover, maintaining multiple AI systems requires a mix of skills (data scientists, ML engineers, DevOps, etc.). If an organization doesn't grow its talent base, it may struggle to support and enhance AI solutions company-wide (Du et al., 2023). Overcoming this barrier has a few dimensions. First is hiring and partnering: hiring more experts, but also leveraging external partners or vendors when needed. Some firms at the scaling stage partner with AI vendors for specific solutions to reduce the internal burden, at least temporarily, while they ramp up internal skills. Second is upskilling non-AI personnel to take on quasi-AI roles. For example, training business analysts in basic machine learning can create a layer of "citizen data scientists" who can handle simpler modeling tasks or serve as liaisons between business units and the core AI team (Farid, 2024). This democratization of AI skills not only increases capacity but fosters a culture of AI fluency across the organization. An interesting practice to address talent shortage is to use centers of excellence and mentoring. The expert data scientists in the CoE can mentor tech-savvy individuals in various departments, accelerating their learning and enabling those departments to handle local AI tweaks or first-level support. Also, cross-training IT staff (who might be experts in software engineering but not AI) in machine learning operations helps to expand the pool of people who can deploy and monitor models (Weber et al., 2023). Organizations might also invest in external training programs or certifications for employees to deepen the talent bench. Some have instituted rotational programs where promising employees from different backgrounds rotate through the AI team for a stint to build expertise, then return to their home department with new skills – seeding AI knowledge throughout the enterprise.

Barrier 4: Organizational inertia and siloed mindsets. Beyond individual resistance, there can be institutional resistance – departments protecting turf, "not invented here" syndrome for solutions coming from outside their group, or simply complacency in processes that have worked historically. Large organizations might have bureaucratic processes that slow down AI implementation or a risk-averse culture that balks at the uncertainty inherent in AI projects (Murire, 2024). Overcoming such inertia often requires change management at the leadership and structural level. Strong executive sponsorship can help break silos: when the CEO or top team clearly makes AI a priority and sets expectations of collaboration, middle managers are more likely to fall in line (Sharma & Reddy, 2024). Some companies set up cross-functional governance for AI, such as an AI steering committee with leaders from multiple divisions, to ensure alignment and break through departmental barriers. This committee can mediate resource sharing (e.g., encouraging one department with success in AI to share best practices and even code with another). Another tactic is to realign incentives. If each department is only rewarded for its own P&L, they may resist cross-department AI that benefits the whole but might inconvenience them or shift budget allocations. Realigning KPIs to include enterprise metrics (like overall efficiency or customer satisfaction) can encourage a more collaborative stance (Horani et al., 2025). For example, if an AI system requires Sales and Operations to share data and coordinate closely, but historically they operated in silos, the company might introduce a joint KPI (like "end-to-end order fulfillment time") that both departments are accountable for. This creates a mutual incentive to cooperate on the AI-driven process that improves that metric.

Barrier 5: Ethical, regulatory, and social concerns. As AI projects grow in scope (especially those affecting customers or public outcomes), concerns about bias, fairness, and compliance can become barriers if not proactively handled. A project could be slowed or halted by legal and compliance reviews, or by public pushback if an AI decision is seen as unfair (Rakova et al., 2020). To overcome this, organizations must bake ethical risk assessments and compliance checks into the AI development life cycle (Rakova et al., 2020; Sharma & Reddy, 2024). This might involve creating bias testing protocols for AI models (e.g., checking model decisions across different demographic groups), maintaining documentation for model decisions to satisfy regulatory audits, and staying updated on AI-related regulations in their industry (which are quickly evolving). For example, a credit lender scaling up an AI underwriting system will need to ensure the model doesn't inadvertently discriminate – implementing bias mitigation techniques and getting legal sign-off before full deployment is part of overcoming this barrier. Openness and stakeholder engagement are also key. Some companies choose to be transparent with users about AI use – for instance, informing customers that an AI is involved in decision-making and providing recourse (like a human review process) if needed. Far from undermining trust, such transparency can build it by showing the company is conscientious. Over time, demonstrating a track record of responsible AI usage can ease internal and external concerns, thus smoothing the path for further adoption (Böhme & Graf-Pfohl, 2025). Driving scalable adoption refers not just to removing barriers, but actively enabling and accelerating the spread of AI throughout the organization. One effective driver is the creation of an AI knowledge-sharing platform or community of practice.

When teams can easily share their AI project experiences, code repositories, and lessons learned, duplication of effort is reduced and late adopters benefit from early adopters' insights (Tomazevic et al., 2024). For example, an internal AI wiki or regular "AI demo days" can highlight what different parts of the company are doing, inspiring others and providing practical guidance. Such cross-pollination can turn isolated wins into company-wide wins. Scaling adoption also benefits from modularizing AI solutions – building some AI components as reusable services that multiple business units can tap into. If the first implementation of, say, an NLP text analytics tool is done in Customer Service for analyzing feedback, the IT/AI team could package that as a service. Then other departments (e.g., HR analyzing employee surveys, or R&D analyzing research papers) can reuse the service for their text analytics needs with minimal extra development. This reuse accelerates adoption because units don't have to reinvent the wheel; it leverages the initial success broadly (Weber et al., 2023). To truly drive adoption at scale, organizations often need to institutionalize AI into the business processes. That means updating standard operating procedures, training new employees on AI tools as part of onboarding, and including AI initiatives in annual business plans. When each department's strategy plan includes AI opportunities and projects – reviewed just like any other key project – it signals that AI is part of the normal course of business. At this point, the company has moved beyond "experimenting with AI" to "operating with AI" as a default. Achieving this state is an indicator that the barriers have been largely overcome and the organization is proficient at integrating AI (Tomazevic et al., 2024; Westover, 2025). Finally, it's important to maintain momentum. Overcoming initial barriers is great, but organizations must avoid plateauing. Regularly revisiting the AI strategy (as mentioned earlier) and scanning for new tech developments or new internal needs keeps the adoption curve moving upward. Leadership can set progressive targets – for instance, "Within 2 years, 50% of customer interactions to be augmented by AI in some form" – to push continued scaling. They should also continue addressing new barriers that might emerge at later stages, like managing the complexity of many AI systems (e.g., which could be tackled by investing in a centralized monitoring platform). In essence, driving scalable adoption is an ongoing leadership task of removing friction and encouraging propulsion of AI usage. Overcoming barriers and scaling AI adoption require both removing impediments and actively fostering enablers. Through trust-building, robust data practices, talent development, cultural and structural alignment, and responsible governance, organizations can convert initial AI wins into a broad transformation. The journey is seldom linear – each barrier might require targeted interventions – but the collective outcome is an organization that can deploy AI in multiple areas effectively and sustainably. As research and practical experiences show, those who navigate these challenges successfully are often the ones who achieve significant competitive advantages from AI, turning it from a buzzword into a deeply ingrained capability of the enterprise (Horani et al., 2025; Sharma & Reddy, 2024). With the barriers addressed and adoption scaled, the organization is positioned to continuously leverage AI for innovation and improvement, fulfilling the strategic promise outlined at the beginning of this chapter.

5. Organizational culture and change management in the AI era

5.1 CULTURAL BARRIERS AND CATALYSTS FOR AI ADOPTION

Organizational culture can significantly impede or accelerate the adoption of artificial intelligence in the workplace. A prevalent barrier is resistance to change rooted in fear – many employees worry that AI-driven automation will render their roles obsolete, leading to job insecurity and anxiety. Such fears of displacement often manifest as pushback against new AI tools or reluctance to fully engage with them. Leadership attitudes can either exacerbate or mitigate this resistance. When top managers are skeptical of AI's benefits or fail to champion its use, their hesitation signals to the rest of the organization that AI is not truly valued, undermining adoption efforts (Zaidi et al., 2025). Conversely, active leadership advocacy – where leaders visibly support AI initiatives and frame them as opportunities rather than threats – can be a powerful catalyst for cultural change. Research indicates that organizations with leaders who communicate a clear vision for AI and emphasize augmentation (using AI to enhance human work) over pure automation tend to cultivate more positive employee mindsets toward AI (Hossain et al., 2025c; Mohan, 2024). In such environments, employees are more likely to see AI as a tool that empowers them rather than replaces them, which reduces change resistance and fosters openness to experimentation.

Another cultural barrier is the presence of organizational silos and lack of collaboration across departments. AI implementation often requires interdisciplinary cooperation – data scientists, IT specialists, and business domain experts must work together. In rigid, siloed cultures where departments operate in isolation, these collaborations falter, impeding AI projects (Budianto et al., 2025). A case analysis of government AI initiatives found that cross-functional teamwork and open communication were critical success factors for making AI "work" in practice. Thus, a culture that encourages knowledge sharing and breaks down silos serves as a catalyst for AI adoption. For example, knowledge-sharing cultures – where employees regularly exchange ideas and learn from each other – can significantly improve AI readiness. One study demonstrated that paradoxical leadership (leaders who can be both directive and flexible) combined with a technophilic attitude (enthusiasm for new technology) led to higher employee knowledge sharing when AI was introduced. In other words, when leaders foster an environment of open learning and simultaneously address employees' concerns, workers become more willing to share insights about AI tools and integrate them into their routines (Hu et al., 2025).

Trust and transparency are additional cultural elements that influence AI uptake. If the workforce perceives AI systems as "black boxes" or inherently unfair, mistrust can become a major hurdle (Zhang et al., 2024). Employees need to trust that AI will make decisions in a just and unbiased manner; otherwise, they may resist using AI outputs or even sabotage AI implementations. Studies on e-government adoption show that explainable machine learning systems can enhance user trust and rational acceptance of AI recommendations. By extension, in a corporate setting, a culture of transparency – where the functioning and purpose of AI are clearly communicated – can assuage fears. Companies that proactively educate employees about how an AI tool works, what data it uses, and how decisions are made tend to see higher trust in those systems (Salem et al., 2024). This transparency must be coupled with ethical safeguards; employees are more receptive to AI when they believe leadership is addressing ethical issues like bias and privacy (Kandasamy, 2024; Wang & Pashmforoosh, 2024). For example, if an organization openly discusses how it is preventing AI bias or how human oversight is maintained, it demonstrates a values-driven approach that aligns AI adoption with core cultural values of fairness and accountability.

Importantly, organizations that have an AI-ready culture and mindset gain a head start in adoption. An AI-ready culture is one characterized by agility, curiosity, and a forward-looking orientation – employees and leaders continuously seek innovative solutions and are comfortable adapting to new technologies. Such a mindset doesn't emerge overnight; it is cultivated through deliberate change efforts. Companies often identify and empower change champions or influencers within teams who can model positive use of AI and mentor their peers (Elsherif, 2024a). These champions help normalize AI by demonstrating small wins and practical benefits, turning abstract technology into relatable improvements in day-to-day work. Research-based frameworks for AI implementation emphasize the role of these internal champions in overcoming cultural inertia (Serikbay & Abdykhalykov, 2024b). In Kazakhstan's project management context, for instance, adaptive leadership strategies included appointing team members to advocate for AI tools, which significantly reduced resistance among colleagues by providing trusted, culture-fit messengers for the change. Alongside champions, providing avenues for employee voice – such as forums to express concerns and feedback about

AI – can convert skeptics into participants in the change process, thereby shifting mindsets over time.

Finally, successful culture change for AI adoption often involves aligning the new technology with the organization's core values and purpose. Employees need to see how AI supports the mission of the company and their own professional growth. When AI initiatives are framed as part of the organization's evolution (rather than an imposed foreign element), employees are more likely to internalize the change. Studies have shown that inclusive and innovative cultures tend to experience more seamless AI integration because their values already promote adaptation and learning (Portillo, 2025c; Nyoto et al., 2024b). In fact, a global rapid review noted that organizations embracing AI often report improvements not just in performance metrics but also in workforce engagement and innovation – suggesting that an AI-positive culture can become self-reinforcing as employees witness positive outcomes. By celebrating quick wins and sharing success stories where AI augmented human capabilities, leaders can reinforce a narrative that resonates with the company's identity (Brillianto et al., 2024). Over time, the employee mindset shifts toward AI as people observe that the technology helps them work smarter, not harder, and that management is committed to investing in their development alongside AI. In summary, tackling cultural barriers to AI requires empathetic leadership and a proactive strategy to turn fears into curiosity, and uncertainty into shared learning. With strong cultural catalysts – trust, transparency, leadership advocacy, and an inclusive mindset – organizations can transform AI from a source of resistance into a source of strategic empowerment.

5.2 CHANGE MANAGEMENT FRAMEWORKS FOR AI IMPLEMENTATION

Implementing AI at scale is not a trivial technical upgrade – it is a transformational change that demands structured change management. Organizations have found value in applying classic change management frameworks (like Kotter's 8-Step model or the ADKAR model) tailored to the digital context of AI projects. These frameworks provide a roadmap to guide employees through the transition and ensure that the human side of AI adoption is addressed systematically. For example, Kotter's model, which calls for steps such as establishing urgency, forming a guiding coalition, and consolidating gains, can be reinterpreted for AI: leaders first communicate a compelling need for AI (urgency), assemble a cross-functional AI leadership team (coalition), and secure short-term wins with pilot AI projects before scaling up. In practice, many companies start with pilot programs or proof-of-concept implementations of AI to demonstrate value quickly and create momentum for broader change (Elsherif, 2024a). These early wins help convince stakeholders of AI's benefits, addressing the inertia or skepticism that often greets new technology. In fact, a practitioner framework for AI leadership strategy stresses the importance of pilot-to-scale methodologies, noting that phased deployments build organizational confidence and competence with AI tools. By celebrating pilot successes and publicizing measurable improvements (e.g., an AI system reducing processing time by 30%), leaders can solidify buy-in for further implementation steps (Madanchian et al., 2024b).

Another widely used model, ADKAR (Awareness, Desire, Knowledge, Ability, Reinforcement), aligns well with AI change efforts. In the awareness phase, companies must communicate why AI is being adopted – linking it to business strategy and competitive necessity – to preempt rumors or misinformation. This is crucial because if employees understand the rationale (e.g., improving customer experience or relieving staff of drudge work), they are more likely to support the change (Brillianto et al., 2024). The desire phase might involve addressing personal WIIFM ("What's in it for me?") concerns, such as explaining how AI will make employees' jobs easier or open new career opportunities, thereby motivating them to participate. Providing education and training addresses the knowledge and ability phases: successful AI rollouts include robust training and support programs to upskill employees on new systems. For instance, when introducing an AI-driven analytics platform, one company scheduled hands-on workshops and peer mentoring sessions so employees could build confidence using the tool. This approach echoes lean change management principles of continuous learning and iteration – instead of one-off training, organizations that excel with AI often create ongoing learning resources (e.g., online tutorials, AI "help desk" support) (Westover, 2025; Tasnim, 2024a).

Finally, reinforcement might involve updating performance metrics and reward systems to encourage the sustained use of AI in daily workflows, ensuring the change "sticks." Without reinforcement, there is a risk that employees revert to old habits after the initial excitement wanes. Studies note that maintaining change momentum is a recurring challenge; frameworks like Kotter's explicitly advise anchoring new approaches in the culture – for AI, this could mean incorporating AI proficiency into job evaluations or continuing to highlight AI success stories in company communications long after launch. Agile change management has also gained prominence for AI projects. Traditional change models can be too linear for the fast-paced, experimental nature of AI implementation. Agile methodology, with its iterative cycles and incremental deployments, aligns naturally with how AI systems are developed and refined (Elsherif, 2024a). Many organizations adopt an agile implementation cycle for AI, essentially treating culture change as a series of sprints: they introduce a small AI feature, gather feedback, adjust the approach, and then expand to the next feature or department. This iterative feedback and adaptation loop is essential because AI technologies often improve through user interaction and because unforeseen issues (like a bias in an algorithm or workflow bottleneck) may only become apparent post-deployment. By using agile principles, change managers remain flexible – they can pivot strategies if employees are struggling or if the technology requires tweaks – rather than rigidly following a predetermined plan. Lean change management similarly emphasizes short cycles of change with constant stakeholder input, which helps avoid "change fatigue." AI initiatives can overwhelm staff if too much is introduced at once; agile/lean approaches mitigate this by focusing on continuous, manageable changes instead of a one-time big bang (Serikbay & Abdykhalykov, 2024b). For example, a bank rolling out AI customer service bots might start with a pilot in one region, learn from that experience, then gradually extend to other regions, allowing employees and customers to adjust in stages. This phased approach is reflected in many AI adoption roadmaps and is cited as a best practice for aligning technology rollout with human readiness.

No matter the framework, stakeholder alignment is a critical component of change management for AI. Successful frameworks ensure that key stakeholders – from executives to front-line employees and even external partners – are engaged and on the same page. Before broad implementation, leading companies form steering committees or AI councils that include representatives from various departments (IT, HR, operations, etc.) to ensure all perspectives are considered (Hossain et al., 2025c). This mirrors Kotter's idea of a guiding coalition and is particularly vital for AI because its impacts cut across traditional organizational boundaries. One study on AI leadership integration found that interdisciplinary collaboration in developing governance models greatly improved the acceptance of AI solutions. When people feel their concerns and insights have been heard in the planning stages, they are more likely to embrace the change. This also helps to surface and address potential roadblocks early – for instance, the HR representative might raise concerns about retraining needs, or the compliance officer might flag regulatory issues with AI usage. Incorporating these insights leads to more robust implementation plans that can preempt resistance (Wang & Pashmforoosh, 2024). Additionally, a well-crafted communication plan is embedded in all effective change frameworks. Regular, transparent communication about the AI project's goals, progress, and successes helps demystify the change and keeps everyone informed. Companies often utilize multi-channel communication: town hall meetings to address broad questions; email newsletters with tips and updates; and internal social platforms where employees can ask questions. This steady drumbeat of communication builds trust and prevents the rumor mill from filling any information void with anxiety.

Finally, modern change management frameworks for AI increasingly incorporate considerations of ethical and sustainable change. It's not enough to deploy AI quickly; it must be done responsibly to gain lasting support. Frameworks now often include steps to ensure ethical guidelines are integrated (e.g., reviewing algorithms for bias, establishing clear data privacy rules) and to promote adaptability in the workforce (Kandasamy, 2024; Madanchian et al., 2024b). For example, a new framework for ethical AI leadership suggests keeping Human Resource Development (HRD) "in the loop" – meaning continuous training and dialogue with employees about ethical AI use is part of the change process (Wang & Pashmforoosh, 2024). By embedding ethics and adaptability into the implementation plan, organizations address two common reasons for AI change failure: moral resistance (employees objecting to AI decisions they see as unfair) and skill obsolescence (employees feeling left behind by new tech). In essence, change management for AI is most effective when it blends the rigor of established models with the agility and empathy required by AI's disruptive nature. A combination of structured steps (to guide the organization) and flexibility (to iterate and learn) has proven to help enterprises manage the transition smoothly, keeping people at the center of the technological transformation (Elsherif, 2024a; Devabhaktuni et al., 2025). With such frameworks in place, companies can navigate the complexities of AI implementation – from initial pilot to enterprise-wide integration – while maintaining morale and productivity, ultimately sustaining change momentum into the future.

5.3 BUILDING AN AGILE AND INNOVATIVE ORGANIZATIONAL MINDSET

The rapid pace of AI development has made agility and innovation not just desirable traits, but essential ones for organizational survival. Building an agile and innovative mindset means reshaping the culture so that continuous improvement, experimentation, and adaptability become core values. In practical terms, this involves encouraging employees to try new ideas (and occasionally fail), empowering teams to make decisions quickly, and fostering an environment where learning is constant. Agile methodologies, originating in software development, have now permeated management thinking because they offer a way to cope with uncertainty – a hallmark of the AI era. An agile organization is one that can rapidly iterate on processes or products in response to feedback and new information, rather than clinging to rigid plans. Research shows that companies that have embraced agile leadership principles tend to handle AI-driven change more effectively. For instance, an agile mindset allows a firm to pilot a new AI tool on a small scale, learn from the results, and either scale it up or pivot as needed. This kind of flexibility was crucial during recent digital transformations: one literature review noted that over 60% of executives recognize AI's potential to improve key performance indicators, but only agile, forward-thinking cultures are positioned to realize those gains fully. In other words, even when leaders see the promise of AI, it is the organizational mindset – whether bureaucratic or nimble – that often dictates success or failure in implementation (Asiabar et al., 2024; Nyoto et al., 2024b).

An innovative mindset goes hand-in-hand with agility. Cultivating innovation requires creating a culture of creativity and experimentation. This means moving away from a punishment-oriented view of failure toward a "fail-fast" ethos where small failures are seen as learning opportunities. Organizations at the forefront of AI adoption often set up innovation sandboxes or labs where employees can play with AI technologies without fear of repercussions if something doesn't work out. Such safe spaces for experimentation are vital – they signal that management values initiative and creative problem-solving. Psychological safety is a key ingredient here: when employees feel safe to voice unconventional ideas or admit mistakes, they are more likely to contribute to innovation. Studies on team dynamics affirm that psychological safety boosts learning behaviors and innovation, which is particularly relevant when teams are figuring out how to integrate complex AI systems (Hu et al., 2025). A paradoxical leadership style – balancing support with challenge – can promote this environment by giving teams autonomy (to spark creativity) while also providing guidance and resources (to channel that creativity productively). For example, a leader might encourage a cross-functional team to brainstorm novel AI applications for improving customer service, explicitly stating that "wild" ideas are welcome, and then offer funding or time for the most promising concepts to be prototyped. Even if a prototype fails, the learning is captured and shared, turning the experience into an asset for future innovation efforts.

In building an innovative organizational mindset, empowerment and autonomy are crucial. Hierarchical, command-and-control management stifles the quick decision-making and experimentation needed for AI projects. Companies are therefore flattening hierarchies and pushing decision-making authority down to agile teams who work closely with AI technologies (Budianto et al., 2025). This empowerment enables those with the most hands-on knowledge (like data scientists or front-line process owners) to iterate and improve AI solutions without waiting for endless approvals. A survey of AI-driven organizations suggests that those that trust and empower their employees see higher innovation outputs and faster problem-solving because teams can adapt on the fly to new data or insights (Spisak, 2024). Indeed, remaining people-centered while innovating with AI is a theme highlighted by leadership experts: organizations should leverage AI to augment human creativity rather than replace human judgment. For example, an AI system might analyze large datasets to surface patterns, but it's often an empowered human team that interprets these patterns in creative ways to devise a new product or strategy. Agile, innovative cultures recognize this complementarity and thus treat employees as creative partners to AI, not cogs to be automated. This perspective encourages employees to view AI as a means to elevate their work – freeing them from rote tasks and giving them more scope to focus on imaginative, high-value activities (Rožman et al., 2023). Empirical evidence supports this: an organizational study found that introducing AI to handle routine workload increased overall performance and freed employees' time for more complex problem-solving. When employees witness such benefits, it reinforces a virtuous cycle – they become more willing to innovate with AI, having experienced how it can amplify their impact.

Another aspect of an agile and innovative mindset is fostering a learning organization. The concept of a learning organization (popularized by Peter Senge) is one where the company continually transforms itself by facilitating the learning of its members. In the AI era, this is absolutely critical; technologies and best practices evolve so rapidly that yesterday's knowledge can become obsolete. Organizations with a strong learning orientation encourage continuous upskilling, knowledge sharing, and reflection. For instance, they might implement peer learning sessions where teams who've tried an AI solution share their lessons with the rest of the company (Soares et al., 2021). Such mechanisms help avoid siloed learning – one of the pitfalls where an isolated team learns something valuable but the insight never propagates. A learning culture also means encouraging questions and intellectual curiosity. Leaders can model this by staying curious themselves: asking for feedback from teams, being open about what they don't know, and actively seeking new ideas from inside and outside the organization. When employees observe leaders engaging in learning behaviors, it legitimizes those behaviors for everyone. A recent study on digital leadership noted that effective leaders demonstrate humility and continuous learning, which in turn cultivates adaptability in their teams (Hossain et al., 2025c). This continuous improvement mindset is essentially the DNA of agility – always iterating and never settling for the status quo. In practice, some companies have adopted techniques like retrospectives (regular team meetings to discuss what went well or poorly in a project cycle) beyond just software teams, using them in marketing or HR after implementing AI tools. These retrospectives institutionalize learning and ensure that each cycle of change yields insights that make the next cycle better.

Building an agile and innovative mindset is not solely an internal affair; it often involves looking outward and embracing external ideas. Organizations that thrive with AI often participate in broader innovation ecosystems – partnering with startups, academic institutions, or industry consortia. This openness to external collaboration can infuse fresh perspectives and prevent inward-looking thinking. Culturally, it sends a message that innovation can come from anywhere and that the company is not "too proud" to learn from others. For example, several large companies have created AI innovation hubs or incubators that host external entrepreneurs on site, blending different cultures of innovation. This cross-pollination fosters creativity and keeps the organization nimble, as it is constantly exposed to new approaches. Interdisciplinary collaboration, both internally and externally, was cited in a systematic review as a key enabler of AI-augmented leadership innovation. Teams comprising diverse expertise (technical, ethical, domain-specific) were more likely to design innovative AI solutions and anticipate potential challenges. Thus, diversity of thought is a pillar of the innovative mindset. Companies must encourage not only diversity in hiring but also diversity in idea generation – ensuring that contrarian or minority viewpoints around AI are heard, as they can often spark breakthrough innovations or highlight risks that the majority overlooked. In summary, forging an agile and innovative organizational mindset for the AI era requires deliberate cultural engineering: promoting flexibility; rewarding creativity; ensuring psychological safety; and making learning a perpetual priority. Organizations that succeed in this transformation position themselves to not only adapt to the future but to actively shape it, leveraging AI as a springboard for human innovation rather than a crutch or threat.

5.4 WORKFORCE ENGAGEMENT AND COMMUNICATION DURING AI CHANGE

Successfully implementing AI in an organization isn't just a technical endeavor – it's a human one. Workforce engagement and clear communication throughout the AI change process are pivotal in turning passive employees into active participants. When employees feel engaged – that is, informed, heard, and involved – they are far more likely to support AI initiatives rather than resist them. One of the first steps in engagement is championing AI literacy and transparency across the workforce. Employees often fear what they do not understand; thus, improving AI literacy (basic knowledge of what AI is, how it works, and what it can and cannot do) can demystify the technology and reduce irrational fears. Companies leading in AI adoption have launched internal education programs: for example, interactive town hall sessions where the AI team showcases new tools, or "AI 101" workshops for non-technical staff. Such efforts build a baseline comfort with AI concepts. In one financial services firm, after a series of AI literacy webinars, employees reported less anxiety and more curiosity about AI, indicating that understanding breeds empowerment (Herlina et al., 2024). Transparency goes hand-in-hand with literacy. Leaders should communicate openly about why AI changes are happening, what the expected impacts are, and how the organization will address any negative consequences. A candid discussion about, say, potential job role changes or re-skilling opportunities can preempt the grapevine of worst-case scenarios. The goal is to replace rumors with facts. Empirical evidence from an employee engagement study suggests that when organizations communicate the purpose and progress of digital transformations clearly, employee trust and morale remain significantly higher. In essence, informed employees are less likely to imagine the worst and more likely to see where they fit in the future vision.

Active employee involvement in the change process is another engagement strategy that pays dividends. Rather than treating staff as passive recipients of AI, progressive organizations invite them to contribute to implementation. This might take the form of user groups or committees that gather front-line feedback on AI tools, pilot user programs that allow a subset of employees to test new systems and suggest improvements, or even innovation challenges that solicit AI use-case ideas from anyone in the company. Such involvement taps into the collective wisdom of the workforce and gives employees a stake in the outcome. A study on AI-driven management found that companies engaging employees through pilot participation and feedback loops saw higher adoption rates and smoother transitions, as employees felt a sense of ownership over the new tools (Tummalapalli et al., 2024). In practice, a manufacturing firm implementing collaborative robots ("cobots") formed a volunteer task force of shop-floor workers to advise on cobot placement, safety protocols, and task assignments. The task force's recommendations not only improved the implementation plan but also turned its members into vocal advocates who then helped win over their peers. This exemplifies how engagement can convert potential critics into change champions. It aligns with research indicating that organizations with strong employee involvement mechanisms often experience better workforce acceptance and even gains in morale during AI rollouts. When people are part of the solution, they are less likely to see themselves as victims of change.

Effective communication during AI-driven change must be two-way. Leadership should not only broadcast information but also listen actively to employee concerns and feedback. Establishing two-way feedback channels – such as Q&A sessions, dedicated email hotlines, or anonymous surveys – shows employees that their voice matters. Early in an AI initiative, these channels can surface legitimate concerns (e.g., "The new AI scheduling system doesn't account for our overtime rules") that leaders can then address, demonstrating responsiveness. Moreover, simply providing an avenue for employees to vent or ask questions can alleviate uncertainty. One global survey found that employees coping with technological change felt significantly less stress when they had a means to provide feedback or influence the change (Nyoto et al., 2024b). Companies are also using modern communication tools to keep the dialogue flowing. Internal social networks (like Slack or Yammer channels devoted to the AI project) allow continuous interaction: employees can raise issues in real time and change leaders or subject matter experts can respond publicly, so everyone benefits from the clarification. These discussions can also serve as informal training; for instance, if someone asks, "Why did the AI make X recommendation?" the answer can educate many readers and build trust in the system's logic. Maintaining visibility of leadership throughout the change is crucial – leadership visibility and support means leaders regularly communicating updates, acknowledging challenges, and reinforcing the vision behind the AI adoption. When employees see leaders actively steering the change (not just delegating it to IT), it signals commitment. A CEO who periodically emails the whole company about progress, lessons learned, or even missteps ("We learned that our first AI model had bias – here's how we're fixing it") will earn credibility and reinforce that the AI initiative is a top priority.

Addressing emotional and cultural aspects directly is a key part of communication during AI change. Employees often have fears beyond just job loss – they may worry about their ability to learn new systems, the impact on team dynamics, or the loss of human judgment in decision-making. Addressing employee AI anxieties openly can prevent these issues from festering. For example, if employees express worry that an AI might make unfair decisions, leadership can respond by explaining the ethical review process in place and perhaps adjusting plans to include a human in the loop for sensitive decisions (Salem et al., 2024). If people fear they won't be able to keep up with the technology, companies can share detailed training roadmaps and success stories of colleagues who successfully upskilled. Communication should thus not shy away from tough topics; instead, it should anticipate and tackle them. One manufacturing company, anticipating anxiety about a new AI-driven quality control system, held small group meetings where managers facilitated frank discussions about "what this change means for our jobs." They coupled this with assurances of no layoffs and clear plans for role transitions. Post-implementation surveys showed a higher acceptance rate and trust in management among employees who participated, compared to those who only received generic communications (Brillianto et al., 2024). The lesson is that building trust during transitions requires empathy and honesty. Leaders who admit that change can be hard and offer support (like counseling or one-on-one check-ins) often foster a stronger bond with employees. Trust is further reinforced by consistent messaging – if leadership promises, for example, that "no one will lose their job; roles will evolve with training," they must follow through. Any breach (like a surprise layoff) can severely damage credibility and engagement. Thus, communication plans are often aligned with HR policies to ensure promises are kept (Hossain et al., 2025c).

A compelling change story and vision is another communication tool that drives engagement. People need to understand not just the nuts and bolts of the change, but the broader narrative – the "why" and the hopeful future it brings. Crafting a story that situates the AI adoption in terms of the organization's mission and values can be highly motivating. For example: "We have always valued innovation and customer service. By embracing AI in our customer support operations, we free our reps to solve complex customer problems and innovate new solutions, which ultimately delivers on our promise of excellence." Such narratives help employees connect the change to a purpose they can get behind. An entrepreneurial tone – highlighting opportunities for growth, market leadership, or personal career development – can also energize the workforce. Indeed, entrepreneurial organizations often rally their teams around the idea that adopting advanced technologies like AI is part of staying competitive and pioneering in the industry, turning the change into a point of pride rather than a trial. Throughout, it's beneficial to celebrate quick wins and milestones publicly. Recognizing teams or individuals who have embraced the AI solutions and achieved positive results not only rewards adopters but also provides concrete examples to the rest of the company. For instance, if an AI prediction tool helped the sales team identify 20% more leads last quarter, highlight that success and credit the team's openness to new methods. Stories of colleagues succeeding with AI can dissipate doubt and create peer influence ("If their team did well with it, maybe ours can too"). Such celebrations, even small ones, maintain morale during the transformation by showing that the effort is yielding fruit.

High engagement and effective communication form the bedrock of managing the human side of AI change. A continuous, open dialogue that educates employees, solicits their input, and addresses their concerns fosters an atmosphere of trust and collaboration. This proactive approach to engagement has tangible benefits: case studies show it leads to higher adoption rates, better performance outcomes, and even increased employee satisfaction as the workforce feels carried along rather than dragged through change (Herlina et al., 2024; Lakshmikanth et al., 2024). When employees become partners in the AI journey – knowledgeable, heard, and motivated – the organization doesn't just implement a new technology; it also strengthens its culture and unity in the process. By treating communication and engagement not as afterthoughts but as strategic priorities, leaders humanize the change experience and set the stage for a workforce that is resilient, informed, and ready to thrive in the AI-enabled future.

5.5 RESTRUCTURING TEAMS AND WORKFLOWS AROUND AI

Adopting AI at scale often necessitates a fundamental restructuring of teams and workflows to fully realize the technology's benefits. AI doesn't operate in a vacuum; it slots into business processes and thus changes how work gets done and who does it. A common shift is the redesign of business processes to integrate AI where it adds the most value. For example, consider a customer service workflow: traditionally, a customer query might go through multiple human agents for resolution. With AI (like a triage chatbot or an AI-assisted knowledge base), the initial steps of that process can be automated – the AI can categorize the issue or even solve simple requests – leaving only complex queries for human agents. To accommodate this, the workflow is restructured so that AI handles front-line triage and humans focus on escalations. Such human–AI task allocation is at the heart of new workflow design (Lai & Rau, 2025). Organizations must analyze each step of key processes and decide: should this task be done by AI, by a human, or collaboratively? The goal is to exploit AI's strengths (speed, data processing, consistency) while leveraging human strengths (judgment, empathy, creativity). An effective allocation often results in AI handling routine, repetitive tasks and generating preliminary outputs that humans then refine.

Evidence from field studies suggests this augmentation approach significantly improves efficiency and decision quality, as seen when algorithmic decision-support systems pre-screen data for managers, who then apply their expertise to the curated information (Miah et al., 2023). Indeed, a recent era in organizational decision-making is described as one where AI filters the noise and extends the rational bounds of managers, allowing humans to focus on higher-order thinking. To support this, companies are redesigning workflows to formally embed AI outputs into human decision loops – for instance, making it a standard step that an AI forecast is reviewed in weekly planning meetings, thereby institutionalizing the AI's role in the process. Restructuring teams themselves is equally important. As AI takes on certain tasks, job roles naturally evolve. Organizations are creating new AI-centric roles and skills requirements while phasing out or reimagining some traditional roles. A clear example is the emergence of roles like data analysts, AI model trainers, or AI ethicists within teams that previously had none. In a marketing department, where once there were only marketing managers and creatives, one might now find a marketing data scientist role focused on leveraging AI analytics for campaign targeting. Interdisciplinary project teams are becoming the norm for AI initiatives, mixing domain experts, IT professionals, and data specialists together (Budianto et al., 2025).

This interdisciplinary approach breaks the mold of homogenous functional teams. It acknowledges that successful AI deployment requires a convergence of expertise – those who understand the technical workings of AI and those who understand the business context must work side by side. As a result, many organizations are reorganizing at least part of their structure into cross-functional squads or "pods" for AI projects, rather than purely functional silos. Tech companies have pioneered this with, for example, "AI product teams" that include engineers, user experience designers, and product managers all in one unit focused on a specific AI-driven feature. Traditional enterprises are following suit; banks might set up multidisciplinary teams for AI in credit scoring, including compliance officers to ensure regulation is met from the start. Flattening hierarchy often accompanies this team recomposition. Since AI systems can empower lower-level employees with insights previously only accessible to management, decision-making can decentralize. Information asymmetry is reduced when an AI can provide real-time analytics to anyone with access (Portillo, 2025c). Thus, some companies find they can "flatten" layers of middle management because AI dashboards enable front-line staff to make decisions that used to require managerial approval. This is not a trivial change – it requires trust in employees and an adjustment of accountability structures – but it can speed up operations and make the organization more responsive.

Anthropological studies of AI integration have observed instances where removing layers between the data (AI outputs) and the action (employee decisions) improved agility and morale, as employees felt more empowered and valued (Van Quaquebeke & Gerpott, 2023). Collaborative human–AI workflows are a hallmark of the restructured organization. Rather than linear processes handed off from person to person, workflows become more dynamic with AI agents working in parallel with humans. For example, in a modern manufacturing setting, a human technician and an AI-driven machine vision system might simultaneously inspect a product for defects – the AI quickly flags anomalies and the human double-checks those flags and decides on corrections. This concurrent collaboration can greatly speed up processes and improve accuracy. To facilitate such workflows, teams may need to adopt new collaboration tools or platforms that integrate AI outputs seamlessly into daily tasks. Project management software might be augmented with AI recommendations, or CRM systems might auto-suggest actions to sales teams.

The team structures might also adapt by pairing roles in new ways: some companies have experimented with a "centaur" model in teams, formally assigning a human–AI pair to tasks (e.g., a human planner working continuously with an AI planning assistant). This effectively treats the AI as a team member – a radical but increasingly common notion. It requires clarity of roles: humans are accountable for final decisions, but they rely on AI for data-driven suggestions and routine actions. Role clarity becomes essential in these hybrid workflows to avoid confusion or over-reliance. Guidelines and training often accompany these changes, teaching employees how to interpret AI outputs (Buçinca et al., 2021b) and where human judgment must intervene. Studies on trust and over-reliance warn that without proper training, humans might either distrust the AI too much or trust it blindly. Therefore, restructured workflows include checkpoints for human validation on critical decisions and fail-safes for AI errors, ensuring that the collaboration augments rather than undermines decision quality.

A notable impact of AI on team structure is the replacement or reallocation of routine management tasks. Routine tasks like scheduling, status reporting, basic analytics, and even initial performance evaluations can be offloaded to AI systems. One sustainability study showed that using AI to reduce employees' administrative workload not only increased performance but also improved employees' perception of work meaningfulness. In management, this translates to team leaders spending less time on bureaucratic chores and more on strategic or people-focused activities. For instance, an AI tool might automatically compile a project's progress report, allowing the project manager to dedicate more time to mentoring team members or refining project strategy. As these tasks shift, teams may find the traditional spans of control and team sizes can change. A manager supported by AI analytics might effectively oversee a larger team because the AI provides real-time insights that previously would have required manual data gathering by a human assistant. Some organizations have leveraged this to streamline structures – reducing middle-management headcount and broadening supervisory responsibilities, with AI as a force multiplier (Rožman et al., 2023). However, this must be done carefully, as leadership and human connection still matter; AI can provide data, but it cannot motivate or understand context in the way a human leader can. Many companies end up redesigning organizational roles rather than removing them outright. For example, a mid-level manager's role might shift from information gatekeeping (gathering and reporting data up and down the chain) to coaching and exception handling (since AI handles routine reporting). Research on leadership in AI-driven enterprises underscores that new competencies – like data interpretation, technological acumen, and emotional intelligence – are increasingly important for these evolved roles (Mohan, 2024). As a result, HR and L&D departments often update job descriptions and competency models when restructuring around AI, to capture the blend of skills needed (technical + soft skills).

Reskilling and role evolution go hand in hand with restructuring. A continuous reskilling initiative is almost always part of the organizational redesign, ensuring that employees whose tasks have been altered by AI can transition into new functions. Companies might set up internal academies or partnerships with online learning platforms focusing on data science basics, AI oversight, or other relevant skills (Sposato, 2024b). This not only equips the workforce to collaborate effectively with AI, but it also signals that the organization is investing in its people, which can mitigate fears and increase buy-in for the change. A prominent example is IBM's approach when introducing AI – they created the mantra "AI will not replace managers, but managers who use AI will replace those who don't," and backed it up with extensive training for managers on using AI tools for decision support (Zaidi et al., 2025). By framing AI as an empowerment tool and giving employees the skills to wield it, IBM effectively restructured roles with minimal layoffs, focusing instead on evolution. Similarly, many financial institutions retrained loan officers to work with AI credit scoring systems: instead of manually evaluating every application (a task largely automated by AI), officers learned to interpret AI risk assessments and focus on complex cases or customer relationship-building. This adaptive role redesign can sustain morale, as employees see a future for themselves in the organization's AI-driven model (Herlina et al., 2024). Moreover, organizations often need new structures for governance around AI – committees or roles dedicated to monitoring AI outcomes, bias audits, and maintenance. These might be entirely new teams (e.g., an AI governance board) that work across existing departments to ensure the AI usage aligns with company policies and ethical standards (Kandasamy, 2024).

Finally, restructuring around AI sometimes means implementing completely new operating models, such as creating an AI Center of Excellence (CoE) or centralized teams that provide AI capabilities as a service to the rest of the company. This can concentrate expertise and avoid duplication of efforts when multiple teams need similar AI solutions. For instance, rather than each business unit hiring its own data scientist, a central CoE might develop common AI models and tools that various units can adapt. This structure requires careful coordination – liaison roles are often established to bridge the CoE with business units, ensuring that solutions meet real needs. The CoE model was cited in transformation case studies as beneficial for scaling AI across a large enterprise because it balances specialization with knowledge sharing (Elsherif, 2024b). It also creates a career path for AI specialists, which helps with talent retention. On the flip side, decentralization of AI capability is another model: embedding data scientists within each business unit so they become intimately familiar with that unit's operations. Some organizations choose this to ensure AI efforts are closely aligned with domain needs. In many cases, a hybrid emerges – a central team sets standards and provides core infrastructure, while satellite experts within departments tailor AI solutions locally. These kinds of structural decisions are strategic and depend on company size, culture, and goals. Regardless of the model, the trend is clear: the traditional organizational chart is bending and flexing under the influence of AI. Roles are less siloed, workflows are more fluid, and human–AI collaboration is explicitly designed into how work gets done. This restructuring is not a one-time event but an ongoing evolution, as organizations continue to learn where AI can create the most value and how humans and machines can best complement each other in the quest for efficiency, innovation, and excellent service delivery.

5.6 GLOBAL PERSPECTIVES – ADAPTING CULTURE ACROSS REGIONS

AI adoption does not happen in a cultural vacuum, and in today's interconnected world, organizations often span multiple regions with diverse cultural norms. Adapting organizational culture for AI across different regions is a nuanced challenge. What works in one country or cultural context may not translate directly to another. Cross-cultural differences in AI adoption stem from varying attitudes toward technology, work, authority, and risk. For example, employees in highly individualistic cultures might readily embrace AI tools that allow them to work independently and demonstrate personal performance, while employees in more collectivist cultures might respond better to AI implementations that emphasize team benefits and communal learning (Soares et al., 2021). Similarly, societies differ in their trust of technology: in some East Asian contexts, there can be a strong public enthusiasm for advanced technology and a cultural narrative of progress through tech, which may facilitate AI acceptance. In contrast, certain European contexts, with strong privacy norms and skepticism of big tech, might exhibit more caution or demand for strict governance of AI (Salem et al., 2024). A bibliometric analysis of AI and leadership literature across regions revealed that research from North America often focuses on efficiency and competitive advantage, whereas studies from Europe and Asia frequently highlight ethical, human-centric issues and the societal impact of AI. These emphases reflect underlying cultural and regulatory landscapes – for instance, the EU's more precautionary approach (e.g., GDPR and AI Act proposals) vs. the US's innovation-driven ethos. Global organizations must reconcile these differences when crafting AI strategies.

Eastern vs. Western leadership styles can influence AI integration approaches significantly. Western leadership frameworks (common in the US or Northern Europe) often stress traits like empowerment, delegation, and transparency. Leaders operating under these assumptions might be quick to delegate tasks to AI or encourage bottom-up experimentation with new tools. On the other hand, Eastern leadership styles (prevalent in parts of Asia) can be more hierarchical or paternalistic, with an emphasis on consensus and senior authority. In such settings, employees may expect top-down directives regarding AI use and could be hesitant to voice concerns or suggestions until leaders have signaled clear support. A case in point is how multinational companies experienced AI rollout in different branches: a study noted that in Japan, securing explicit executive endorsement and framing AI in line with company values of harmony and quality was crucial for employee buy-in, whereas in the US branch of the same company, employees responded more to pilot results and data showing AI's effectiveness (Dissanayake & Keppetipola, 2024b). Neither approach is "better" universally; each is tailored to cultural expectations of leadership. Thus, multinational organizations often adopt a glocal strategy – globally unified in technology standards but locally adapted in change management. For example, a global bank might have a central AI system for fraud detection, but the training and implementation in its Southeast Asian offices will be led by local managers in the local language, possibly incorporating more group-oriented workshops, whereas in North America the rollout might lean on self-service training portals and individual certification.

When considering local vs. global AI strategies, companies must also navigate regulatory and market differences. Some regions have strict regulations that require cultural adaptation: for instance, using AI in HR processes might be accepted in one country but face legal barriers in another due to employment laws or data protection rules. Culture interacts with these regulations; for example, strong union cultures in parts of Europe mean that introducing AI to automate tasks might necessitate negotiations and assurances to workers far more than in countries with a more laissez-faire labor market. Global change management case studies highlight that misreading local cultural cues can derail AI projects (Elsherif, 2024b). One notable example involved a US-based tech firm implementing an AI-driven performance management system in its European subsidiary. The system provided granular performance analytics on employees. While it was well received in the US as a high-tech enhancement to meritocracy, European employees (operating in a culture valuing privacy and equality) reacted negatively, perceiving it as intrusive surveillance and a threat to collegial workplace culture. The company had to pause and redesign the system with anonymized data and heavier employee consultation in Europe to rebuild trust. The lesson is clear: organizations must adapt communication and implementation tactics across cultures, even if the core AI technology is the same. In high-context cultures (where communication relies on implicit understanding and context), change leaders may need to invest more in relationship-building, face-to-face meetings, and storytelling to convey the purpose of AI changes. In low-context cultures (where direct communication is valued), straightforward messaging and detailed documentation might suffice . Cultural dimensions in the AI context – such as power distance, uncertainty avoidance, and long-term orientation (Hofstede's dimensions) – provide a framework for understanding differences in AI adoption. High power distance cultures, where inequality is accepted and subordinates are less likely to question superiors, might see less open pushback on AI initiatives (employees may not voice doubts openly). However, this does not mean genuine acceptance; concerns might be unspoken. Leadership in these contexts might misread silence as agreement, so they must proactively seek out hidden concerns (perhaps via anonymous feedback) and provide strong reassurance from the top. In low power distance settings, employees may expect to be consulted and could resist if they feel AI is being imposed without their input (Pavitra et al., 2024).

Uncertainty avoidance is another key factor: cultures with high uncertainty avoidance (e.g., many Latin European and some Asian cultures) prefer clear rules and risk mitigation. For AI, this means employees and regulators in such cultures will be more cautious, demanding detailed guidelines for AI use, ethical guardrails, and perhaps phased implementations with contingency plans. Adapting to this might involve piloting AI in low-risk areas first, or providing very explicit SOPs (standard operating procedures) for AI decisions to satisfy the need for certainty (Alghowinem et al., 2024). Conversely, cultures comfortable with ambiguity (e.g., Anglophone or Nordic countries) might be more willing to experiment with AI and iterate as they go. Here, change agents can leverage that comfort by launching minimal viable products and refining them with user feedback, a practice that might terrify employees elsewhere who expect more predictability.

An interesting global perspective is how differing cultural attitudes toward authority and expertise affect trust in AI. In societies where authority is respected (and perhaps not to be questioned), if leadership endorses an AI system, employees may grant it instant legitimacy. On the other hand, if an AI is seen as an "outsider" technology not backed by a familiar authority or tradition, it might be met with skepticism. Some East Asian companies have successfully framed AI as an extension of revered principles (e.g., tying AI-driven quality control to the long-held cultural value of craftsmanship and perfection) to make it culturally palatable. In contrast, Western cultures that have a healthy skepticism of authority might require more evidence and peer-level testimonials to build trust in AI (Noponen et al., 2023). For instance, American tech workers might be more inclined to trust an AI tool after an internal pilot shows improved outcomes and colleagues vouch for it, rather than simply because the CEO said "we're doing AI." Global leadership competencies thus need to include cultural intelligence – the ability to understand and adapt to local cultural expectations when driving AI integration (Serikbay & Abdykhalykov, 2024). Leaders of multinational teams must be adept at reading cultural signals: a nod in one culture might mean agreement, whereas in another it's merely a sign of listening. Virtual global teams implementing AI have to navigate time zones and cultural contexts, which means communication needs to be crystal-clear and inclusive. Some companies rotate meeting times to accommodate different regions and have bilingual materials for major announcements to ensure nothing is lost in translation.

Intercultural training for digital change is emerging as a specialized area. This involves training change leaders (and even AI itself, in user-facing roles like chatbots) to be culturally sensitive. For instance, an interculturally trained change manager would know to involve works councils and observe formal protocols in Germany, to emphasize group consensus and face time in Japan, to highlight career growth and innovation in the US, and to address job security forthrightly in France. They might use different metaphors or success stories tailored to each audience's values – citing local examples of companies benefiting from AI can be more persuasive than global generalizations. A continuous feedback mechanism from regional units to headquarters also helps adjust the approach. It's not uncommon for global firms to pilot an AI program in one region, then incorporate feedback and cultural learnings before rolling it out globally. This phased approach effectively treats each major culture as a testbed to refine the overall strategy (Arar et al., 2025). It respects the notion that one size does not fit all in cultural terms. The ultimate goal is a cohesive transformation that still honors local identities – a balancing act of standardization and localization. Organizations that strike this balance often find that AI adoption can actually be a force for unity rather than division: employees in different countries see that they are all part of the same forward-looking evolution, just approached in culturally resonant ways. In conclusion, from a global perspective, successful AI integration demands cultural adaptability. Strategies must be flexed to align with local values, communication styles, and regulatory environments. By doing so – by meeting people where they are culturally – an organization can harness the full power of AI across all its regions, avoiding the pitfalls of cultural resistance and instead benefiting from the rich diversity of ideas and acceptance that a culturally intelligent approach brings.

5.7 CROSS-CULTURAL LEADERSHIP STYLES AND AI INTEGRATION

Leadership style profoundly shapes how AI is integrated into organizations, and these styles themselves are deeply influenced by culture. When we look across cultures, distinct leadership paradigms emerge – each with implications for AI adoption. One important dimension is high-context vs. low-context communication as it pertains to leadership in AI projects. In high-context cultures (found in many Asian, Middle Eastern, and Latin American societies), effective leadership communication is subtle, relying on shared understanding, indirect cues, and relationship history. Leaders in such cultures might introduce AI in a more roundabout way – perhaps by first building consensus informally, or by framing it as aligned with the group's long-term harmony and success, rather than bluntly announcing a change. For example, a high-context leader might say, "We have always valued precision and care; this new tool can help us uphold those values," implying the AI is a natural extension of what the team already believes in. This indirect approach can ease AI into the workflow without jarring the team's communication norms (Mariyono et al., 2024). Conversely, in low-context cultures (common in North America and much of Northern Europe), leaders tend to be direct, explicit, and transparent in their communication. A leader in a low-context setting might openly articulate the reasons for adopting AI, the expected outcomes, and the plan forward in a detailed meeting or memo. They will encourage questions in a straightforward manner. The advantage here is clarity – everyone knows what the AI initiative entails – but it might come at the expense of not tapping into the rich subtext and unspoken concerns that a high-context approach would surface. Effective cross-cultural leadership recognizes these differences: a skilled leader will adjust their communication strategy when managing international teams, perhaps combining both approaches. They may provide clear, written details for those who expect it, while also engaging in relational, behind-the-scenes discussions with those who value a personal touch.

Power distance is another crucial factor in leadership and AI integration. In high power distance cultures, leaders are expected to make decisions with authority and subordinates are less likely to challenge or offer input to those decisions. In such contexts, the integration of AI might be very top-down: if the leader decides to implement an AI system, the team will likely accept it with minimal outward dissent. The upside is that change can be swift and coordinated under a strong directive. However, there's a risk that important feedback from lower levels (who may see practical issues or ethical concerns with the AI) is not voiced due to deference. For instance, a junior analyst might notice the AI software misclassifying data but might hesitate to speak up in a culture where questioning decisions is not the norm. A cross-cultural leader in a high power distance setting should take extra steps to encourage feedback, perhaps by explicitly inviting critique or creating safe channels for it (Herlina et al., 2024). By doing so, they compensate for the cultural tendency to stay silent and ensure the AI integration benefits from ground-level insights. In low power distance cultures, leadership is usually more consultative and egalitarian. Team members expect to be involved in decisions and feel comfortable providing input, even to leaders. Here, AI integration might involve workshops or democratic discussions on how to implement the technology. Employees might openly debate the merits of different AI tools and voice their personal comfort levels. The leader acts more as a facilitator than a director in such scenarios. The benefit is a rich pool of input and possibly more buy-in since everyone had a say. The challenge is that consensus-building can be slow. A cross-cultural leader in a low power distance environment must manage the process to avoid analysis paralysis – perhaps by setting clear decision criteria or timelines for deciding on the AI adoption after sufficient discussion (Pavitra et al., 2024).

Individualist vs. collectivist orientations also color leadership and AI dynamics. In individualist cultures (e.g., the US, the UK, and Australia), leadership often appeals to personal achievement and autonomy. A leader might encourage AI adoption by highlighting how it will help each person perform better, develop new skills, or gain recognition for innovation. The narrative might be: "This AI tool will make you more productive and free you up for creative work." Leaders may also allow individuals or sub-teams to experiment in their own way with the AI, fostering a sense of personal ownership over the change. People in these cultures may be more willing to tinker with a new system independently and even compete in a friendly way to extract the most value from AI (Vivek & Krupskyi, 2024). On the flip side, in collectivist cultures (common in Asia, Africa, and Latin America), leadership frames changes in terms of group benefit, harmony, and collective growth. A leader would stress how AI will help the team or organization succeed and how everyone will need to support each other in learning and using the new tools. The introduction of AI might be accompanied by group training sessions where the emphasis is on moving forward together so that no one is left behind (Hu et al., 2025). Employees might be less inclined to stand out as "super users" of the AI and more focused on ensuring team members are coping well. Cross-cultural leaders who understand this will tailor their incentives and recognition accordingly: in collectivist contexts, praising the whole team for AI adoption success can be more effective than singling out individuals (which might even cause embarrassment). In individualist contexts, recognizing star performers who championed the AI can accelerate cultural uptake by appealing to others' competitive spirits or personal ambitions.

Cultural values and tech trust vary widely – some cultures have an inherent trust in technology and innovation, while others are more cautious, valuing tradition. For example, countries like South Korea or Singapore have public narratives of technology as a means of national progress, which can make workforces generally more receptive to AI innovations (Ejjami, 2024a). Leaders in such environments might find employees eager to try AI, even pushing leadership to adopt more cutting-edge tools. The leadership style thus can be more exploratory and ambitious, setting bold tech visions, knowing the cultural current supports it. Contrast this with cultures that place a premium on human touch and tradition (perhaps some family-business-dominated cultures or those with skepticism of Western tech influence). There, a leader might need to adopt a more assurance-based leadership style, constantly reaffirming that AI will not replace human wisdom and that it will be implemented in a way that respects local customs or long-standing practices (Maddula, 2018). For example, in a culture with a tradition of apprenticeship and senior artisans (like certain crafts or industries in parts of Europe or Asia), a leader integrating AI might do well to have the respected master craftsmen involved in selecting or validating the AI – thus blending new tech with revered human expertise to gain trust. Cross-cultural competency also extends to recognizing global leadership competencies needed in an AI-driven world. These include adaptability, cultural intelligence, and inclusive decision-making (Subrahmanyam, 2025b). Leaders must be able to switch between leadership modes – autocratic when quick decisions are needed and the culture permits, democratic when buy-in is crucial and culture expects participation, task-focused in some settings vs. relationship-focused in others – all while steering the organization toward successful AI use. This is a tall order and suggests that training for leaders in the AI era should incorporate cross-cultural scenarios and feedback. Programs that develop leaders' ability to read cultural cues and adjust their approach (e.g., situational leadership models enriched with cultural dimensions) will be invaluable.

Adapting leadership training to culture is already happening in global organizations. Companies are customizing their AI leadership workshops regionally. In some Asia-Pacific divisions, training might involve more group activities, emphasize consensus and senior endorsement of AI principles, and include family or community considerations (since work and family are tightly knit in some cultures – e.g., how AI might improve work–life balance for everyone). In North America or Europe, the same training might be more individual-centered, encourage debate, and highlight how AI skills benefit one's personal career. The content must also consider differing baseline familiarity with AI; some cultures with advanced tech infrastructure might have many employees already savvy with AI concepts, whereas others might be encountering these ideas formally for the first time. Leaders must gauge their team's starting point and adapt communication accordingly to avoid talking down or over people's heads. Multinational team collaboration introduces another layer of complexity: teams composed of members from multiple cultures (often the case in global firms or remote cross-border projects) face internal cultural frictions or misalignments in their approach to AI. A leader of such a team has to establish team norms that bridge cultural gaps – for instance, explicitly agreeing that all voices will be heard (to encourage those from high power distance or collectivist backgrounds to speak up) but also setting a respectful structured meeting protocol (to manage those from more outspoken cultures). They may find themselves mediating misunderstandings: a direct critique of the AI system by a German team member might alarm a Japanese colleague who perceives it as conflict; the leader might then clarify intentions and reframe comments in culturally neutral terms.

Cultural intelligence in AI projects means being aware of these subtleties and coaching the team to value their diversity as a strength. One cross-cultural implementation case described how a global IT company rolled out an AI-driven process tool to a team distributed across India, France, and the US. Initially, there was confusion – the American members kept suggesting changes to the tool (normal in their culture), the French members raised theoretical concerns about data privacy (reflecting their social priorities), and the

Indian members, out of respect, tried to implement the tool as instructed without objection (aligning with a more deferential style). The project's leader realized the need to align these differences: they established a rotating feedback leadership where each culture's members took turns leading the discussion on improvements (so everyone had equal voice), they addressed privacy concerns by involving an EU legal expert to satisfy the French team, and encouraged the Indian team members to share the on-the-ground challenges they faced when using the tool, ensuring them that honesty was needed not insubordination. The result was a more cohesive integration and even some innovative modifications to the AI tool that benefited all, born from this cross-cultural collaboration. Thus, when successfully managed, cross-cultural teams can generate richer solutions for AI integration than any single-culture team, because they combine the best of multiple perspectives and avoid cultural blind spots. Cross-cultural leadership in the AI era, therefore, is about weaving a global mindset – understanding and leveraging cultural differences to enhance, rather than hinder, the uptake of AI across the organization. Leaders who can navigate this tapestry will enable their organizations to implement AI in a way that resonates with diverse workforces and maximizes the technology's positive impact worldwide.

5.8 CONTINUOUS LEARNING CULTURE IN THE AGE OF AI

In the AI era, perhaps nothing is more important than fostering a continuous learning culture within organizations. The reason is clear: AI and related technologies evolve rapidly, rendering specific skills or knowledge obsolete at an unprecedented pace. To remain competitive and innovative, companies and their people must be in a state of perpetual learning, continually refreshing their capabilities and understanding. This is often framed as promoting lifelong learning in the digital era. Lifelong learning isn't a new concept, but AI has made it an imperative at all levels of an organization, from the C-suite to the newest hire. Organizations thriving with AI encourage their employees to view careers as journeys of ongoing development rather than a static set of duties. They invest in AI-based workforce reskilling and upskilling programs that personalize development. For instance, using AI-driven learning platforms, companies can offer adaptive training courses – algorithms can assess an employee's current skill set and learning style, then recommend tailored modules to close knowledge gaps or prepare for new roles. Such platforms often use spaced repetition, microlearning, and interactive simulations (sometimes leveraging VR/AR) to make learning engaging and effective (Sposato, 2024b). A culture that embraces these tools signals to employees that learning is not just an occasional HR exercise, but a core part of work life. Research by

Westover (2025) highlights that organizations which cultivate leadership intelligence through continuous learning are better at building "tomorrow's leaders" who can integrate AI effectively. Leaders set the tone: when they actively participate in learning (e.g., attending workshops, openly reading up on AI trends, discussing books or courses they took), it legitimizes continuous education for everyone else (Tasnim, 2024a). It becomes normal for an engineer to take a day off to attend an AI ethics course or for a marketing analyst to spend an hour each week on a data science MOOC – because the culture supports development time as part of the job, not apart from it.

A continuous learning culture also highly values knowledge sharing. In a fast-learning organization, what one person learns about a new AI process is quickly disseminated to others. This can be facilitated both socially and technically. Socially, companies encourage communities of practice, like internal forums or guilds (e.g., a Data Science Guild or an AI-in-Marketing roundtable) where employees regularly meet (virtually or in person) to discuss new insights and techniques. These forums break down silos and prevent knowledge "islands." Technically, some organizations deploy knowledge management systems or even AI-powered knowledge bases that capture lessons learned from projects. Imagine an internal wiki where every AI pilot project team documents what worked, what didn't, and tips for future teams – enriched by an AI assistant that helps employees query this repository in natural language. When an employee wonders "Has anyone used AI to improve supplier delivery times?," the system could pull up relevant project summaries, contacts of experts in-house, and even recommend best practices extracted from those experiences (Hu et al., 2025). This level of knowledge sharing dramatically accelerates learning cycles, as people can build on each other's experiences rather than reinvent the wheel. A telling indicator of success in this realm is when employees begin to not only consume knowledge but actively contribute to these knowledge systems, showing that continuous learning has been internalized as a shared responsibility and norm.

Central to the learning culture is promoting a growth mindset among employees (a term popularized by Carol Dweck). A growth mindset is the belief that abilities and intelligence can be developed through dedication and effort. In contrast, a fixed mindset assumes abilities are static. In the context of AI, a growth mindset culture helps dispel the fear that "if I'm not good at tech now, I never will be." Instead, it instills the outlook that anyone can become adept with AI tools through learning and practice. Leaders can nurture this by praising effort, learning, and improvement, not just innate skill or immediate results. For instance, if a finance team member from a non-technical background takes the initiative to learn basic coding for an AI process automation, the organization should recognize that effort – regardless of whether their first prototype succeeds. Celebrating learning-oriented achievements (like completing a certification or experimenting with a new solution) signals that growth is valued. Studies have found that organizations where the growth mindset is prevalent see higher innovation and resilience because employees are less afraid of failure and more motivated to tackle new challenges (Westover, 2025; Vivek & Krupskyi, 2024). In these environments, AI is less intimidating; it's simply another area in which one can grow. A practical measure some companies use is including personal development goals in performance reviews – not just what you achieved, but what you learned. Over time this embeds a norm that stagnation is the only real failure.

Mentorship and coaching with AI are emerging as innovative ways to reinforce continuous learning. Some organizations pair less experienced employees with mentors specifically to help guide them through developing AI-related skills or understanding how AI affects their career path. In addition, AI itself can be a coach: there are AI-driven coaching bots that can give managers feedback on their leadership communication (based on analysis of meeting transcripts or emails), or coach employees on public speaking by analyzing practice session videos. These AI coaches can provide immediate, private feedback, complementing human mentors by covering day-to-day micro-improvements. For example, an AI communication coach might tell a customer service agent that in a recent call they spoke a bit too quickly and interrupted the customer twice, suggesting some techniques to improve. The agent can work on these suggestions and perhaps review progress with their human coach or manager later. The synergy of human and AI coaching accelerates learning – AI provides real-time, objective insights, while human mentors provide context, encouragement, and deeper discussion (Lakshmikanth et al., 2024). A continuous learning culture is excited about using all these tools to develop people, rather than viewing development as remedial or optional. It's common in such cultures to see employees proactively seeking mentors and also volunteering to be mentors once they've gained expertise, creating a virtuous cycle of learning and teaching.

Furthermore, a culture of continuous learning in the AI age needs to be supported by learning metrics and incentives aligned with it. Traditional metrics might focus purely on performance outputs, but progressive companies also track learning inputs and outcomes. They might measure how many hours of training employees log, how many new skills are acquired organizationally each quarter, or even use competency assessments to see skill growth over time. Some incorporate these into KPIs: for instance, a tech consulting firm might set a goal that 80% of their workforce earns a particular AI certification by year's end and tie a portion of bonuses or rewards to achieving it. Incentives could include tangible rewards like tuition reimbursement, promotion pathways for those who expand their skill sets, or hackathon prizes for innovative uses of newly learned techniques (Tummalapalli et al., 2024). Importantly, not all incentives are financial – recognition is huge. Showcasing "Learner of the Month" or success stories of career transitions (like a call center rep who became a data analyst through the company's learning programs) can motivate others and normalize continuous evolution. When employees see colleagues being celebrated for reinventing themselves or mastering new domains, it reinforces that the company truly values growth. This also helps alleviate the fear that AI will automate jobs away – in a strong learning culture, people see that the company is willing to invest in them to take on new, more sophisticated roles as automation changes old ones (Sinshaw et al., 2021). The implicit promise is: as the company grows with AI, so will you. That psychological contract encourages employees to stay engaged and forward-looking rather than fearful and resistant.

In sum, continuous learning culture has an outward-facing aspect: openness to new ideas from outside the organization. This might involve attending industry conferences, collaborating with academic institutions for the latest research, or participating in open-source AI projects. Employees in a true learning culture are not confined to internal knowledge – they are encouraged to tap into global communities of practice. A company might sponsor online course subscriptions for staff or provide time off for attending workshops, understanding that the infusion of fresh ideas keeps the organization ahead of the curve (Alghowinem et al., 2024). In sum, a continuous learning culture in the AI era is one where curiosity, adaptability, and knowledge sharing are ingrained values. It's a place where employees at all levels feel safe admitting "I don't know – let's find out," and then have the resources and support to indeed find out. Such a culture doesn't just react to the future – it actively creates the future by constantly upgrading the collective capacity of its people. This stands in stark contrast to static cultures of the past, and the difference is evident in outcomes: companies that have embraced continuous learning are demonstrably more innovative, have higher employee engagement, and adapt faster to market changes. As AI continues to advance, the organizations that will thrive are not necessarily the ones with the most advanced algorithms, but the ones with the most agile learners. They will turn the challenge of constant change into an engine of constant growth, ensuring that both technology and talent develop in tandem toward shared success.

6. People, teams, and talent in an AI-augmented workplace

6.1 AI IN TALENT ACQUISITION AND PERFORMANCE MANAGEMENT

AI technologies are rapidly reshaping how organizations recruit talent and evaluate performance. Talent acquisition processes now often begin with algorithms: automated systems screen résumés and rank candidates, leveraging natural language processing to identify keywords that match job requirements. This automation accelerates hiring by sifting through thousands of applications in a fraction of the time it would take a human recruiter. The efficiency gains are significant – recruiters are freed from tedious initial screenings to focus on higher-value tasks like engaging with top candidates. For example, AI-driven applicant tracking systems can filter résumés and even interact with applicants via chatbots for initial Q&A, streamlining early-stage recruitment. Predictive hiring analytics go a step further by using machine learning models to forecast a candidate's success or tenure at the company based on past hiring data and performance indicators. These models might analyze attributes of previously successful employees to predict which new applicants could be high performers, ostensibly improving hiring quality. However, these benefits come with critical caveats. Studies warn that if not carefully managed, AI hiring tools can inadvertently reinforce biases present in historical data. A famously cited case involved an AI résumé screener that favored certain demographics because it was trained on data reflecting past hiring biases – a stark reminder that algorithms carry the risk of automating old prejudices.

Ensuring fairness requires diligent oversight: researchers emphasize the need for HR professionals ("keeping HRD in the loop") to monitor AI decisions for bias and to maintain transparency in how the algorithms evaluate candidates. In fact, a new framework for ethical AI in HR has been proposed to address these issues, highlighting fairness and human accountability as key pillars. As Wang and Pashmforoosh (2024) note, HR departments must remain actively involved in AI deployment, verifying that automated screening criteria are job-relevant and free from unlawful discrimination (Wang &

Pashmforoosh, 2024). This human oversight is vital for trust – both candidates and hiring managers need to trust that the AI's recommendations are unbiased and valid. Beyond recruitment, AI is transforming performance management. Traditional annual performance reviews are giving way to continuous, data-driven evaluations assisted by AI analytics. Many organizations now collect real-time performance data – sales figures, customer feedback, project delivery metrics – and use AI to analyze patterns and outliers. Real-time performance analytics dashboards driven by AI can alert managers to an employee's achievements or struggles in the moment, enabling more timely feedback and coaching. For instance, an AI system might flag that a customer service agent consistently excels at resolving complaints on first contact, prompting management to recognize and reward that strength promptly, or to tap the agent's insights for training others. Conversely, if an employee's productivity drops, AI analytics might detect this early and suggest interventions or additional support. Such continuous monitoring has a clear upside for development – problems are addressed before annual reviews, and good work is acknowledged when it happens, boosting engagement (Pei et al., 2024). Research by Pei et al. (2024) found that AI-generated feedback, when used appropriately, can enhance employee performance and satisfaction by providing timely, constructive inputs that employees perceive as supportive rather than punitive. In other words, AI can help managers "save face" in delivering negative feedback – the system identifies areas for improvement objectively, which managers can then discuss with employees, reducing personal biases and emotional tension in feedback conversations (Pei et al., 2024).

AI's growing role in performance management also includes intelligent employee monitoring systems. These range from benign tools that track work objectives and progress, to more intrusive software that can log keystrokes or screen time. When used ethically, moderate monitoring can help employees prioritize tasks and maintain focus, or help remote teams stay aligned. For example, some companies use AI to analyze how employees allocate their time (e.g., time spent on emails vs. creative work) to identify inefficiencies and coach better work habits. Yet the line between helpful insight and surveillance is thin. Excessive monitoring can erode trust and damage the employee experience if people feel constantly watched or reduced to data points. There is evidence that maintaining human-centered leadership in deploying these tools is crucial – leaders must clearly communicate the purpose of monitoring (to support productivity and well-being, not to micromanage) and set boundaries to protect privacy (Kandasamy, 2024; Wang & Pashmforoosh, 2024). Ethical leadership in the AI era emphasizes transparency and fairness. Employees are more likely to accept AI-based evaluations when the criteria are transparent and they feel the system is fair and unbiased (Kandasamy, 2024). Thus, many organizations are establishing AI ethics guidelines within HR to govern how monitoring and analytics are implemented (Wang & Pashmforoosh, 2024).

Another emerging application is using AI in succession planning and talent management. AI tools can analyze employee performance data, skills, and even social network graphs within the company to identify high-potential individuals for future leadership roles. Rather than relying solely on managerial intuition or static talent reviews, companies leverage algorithms to surface "hidden gems" deep in the organization – those who consistently perform well, learn quickly, or demonstrate leadership behaviors in peer feedback. Research in education administration has begun to integrate AI into succession planning models, showing promise for broader organizational use. For example, At-tamimi et al. (2024) describe how an AI-driven approach in a university setting could match academic staff profiles with leadership competency requirements, streamlining the pipeline for administrative roles. In a corporate setting, a similar AI system might flag a mid-level engineer with strong project mentorship feedback and high innovation metrics as a candidate for accelerated management training. By illuminating data-backed trajectories for employees, AI supports more objective and strategic succession planning.

These talent analytics extend to employee retention as well. AI can parse through indicators like job tenure, promotion wait times, engagement survey scores, and even sentiment in internal communications to predict who might be at risk of leaving. Early warning of flight risk enables HR to proactively engage those employees – perhaps offering new growth opportunities or addressing workplace issues – thus improving retention. For instance, if an algorithm detects that an employee's engagement has dipped (maybe their project satisfaction scores and mentorship interactions have declined), it could alert HR to check in with that individual. Some companies have reported lower turnover after implementing predictive retention models, as interventions can be timed before an employee has one foot out the door (Aziz et al., 2024d). Still, caution is warranted: a false prediction could stigmatize a loyal employee if misused. Therefore, best practices again call for human verification of AI insights – a manager or HR professional should validate any AI-derived red flag through conversation and context, rather than acting on it blindly (Aziz et al., 2024d).

Finally, AI is augmenting the HR team itself through chatbot-based HR assistants. These AI assistants handle routine inquiries – from answering questions about benefits and company policies, to guiding candidates through application steps. They operate 24/7, providing instant responses and freeing HR staff from a deluge of repetitive queries. A new hire might interact with a chatbot named "AskHR" to learn how to enroll in health insurance or find the employee handbook. In recruitment, chatbots can engage candidates with pre-screening questions or schedule interviews, enhancing the candidate experience with prompt communication. Organizations have found that these AI agents improve responsiveness and consistency in HR services (Lakshmikanth et al., 2024). However, while convenient, they must be carefully designed to align with the company's tone and values – a cold, robotic answer can alienate employees or applicants. Empathy and nuance, often hallmarks of HR, are challenging to embed in a bot. Some advanced systems attempt to detect sentiment and adjust their replies accordingly, but they are not foolproof. Thus, many companies keep a hybrid approach: chatbots for straightforward Q&A, with easy escalation to a human HR representative for complex or sensitive issues. This approach leverages AI's efficiency without sacrificing the human touch in people management (Lakshmikanth et al., 2024). AI in talent acquisition and performance management offers a potent mix of speed, data-driven insight, and scalability. Organizations can recruit smarter and manage performance more dynamically by utilizing AI tools to augment human decision-making. Early evidence suggests tangible benefits – better hiring outcomes, more timely feedback, and identification of talent patterns that humans alone might miss (Frimpong & Wolfs, 2024). Yet, the human element remains paramount. Ethical considerations such as bias mitigation, transparency, and employee trust form the crux of sustainable AI–HR integration. HR leaders are thus evolving into "AI custodians," ensuring that algorithmic decisions are fair and aligned with organizational values (Kandasamy, 2024). When done right, AI can become a trusted partner in managing people – handling the heavy data crunching while humans drive the empathetic, strategic, and ethical aspects of talent management (Dwivedi, 2025a; Kandasamy, 2024). The goal is not to replace HR professionals, but to empower them with richer information and more time for human-centered work. As one systematic review put it, AI's strategic use can enhance decision-making and organizational agility, but only if balanced with fairness and human oversight (Madanchian et al., 2024b; Wang & Pashmforoosh, 2024). That balance defines the new era of talent management in an AI-augmented workplace.

6.2 AI-POWERED LEARNING AND DEVELOPMENT PROGRAMS

As the shelf-life of skills shortens in the digital age, organizations are turning to AI to revolutionize learning and development (L&D). Traditional one-size-fits-all training modules are being replaced or supplemented by personalized learning pathways curated by intelligent algorithms. These AI-driven platforms assess each employee's current skills, performance data, and even learning style to tailor training recommendations. The result is a customized curriculum for each individual – for example, a marketing specialist might automatically receive suggestions for brief courses in data analytics if the AI notices a skill gap in handling campaign metrics, while a software engineer might be guided to advanced courses on a new programming framework. Research emphasizes that personalized, adaptive learning can significantly improve knowledge retention and engagement. By leveraging AI to adjust content difficulty and modality (text, video, interactive simulations) based on user feedback and quiz performance, companies create a more responsive learning environment that keeps employees in their optimal learning zone (Chen, 2024). Chen (2024) notes that AI-enabled training systems can offer real-time formative feedback – much like a personal tutor – which helps learners correct mistakes on the fly and deepens understanding in a way static modules cannot. This responsiveness transforms learning from a periodic, generic event (e.g., annual workshops) into an ongoing, dynamic journey for each employee.

AI-driven training platforms often serve as the hub of this modern corporate academy. These platforms employ algorithms to recommend training content just as Netflix recommends movies – by analyzing user behavior and peer learning trends. If many product managers in a firm are taking a certain course on agile methodology and giving it high ratings, the system will suggest it to others in similar roles. The platform might also detect when an employee's role is about to change or a new project demands unfamiliar expertise, and proactively push relevant training resources. Sposato (2024b) describes how "leadership training and development in the age of AI" involves blending traditional development models with AI's predictive and adaptive capabilities. It's not merely about digitizing content, but using AI to identify developmental needs and match them with tailored interventions (Sposato, 2024b). This can include microlearning modules delivered in the flow of work – for instance, a five-minute tutorial video popping up when an employee encounters a problem in a software tool, guided by an AI that senses the user's struggle. Such timely assistance makes learning seamless and reduces the frustration that can occur when new technology or processes are introduced (Alghowinem et al., 2024).

A particularly exciting innovation in this space is the use of virtual coaching assistants. These are AI-powered "mentors" that can engage in natural language conversations with employees about their career goals and challenges. Consider a scenario: an employee could chat with an AI coach about improving their public speaking skills. The AI might analyze the employee's past presentation videos (with permission) to give specific feedback on pacing and tone, then recommend targeted exercises or courses to address weaknesses. Over time, the AI tracks progress and adjusts its coaching style – a truly personalized mentor available on-demand. Early implementations of this concept show promise, especially when combined with human coaches. For example, an AI coach might handle routine check-ins and skill exercises, escalating to a human mentor when deeper insight or empathy is needed. This hybrid coaching model scales leadership and professional development by allowing a smaller number of human coaches to effectively guide a larger workforce

(Westover, 2025). Westover highlights how AI, paired with human leadership intelligence, can accelerate the development of tomorrow's leaders by offering continuous, data-informed guidance that was previously impractical at scale.

In tandem, immersive technologies like VR/AR (Virtual Reality/Augmented Reality) are being supercharged by AI to create realistic, interactive training simulations. AI can adapt scenarios in real time within VR training modules – for instance, in a leadership training simulation, an AI-driven virtual "employee" might respond differently to the trainee's management style, presenting tougher challenges if the trainee is performing well, or offering hints if the trainee is struggling. These intelligent simulations build competencies in a safe sandbox, whether it's practicing difficult conversations, negotiating deals, or even medical and safety training. Arar et al. (2025) note that integrating AI into educational leadership and management training helps create more engaging and impactful learning experiences, allowing leaders to practice navigating complex situations in a low-risk virtual environment (Arar et al., 2025). The AI ensures that scenarios remain dynamic and realistic by controlling virtual characters and environmental variables, effectively "learning" from the trainee's actions and adjusting the difficulty level (Alghowinem et al., 2024). The outcome is a more resilient and adaptable learner, better prepared for real-world challenges after having battled life-like simulations.

Microlearning and AI curation go hand in hand to support continuous skill development. Microlearning involves bite-sized lessons or exercises – think of a daily two-minute quiz, a single concept video, or a short article summary. AI excels at curating and delivering these in a cadence optimized for each individual. If an employee has 15 minutes free between meetings, an AI might suggest a quick module from their learning path to reinforce a concept they were studying last week. Over time, the system can space out repetition of key points (leveraging spaced learning theory) and introduce new material when the learner is ready. By analyzing which questions an employee got wrong in a micro-quiz, the AI knows which areas to reinforce next time (Chen, 2024). The result is a learning loop that is highly personalized: it fills knowledge gaps and builds mastery incrementally without overwhelming busy professionals. This method also respects adult learning preferences – short, relevant pieces of learning that can be immediately applied at work are more appealing than day-long seminars that employees often find too abstract or time-consuming. Indeed, organizational case studies have observed higher voluntary participation in training when using AI-curated microlearning, as employees appreciate the flexibility and relevance (Sposato, 2024b).

Gamification is another trend amplified by AI – turning learning into a game-like experience with points, badges, and leaderboards. AI can enhance gamified learning by adjusting game difficulty in real time and personalizing challenges to keep learners in a state of flow. For example, an AI in a cybersecurity training game might present easier puzzles to a novice IT technician to build confidence, but give a senior analyst more complex cyberattack scenarios to solve. By mining data on user engagement, the AI learns how to keep each individual optimally challenged and motivated, thereby preventing both boredom and overwhelm. Such approaches have been linked to higher engagement and completion rates in corporate learning programs (Alghowinem et al., 2024). They also introduce a fun, competitive spirit among teams when AI-curated leaderboards showcase progress – adding a social learning element as colleagues cheer on or playfully compete with each other to earn certifications or expertise levels.

One critical aspect of AI-powered L&D is skill gap analysis at the organizational level. AI systems can aggregate data from performance reviews, project outcomes, and industry trends to identify what skills the company is lacking for its strategic goals. For instance, an AI might analyze the organization's competencies and reveal that while technical expertise is high, skills in creative problem-solving or cross-cultural communication are comparatively weak. Armed with these insights, L&D leaders can craft development programs targeting those specific gaps, ensuring the workforce is future-ready. Portillo (2025c) emphasizes the transformative role of AI in management development – by providing a data-driven map of organizational competencies, AI allows leaders to align training initiatives with the company's evolving needs. This way, training is not happening in a vacuum, but directly supporting strategic workforce transformation. Some forward-thinking enterprises even use AI scenario planning to anticipate new roles or skills that will be needed two–three years down the line, then begin training employees in those areas now (Budianto et al., 2025). The result is a more agile and resilient workforce, capable of adapting to technological disruptions because continuous reskilling has been woven into the company's fabric.

AI doesn't just identify gaps – it also measures the effectiveness of learning interventions through real-time feedback systems. Imagine an AI that observes how employees apply newly learned skills on the job (via project management tools, sales metrics, code quality, etc.) and correlates that with their training history. If a software developer took an AI-driven course on secure coding and subsequently the AI notes a drop in security issues in that developer's code commits, it's a strong signal the training worked. Conversely, if no improvement is seen, the AI might recommend a different approach – perhaps pairing the developer with a mentor or a more advanced course. This feedback loop closes the gap between learning and performance, creating a culture of evidence-based training. As Sposato (2024b) highlights, L&D programs must integrate closely with practice – the goal is not training for training's sake, but tangible improvement in leadership and work outcomes (Sposato, 2024b). AI's analytic power makes it possible to measure those outcomes quickly and adjust programs accordingly, something traditional L&D evaluations (like end-of-course surveys) often failed to capture in depth.

Implementing AI-powered L&D does raise important considerations. There's the challenge of ensuring content quality – algorithms might recommend popular courses that are engaging but not rigorous, so human oversight in content curation is still needed (Goryunova & Jenkins, 2024). Data privacy is another concern: personalized learning requires collecting data on employees' performance and even behaviors (like which pages of an e-learning they spent most time on). Organizations must handle this data ethically, securing it and being transparent about how it's used (Chen, 2024). Employees should feel that the data gathered is used to help them grow, not to penalize them for what they don't know. A humanized approach to AI learning programs means communicating the benefits to employees – that the company is investing in them by providing a "personal trainer" for their career development, not spying on their every mistake. Studies suggest that when framed positively and used in a supportive manner, employees appreciate AI learning tools and show greater engagement in development activities (Dwivedi, 2025b; Vivek & Krupskyi, 2024). For example, Dwivedi (2025b) discusses integrating emotional intelligence considerations into AI training tools, ensuring the tools encourage and motivate learners, fostering an encouraging atmosphere rather than a judgmental one.

AI is injecting new life and scale into corporate learning and development. It enables continuous, customized learning at an unprecedented scale – something that traditional training departments could scarcely achieve due to resource limits. From personalized learning paths and virtual coaches to adaptive simulations and microlearning bursts, AI makes learning more integrated with work and more responsive to individual needs (Alghowinem et al., 2024; Sposato, 2024b). The outcome is a workforce that is continually evolving, readily upskilling to meet emerging challenges. Importantly, AI-powered L&D also helps develop the very competencies that the AI era demands: digital literacy, adaptability, and a continuous learning mindset among employees and leaders. As one review put it, successful leadership in the AI era hinges on continuous learning and tailored training interventions (Tasnim, 2024a; Westover, 2025). By embedding those principles into daily work life through AI, organizations cultivate not just skills, but a culture of growth and agility. In the AI-augmented workplace, learning is no longer an occasional activity – it's a constant, AI-orchestrated symphony of development that keeps both people and companies in tune with the future.

6.3 DEVELOPING AI-READY LEADERSHIP COMPETENCIES

The rise of AI in the workplace is not only reshaping processes and teams – it's also redefining what it means to be an effective leader. Leadership competencies for the AI era blend traditional skills with new capabilities tailored to a tech-driven environment. To lead in an AI-augmented workplace, executives and managers must cultivate a portfolio of "AI-ready" competencies. One fundamental area is digital literacy and technological acumen. Leaders don't need to be coding experts, but they must be fluent in the language of data and AI. This means understanding, at a conceptual level, how AI systems work, what analytics reports indicate, and where AI can best augment human efforts. Leaders adept in data-driven decision-making can leverage AI insights to complement their intuition, rather than being either blindly led by algorithms or ignorantly dismissive of them (Tasnim, 2024a). As Tasnim (2024a) outlines, competencies such as data literacy and computational thinking are becoming as essential for leaders as financial literacy was in prior decades. The ability to interpret an AI's output – say, a predictive trend analysis – and integrate it into strategic planning is now a hallmark of effective leadership (Budianto et al., 2025).

Crucially, strategic foresight and adaptability have taken on new urgency. AI's rapid evolution means leaders face continuously shifting landscapes. Competent AI-era leaders are those who can anticipate technological trends and proactively adapt their strategies. This might involve scenario planning with AI – envisioning multiple futures with different tech assumptions – and preparing the organization for each. It also means being ready to pivot operations or business models when AI disruptions occur. We see this in leaders who, for example, swiftly embraced automation in supply chains or customer service bots ahead of competitors, turning potential disruption into a competitive advantage. A systematic literature review by Aziz et al. (2024b) found that the most frequently cited leadership qualities in the context of AI were adaptability and openness to innovation (Aziz et al., 2024b). In practice, adaptability might manifest as a leader's willingness to experiment with pilot projects using AI, learn from failures, and scale up successes. Continuous learning is part and parcel of this adaptability – leaders must model the growth mindset they wish to see in their teams, remaining curious and updating their own skills continuously (Sposato, 2024a). This could mean a CEO taking an online course on AI ethics or a sales director learning about the latest AI-driven CRM tools alongside her staff. When employees see leaders learning, it normalizes change and encourages organization-wide agility.

While being tech-savvy is important, the human-centric skills of leadership are perhaps even more critical in an AI context. Paradoxically, the more we integrate AI, the more a leader's human qualities stand out as a differentiator. Emotional intelligence (EI), for instance, becomes a defining competency in the age of intelligent machines. Why? Because AI, for all its prowess, lacks true empathy and social understanding. Leaders with high emotional intelligence can fill this gap by being attuned to their team's morale, fears, and motivations – especially as employees navigate changes brought by AI (Dwivedi, 2025a). Dwivedi (2025a) argues that integrating emotional intelligence with AI strategies is key to leadership excellence, as it fosters trust and a supportive environment for innovation. For example, an empathetic leader will recognize if employees are anxious about a new AI system and will address those concerns through open communication and reassurance, rather than just mandating the change. Such a leader might organize listening sessions or provide additional training to help the team gain confidence in using the AI. This builds trust in leadership and in the AI itself, creating a smoother adoption curve. Vivek and Krupskyi (2024) similarly emphasize that EI – coupled with understanding AI – shapes how future leaders will succeed, by enabling them to balance automated decision inputs with compassion and ethical judgment (Vivek & Krupskyi, 2024).

Hand in hand with EI is ethical reasoning and judgment. AI can introduce complex moral dilemmas, from bias in algorithms to privacy concerns and impacts on jobs. Leaders must have a strong ethical compass and the competency to navigate these issues. This includes being able to ask the right questions about an AI system: "Could this decision model be unfairly disadvantaging a group?" or "How do we ensure transparency so our employees understand how AI affects them?" An AI-ready leader is proactive in establishing ethical guidelines and governance for AI use (Kandasamy, 2024). They don't leave ethical considerations as an afterthought or solely to technical teams; instead, they spearhead cross-functional ethics committees or frameworks (Kandasamy, 2024). In essence, they champion responsible AI use, understanding that long-term trust in AI (both by employees and customers) hinges on ethical leadership. Competencies here include a solid grasp of AI ethics principles (fairness, accountability, transparency) and the courage to make decisions that might sacrifice short-term gains for long-term integrity. For example, a sales leader might decide not to implement an AI lead-scoring tool upon discovering it uses personal data in ways that violate customer trust, even if it promised a conversion boost. Such choices require ethical leadership fortitude.

Another emerging competency is the ability to collaborate with digital agents – essentially, being skilled at leading hybrid teams of humans and AI (which ties into section 6.4). Leaders must learn how to treat AI as a sort of team member or advisor. This involves a mindset shift: recognizing the AI's role, respecting its inputs, but also setting appropriate boundaries. A capable leader knows when to rely on AI and when to lean on human judgment – a skill that comes from experience, understanding AI limitations, and confidence in one's team. Lai and Rau (2025) provide an interesting perspective by studying scenarios of AI as a "co-leader," finding that human leadership behaviors had to adjust when an AI took on structured decision roles (Lai & Rau, 2025). Their findings suggest that leaders need to communicate clearly about how decisions are made in concert with AI and ensure team members still feel valued and heard when an algorithm is in the loop (Lai & Rau, 2025). Thus, competencies in communication and transparency about AI's function are vital. A leader might say to the team, "This forecasting AI will give us data-driven projections, but we will discuss and decide on the strategy together." That clarity helps maintain trust and team coherence.

AI-ready leadership also requires a high degree of creativity and innovative thinking. Ironically, while AI can be great at optimizing and analyzing patterns, it's not so good at out-of-the-box creativity or dealing with unprecedented situations. Leaders, therefore, should sharpen their creative problem-solving skills to complement AI's strengths. Those who can pose the right creative questions will get the most out of AI tools. For example, a leader who asks, "How might we use AI to not just speed up our current process, but to reinvent it entirely?" is likely to drive more transformative outcomes than one who only uses AI to make an existing workflow faster. Westover (2025) discusses "leadership intelligence" in the AI era as a synergy of human creativity and AI's analytical power, suggesting that visionary leaders leverage AI to amplify their imaginative strategies rather than letting AI confine them to existing patterns (Westover, 2025). Innovative thinking also ties to risk tolerance – the willingness to pilot new ideas with AI, accept failures, and learn. Leaders must become comfortable with iterative experimentation, a core principle from agile and design thinking methodologies now permeating leadership in tech-driven contexts.

Resilience and change leadership form another competency cluster. The AI-augmented workplace is characterized by frequent change – new systems, new team structures, evolving job roles. Leaders must be personally resilient to stress and uncertainty, and also skilled in guiding their teams through change (Tasnim, 2024a). This includes mastering change management techniques (some covered in Chapter 5) and being able to articulate a compelling vision of how AI will benefit the team. An AI-ready leader frames change positively: "This automation will relieve us of grunt work so we can focus on more creative tasks – let's grow into those opportunities together." They also show resilience by staying calm and solution-focused when AI projects encounter setbacks (which they inevitably do, given the experimental nature).

Their steadiness provides psychological safety for the team to adapt and continue learning. Leaders who demonstrate this resilience encourage a culture where AI is seen not as a threat but as an evolving tool that everyone can shape and improve.

To develop these competencies, many organizations are overhauling their leadership development programs. Traditional programs centered on communication, delegation, and business acumen are being updated to include modules on data analytics, AI ethics, human–machine collaboration, and adaptive thinking (Sposato, 2024a). Sposato (2024a) describes new training approaches for developing digital leadership skills, such as immersive simulations where leaders must manage AI-integrated projects, or action learning assignments where upcoming leaders implement a small AI tool and reflect on the experience (Sposato, 2024a). The idea is to provide emerging leaders with hands-on exposure to AI in a controlled environment, building their confidence and competence. Alghowinem et al. (2024) even detail an interactive, experiential learning approach in which professionals engage with AI tools directly as part of their leadership courses, ensuring that abstract concepts are tied to practical skill use.

Peer learning is another powerful method: companies are creating internal forums for leaders to share experiences about using AI in their departments (Elsherif, 2024a). These communities of practice allow leaders to teach each other – a sales manager might share how they used AI to predict customer churn, while an operations manager explains how they used AI for demand forecasting. Such cross-pollination spreads AI readiness across the leadership bench. It's also humanizing: leaders learn not just technical tips but also how others handled the people side of AI changes (e.g., overcoming team skepticism).

In evaluating whether a leader is "AI-ready," some organizations have begun incorporating assessment tools that measure these new competencies. For instance, scenario-based assessments might present a leader with an AI-related ethical dilemma or a data-driven decision scenario to see how they respond. Feedback from these assessments helps identify areas for further development, ensuring leaders don't just assume they have the skills but actually demonstrate them. As noted in a comprehensive review by Sejera and Bocarnea (2022), we may need to reconceptualize what leadership effectiveness means in AI environments, blending human and machine collaboration metrics. This could include evaluating how well a leader integrates AI advice into decisions, or how effectively they manage team dynamics when AI is a team participant. These are novel metrics that organizations are still exploring, but they underline the shifting competency model.

Ultimately, developing AI-ready leadership competencies is about balance and integration. The best leaders of tomorrow will be those who can integrate the analytic with the empathetic, the strategic with the ethical, and technology with humanity. They will use AI as an "extra brain" – superb at data and pattern recognition – while they themselves focus on the "heart and soul" of leadership: inspiring people, exercising judgment, and ensuring purpose and values guide every tech-enabled decision. As Portillo (2025c) notes, AI can be a strategic pillar for leadership, but it does not replace the need for human judgment and values; rather, it elevates the importance of those human qualities in guiding AI's use. Preparing leaders with this blend of competencies is an ongoing journey, requiring updated development practices and a commitment to continuous learning (Tasnim, 2024a; Westover, 2025). The organizations that succeed will be those led by individuals who are as adept at reading a room as they are at reading a data dashboard – truly centaur leaders, half human and half machine in capability, guiding their teams with wisdom in one hand and technology in the other.

6.4 MANAGING HYBRID TEAMS OF HUMANS AND AI AGENTS

In the AI-augmented workplace, the very definition of a "team" is expanding. It's no longer only flesh-and-blood colleagues collaborating to achieve goals; increasingly, AI agents are embedded as members of the team, contributing alongside humans. These might be algorithms making recommendations, robotic process automation bots handling workflow steps, or physical robots working beside humans on a factory floor. Managing such hybrid teams – part human, part AI – is a new frontier for leaders and presents unique challenges and opportunities.

A key aspect of managing hybrid teams is clarifying the roles of AI agents vs. humans. Just as one would define roles and responsibilities for human team members, managers must deliberately define what the AI's role is on the team. Is the AI a tool used by the team, a semi-autonomous assistant, or an autonomous decision-maker in certain domains? Clarity on this prevents confusion and helps set expectations. For example, in a customer support team that includes an AI chatbot, the manager might establish that the chatbot handles all Tier-1 simple queries, while humans handle more complex cases or any escalations from frustrated customers. This role clarity avoids duplication of work (humans redoing what the AI did) and also prevents things from "falling through the cracks" because each task is assigned to either a human or AI explicitly (Elabied, 2024). Elabied (2024) discusses new paradigms of collaborative leadership with AI in a university administration context, highlighting that when leaders clearly delineate tasks between AI and staff, the team as a whole operates more smoothly and with less resentment or friction (Elabied, 2024).

Human–AI team coordination hence becomes a managerial competency. It involves scheduling and orchestrating workflows so that humans and AIs hand off tasks efficiently. Take the scenario of a hybrid analytics team: an AI system crunches raw data and generates a report, then a human analyst interprets that report and presents insights to stakeholders. A manager must ensure the timing and integration of these tasks – perhaps by scheduling the AI to run analyses overnight so humans have results ready in the morning, and setting up a process where analysts can feed back into the AI any new variables or corrections needed. Dynamic task allocation might even be aided by AI itself: some advanced project management systems can automatically assign tasks either to a human or a bot depending on which is better suited or available (Lai & Rau, 2025). But ultimate oversight of that allocation falls to managers, who need to verify that the right balance is struck and adjust if, say, the AI is overburdening humans with too many alerts or the humans are overriding the AI too frequently.

One of the thorniest issues in hybrid teams is building and maintaining trust – in both directions. Humans need to trust their AI collaborators, and similarly, AI systems (in a metaphorical sense) "trust" the input and supervision from humans – meaning they function best when humans use them as intended. Trust from humans comes through experience and transparency. Early on, team members might be skeptical of an AI's suggestions ("Can we really trust this hiring algorithm's ranking of candidates?" or "Is the sales forecast AI accurate?"). As a manager, facilitating small wins can help – encourage the team to test the AI on lower-stakes decisions or run it in parallel with human judgment to compare results. Over time, as the AI proves reliable, trust grows. Lai and Rau's (2025) study on AI as a co-leader found that when the AI's "behavior" in decision-making was transparent and aligned with team goals, human participants were more likely to accept its recommendations (Lai & Rau, 2025). Thus, managers should insist on a degree of explainability from AI tools: when an AI provides an output, it should come with rationale or at least be open to interrogation by the team (why did the logistics AI reroute shipments this way?). Many AI vendors now include explainable AI features precisely because organizations realize how important this is for adoption (Kandasamy, 2024). A transparent AI is a trustworthy AI in the eyes of team members (Kandasamy, 2024).

On the flip side, humans need to be able to trust that their own roles remain meaningful. If people fear that the AI is gunning for their jobs or that their contributions are undervalued compared to the algorithm's, morale will suffer. A savvy manager addresses this by humanizing the AI's role: framing the AI as a support tool that amplifies the team's capabilities, not a rival. For instance, calling an AI system "your digital analyst" or "co-pilot" positions it as an assistant to the human team members. Managers can highlight how the humans ultimately make the key decisions or handle the relationships that the AI can't – reinforcing each person's importance. Noponen et al. (2023) explore the search for authenticity in AI-enhanced leadership, effectively noting that teams respond best when leaders remain authentic and emphasize human values, even as they incorporate AI (Noponen et al., 2023). In practice, this could mean a leader openly acknowledging an AI's contribution ("Our scheduling AI did a great job optimizing shifts – let's appreciate that tool. And a special kudos to Maria for handling the complex exceptions the AI couldn't address."). This balanced credit helps the team see AI as an assistant, not a threat.

Now consider the "AI perspective": while AIs don't have feelings, they have performance reliability which can be undermined by misuse. If humans constantly feed poor data or ignore the AI's outputs, the effective functioning of the hybrid team suffers. So managers must train their teams on how to work with the AI properly – for example, logging information consistently so the AI has good data, or following through on AI alerts instead of dismissing them without investigation. One might think of this as getting the team to "earn the AI's trust" in a playful sense – by being good stewards of the AI's inputs and outputs, they keep the human–AI partnership strong.

Communication norms in hybrid teams need careful design. Communication in human–AI teams might involve dashboards, alert systems, or chat interfaces where AIs "speak" through notifications and humans respond. Setting up clear protocols here is key: for example, when the AI flags an anomaly, who on the team addresses it? How should they report back if it was a false alarm or a true issue? Some organizations develop a sort of etiquette manual for interacting with AI systems – analogous to guidelines for interpersonal communication. It might specify things like: always review the AI's reasoning provided before overriding a decision, or always tag the AI in a project management chat when manual changes are made to data so it can update. These might sound technical, but they shape the collaboration flow. Budianto et al. (2025) highlight that transforming organizations with AI means redesigning workflows for this very coordination – ensuring that the interplay of human creativity and machine efficiency is smoothly orchestrated (Budianto et al., 2025).

A particularly intriguing aspect of managing AI agents is considering the "personality" or interaction style of AI in teams. While AI doesn't have a true personality, designers often imbue chatbots or virtual assistants with a certain tone – formal, friendly, humorous, etc. A manager implementing a customer service bot, for instance, might have a say in whether the bot uses colloquial language or sticks to strictly professional responses. This matters because it affects how human team members perceive and collaborate with the AI. If the AI is too stiff, humans may not engage with it fully; if it's too quirky, they might not take it seriously. Some companies have even held little "introductions" for a new AI agent, like sending a note to the team: "Meet Cora, our new AI assistant. She's here to help with data analysis – she's super fast and detail-oriented, but please forgive her if she sounds a bit formal at times!" This lighthearted humanization can lower resistance and give team members permission to incorporate the AI into their social fabric, to an appropriate extent. Hwang's (2024) comparative study on AI-assisted decision-making indicates that teams perform best when they feel a sense of familiarity and predictability in how the AI behaves, much like understanding a teammate's quirks builds trust (Hwang, 2024).

Of course, with AI agents involved, accountability in teams gets complicated. If an AI-driven recommendation goes wrong, who is responsible – the AI, the manager, the team member who acted on it? Best practice leans toward shared accountability but ultimate human ownership. Managers should establish that while AI contributes, a human will always review critical decisions. For example, a hybrid investment team might use an AI to flag trades, but a human portfolio manager signs off on each trade – and therefore, takes responsibility for the outcomes (Devabhaktuni et al., 2025). This aligns with emerging governance perspectives that keep humans "in the loop" for accountability (Devabhaktuni et al., 2025). It's important to communicate to the team that the AI is there to assist, not to take the fall for mistakes. If something does go awry due to an AI suggestion, effective leaders treat it as a system learning opportunity rather than shifting the blame to the machine (which solves nothing). They'll investigate why the AI erred – was the data faulty? Was the model not accounting for a scenario? – and adjust either the AI or team procedures accordingly, demonstrating a focus on solutions over scapegoating.

Best practices for hybrid teamwork are beginning to emerge from various case studies and research. One such practice is the concept of feedback loops between human and AI. For instance, when human team members disagree with an AI output and override it, having a mechanism to feed that decision back into the AI system can be invaluable. It's analogous to mentoring a junior employee – if they make a recommendation and you correct it, you'd explain why so they learn. Similarly, teams are encouraging a culture of "teaching the AI." If the AI suggests restocking a product and the supply chain manager knows there's a supplier issue not reflected in the data, the manager overrides but also inputs a note explaining the situation. Over time, if the AI system is capable of learning (via machine learning updates), it can incorporate such human insights and improve. This continuous improvement cycle strengthens both the AI and team's performance. Another best practice is ensuring diverse input into the AI's functioning. In a human team, diversity of perspectives yields better decisions; likewise, if an AI's parameters or training data are vetted by a diverse group of team members, it's less likely to embody one person's blind spots or biases. A practical example: in a marketing team using an AI to draft social media posts, having team members from different demographics review the AI's content suggestions can catch if the tone or references might not resonate with certain audiences. This way, the AI becomes more attuned to the team's collective intelligence rather than a narrow viewpoint. Training employees to work effectively with AI is a crucial management task as well. It's unrealistic to assume everyone instantly knows how to interpret a confusion matrix or adjust to an AI colleague's "moods" (like occasional errors or downtimes). Managers should facilitate training sessions or resource guides on how the AI systems work, their limitations, and how to troubleshoot basic issues. For example, a manager might run a workshop on "How our AI forecasting tool makes predictions and what to do when its prediction seems off."

Empowering team members with this knowledge reduces frustration and dependency on specialists. It also fosters a sense of co-ownership of the AI among the team, rather than treating it as some alien gadget dropped into their midst. When team members better understand the AI, their collaboration with it becomes more fluent – akin to knowing a teammate's strengths and weaknesses. Managing hybrid teams also requires emotional and cultural intelligence from leaders. Leaders need to navigate these feelings with empathy, framing the AI as augmenting, not questioning, their expertise. It helps to involve such experienced team members in refining the AI – perhaps through a formal role like "AI liaison" or similar, where they can channel their knowledge into improving the system's rules or models. This inclusion can transform a skeptic into a champion, as they see their input reflected in the AI's improved performance (Vivek & Krupskyi, 2024).

In terms of outcomes, well-managed human–AI teams can achieve productivity gains and quality improvements that neither humans nor AIs could reach alone. Studies have shown, for instance, that in medical diagnostics, a human doctor and an AI working together make more accurate diagnoses than either alone. In business contexts, centaur teams (as they're sometimes called) have led to faster decision-making with robust analysis and creative insight combined (Nyoto et al., 2024b). Budianto et al. (2025) note improved operational efficiency and team dynamics in organizations where AI was thoughtfully integrated into teams, essentially acting as a catalyst that enhances human teamwork rather than replacing it (Budianto et al., 2025). Imagine a project meeting where an AI dynamically updates project metrics on a screen in real time as team members discuss options – the conversation stays grounded in data, reducing meeting time and preventing decisions based on outdated information. Or consider product development sprints where an AI instantly prototypes design variations based on the team's brainstormed ideas, allowing immediate feedback and iteration. These synergies illustrate the potential for hybrid teams to be more than the sum of their parts. Of course, not every task is ideally suited for AI involvement, and part of managing hybrid teams is knowing where to draw the line. Leaders must decide which team processes remain strictly human (perhaps brainstorming creative concepts with no AI to encourage uninhibited imagination) and which are AI-supported (such as data analysis or routine report generation). The craft of leading hybrid teams lies in continuously tuning this balance as both the people and technology evolve. Regular team retrospectives that include evaluating the human–AI collaboration can be invaluable: ask questions like "Did the AI help us this sprint? Where did it hinder? What can we adjust?" This reflective practice treats the AI as a permanent team fixture that everyone has a stake in improving.

Managing teams composed of humans and AI agents is about fostering collaboration, trust, and clarity across the biological–artificial divide. Leaders who excel will create an environment where AI is a welcome partner – reliable, understood, and integrated into the team's rhythms – and where human team members feel empowered by the new capabilities at their disposal (Lai & Rau, 2025; Noponen et al., 2023). Hybrid teams challenge managers to elevate their coordination and communication skills to a new level, but they also offer a glimpse of incredible efficiency and creativity. As one leadership study succinctly put it, collaborative leadership models that integrate human and AI capabilities encourage shared decision-making and problem-solving, unlocking outcomes neither could achieve alone (Budianto et al., 2025; Elabied, 2024). The effective manager of an AI-augmented team will be part coach, part translator (between human and AI "language"), and part guardian of team cohesion. When those pieces come together, hybrid teams can become true powerhouses of innovation and productivity – a living testament to the idea that centaurs (half-human, half-machine teams) can outpace any purely human or purely AI group in the race for organizational excellence.

6.5 EMPLOYEE EXPERIENCE AND WELL-BEING WITH AI AUTOMATION

The infusion of AI and automation into the workplace is transforming the daily experience of employees in profound ways. At its best, AI promises to relieve workers of drudgery and enhance job satisfaction by allowing them to focus on more meaningful tasks. At its worst, it threatens to introduce stress, surveillance, and the specter of job insecurity. Navigating this dual-edged sword is a central challenge for modern organizations aiming to support employee well-being in an AI-driven world.

One immediate impact of AI automation is on job satisfaction and workload. By automating repetitive and mundane tasks, AI can significantly reduce the workload burden on employees. For instance, consider a financial analyst who used to spend hours manually reconciling data from different spreadsheets – an AI script can now do that within minutes, freeing the analyst to concentrate on interpreting results and strategizing. Such workload reduction benefits can lead to higher job satisfaction because employees spend more time on intellectually stimulating and creative aspects of their jobs. As one study found, when employees perceive AI as a supportive tool that takes care of grunt work, they report improved job performance and satisfaction (Pei et al., 2024). Pei et al. (2024) noted that leveraging AI to handle negative feedback or routine tasks allowed employees to "save face" and focus on improvement, enhancing their overall engagement and morale. Indeed, many workers enjoy their jobs more when freed from what they often call "busy work" – the manual, monotonous tasks that don't fully use their skills. In this sense, AI can act as a liberator, granting employees more autonomy and purpose in their roles by shifting their effort to strategy, relationship-building, and other uniquely human endeavors (Ateeq et al., 2025).

However, this positive scenario hinges on thoughtful job redesign. The redesign for meaningful work is critical: simply cutting out tasks via automation without reshaping roles could leave employees feeling aimless or, paradoxically, less essential. The goal should be augmentation, not subtraction – when automation removes one set of duties, managers should collaboratively identify how the employee's role can expand in more rewarding dimensions. For example, if an AI system handles 50% of incoming IT support tickets automatically, the IT staff should then be empowered to use that saved time on proactive infrastructure improvements or deeper problem-solving for the tougher tickets. This not only keeps their workload fulfilling but also signals that the organization values their higher-level contributions. Research on organizational behavior suggests that when technology implementations are paired with initiatives to enrich remaining jobs (like new projects, cross-training, or innovation time), employees experience greater engagement rather than the boredom or frustration that can occur if their roles shrink (Pavitra et al., 2024; Duffour, 2024). As Pavitra et al. (2024) highlight, a socio-technical approach that considers both technical efficiency and human fulfillment leads to improved employee engagement during AI integration.

Another dimension of well-being is stress and mental health. AI can impact this in complex ways. On one hand, certain AI tools act as support systems that reduce stress – like an AI scheduling assistant that helps an overworked employee manage their calendar better, or an AI-driven wellness app that monitors work patterns and prompts breaks before burnout sets in. There are even AI programs now that analyze indicators (such as typing speed, language tone in emails, or meeting schedules) to infer when an employee might be fatigued or stressed, gently suggesting they take a rest or offering resources for help. In theory, such tools exemplify a caring use of AI to promote digital well-being and burnout prevention. For example, if an AI notices an employee sending emails at midnight repeatedly, it might flag this to the employee or HR as a sign of potential overwork. Herlina et al. (2024) found that implementing "intelligent experience" systems – essentially AI that helps manage workloads and sustainable practices – was associated with higher work engagement among employees, as it seemed to mitigate extreme stressors (Herlina et al., 2024). The Indonesian companies in their study that introduced AI to optimize work scheduling and load saw employees more energized and involved in their work (Herlina et al., 2024). This suggests that well-calibrated AI interventions can indeed serve as a buffer against overwork.

On the other hand, AI can also be a source of stress if not handled carefully. The phenomenon of "augmentation anxiety" – where employees are anxious not only about outright replacement (more on that soon) but about having to constantly upskill to keep up with AI – is real. An employee might worry: "The AI automates part of my job today, what if tomorrow it can do even more and I can't keep up?" This creates an undercurrent of tension. Additionally, if AI tools are perceived as surveillance (e.g., software tracking keystrokes or capturing webcam photos to ensure remote workers are at their desks), employees can experience increased stress and a sense of invasion, harming trust and morale. One must recall the strong reaction many companies faced when they introduced AI-based monitoring during the shift to remote work – some employees reported feeling like they were treated as machines themselves, with every minute accounted for by an algorithm. This clearly detracts from well-being, leading to pressure and resentment. Thus, trust in AI from the employee's perspective is crucial: they need to trust that the AI is there to help, not to police or judge them unfairly.

How can organizations ensure AI supports rather than erodes well-being? A key strategy is embracing human-centric automation design. This means designing and implementing AI with the end-user (the employee) in mind: their psychological comfort; their sense of control; and their ability to derive positive meaning from the change. For instance, involving employees in the selection or configuration of an AI tool can increase their sense of control and acceptance. A company might pilot a new AI workflow assistant with a volunteer group of employees, gather their feedback on the experience, and adjust the tool's settings or the way it's integrated based on that input before a full rollout. This inclusive approach can transform wary employees into proud co-creators of the new process, significantly reducing anxiety. Moreover, transparency is paramount. If an AI is making decisions that affect employees (like how tasks are assigned or how performance is measured), explaining those algorithms in understandable terms can alleviate fears of secret unfairness. Kandasamy (2024) stresses that fairness and transparency in AI deployment are not just ethical moves but also directly tie into employee trust and acceptance (Kandasamy, 2024). Knowing that an AI scheduling system evenly distributes unpopular night shifts, for example, or that the AI evaluating support tickets for escalation is blind to who handled the ticket (preventing personal bias) can reassure employees that the tech is impartial and beneficial.

Trust in AI intersects deeply with well-being. When employees trust the AI tools they work with, they experience less stress and ambiguity. They can confidently delegate tasks to AI and focus on what they do best, leading to a state of flow rather than anxiety. To build this trust, some organizations have introduced AI slowly, demonstrating quick wins and accuracy in supporting roles before expanding AI's responsibilities. Think of a warehouse where initially the AI only suggested pick paths (routes for workers to collect items) and employees could compare and follow them if they agreed. Once they saw that following the AI's suggestion indeed saved them time and effort consistently, they began to rely on it, and the suggestions became an accepted, trusted part of their routine. This incremental approach gave employees evidence of the AI's reliability and a chance to acclimate, improving their comfort and reducing the fear of the unknown.

We must address the elephant in the room: replacement anxiety and job security. One of the greatest sources of stress related to AI at work is the fear that automation will make one's role obsolete. Historically, technological changes have always spurred such fears – from factory machines to early computers – but AI's broad capabilities rekindle them strongly. It's crucial for leadership to tackle this head-on with empathy and honesty. Blanket reassurances that "no jobs will be lost" can ring hollow if not true; instead, emphasis on redeployment and reskilling is more productive. Wang and Pashmforoosh (2024) argue for keeping HRD in the loop specifically to manage such transitions – meaning companies should actively plan for how to develop and move talent as AI takes over certain tasks (Wang & Pashmforoosh, 2024). In practice, this might mean offering training programs for employees whose current tasks are heavily automated, preparing them for more advanced roles, or even entirely new positions created by AI growth. A positive case is often cited from companies that embraced automation but did so by reskilling their workforce – for example, a bank that used AI to automate some clerical work but retrained those employees to become client advisors or data analysts, ultimately keeping them employed in more enriching roles. When employees see a clear path for themselves in the AI future, their anxiety diminishes and even turns into excitement for learning new skills (Ateeq et al., 2025). Ateeq et al. (2025) observed that organizations which provided strong support for learning and ethical integration of AI saw employees remain engaged and even have higher performance, as they felt part of the innovation rather than victims of it (Ateeq et al., 2025).

Another angle on well-being is how AI influences work–life balance. Ideally, automation should reduce overwork – if AI can handle tasks while you are away, you don't need to stay late to finish everything. There are optimistic visions where AI acts like a diligent assistant that continues working (within limits set by you) after you log off, and by morning you find a lot of prep work done. For example, an AI might draft a report overnight based on data updates, so you just refine it in the morning rather than starting from scratch. When implemented with respect for boundaries, AI could indeed help employees reclaim time. In reality, however, there's a risk that organizations simply raise expectations: if AI makes someone 20% more efficient, perhaps the company assigns 20% more work rather than letting the person go home earlier. That's a cultural choice. Progressive organizations consciously use AI gains to promote flexibility – maybe allowing a four-day workweek with the aid of AI maintaining outputs, or at least encouraging employees to use saved time for creative projects, upskilling, or rest. Augmentation should ideally translate to a more sustainable work pace. Leaders play a role here by not automatically filling every freed minute with new tasks, but recognizing the value of giving employees headspace – which often leads to innovation and better mental health.

Employee empowerment through AI tools is a positive narrative for wellbeing. When people feel capable of doing more and making a bigger impact because they have AI "superpowers," their job satisfaction and confidence can soar. For example, a junior data analyst might be able to produce insights that previously only a senior statistician could, by using an AI analytics platform – this can be incredibly empowering and motivating for that employee. They may feel a greater sense of accomplishment and recognition, knowing they contributed at a higher level than their experience alone would allow. Lakshmikanth et al. (2024) found that tailoring leadership styles with AI inputs led to higher employee engagement and performance, suggesting that when leaders use AI to better support each team member's success, employees feel more empowered and engaged (Lakshmikanth et al., 2024). One can imagine a scenario where a manager uses an AI tool to identify an employee's strengths and interest areas (perhaps through analysis of project performance data), and then assigns them a special task that plays to those strengths. The employee, seeing that the manager and the data have confidence in them, may feel a boost in their own self-efficacy. Empowerment only occurs if the introduction of AI is accompanied by trust and autonomy. If every AI suggestion is mandated with no room for human discretion, employees won't feel empowered; they'll feel controlled by the machine. So maintaining a balance where employees can override or question AI – and are encouraged to use their judgment – is vital. This not only yields better results (because human insight can catch AI errors) but also keeps employees psychologically in the driver's seat. Herlina et al. (2024) mention "intelligent experience" combined with sustainable practices – likely hinting at the idea that smart tools should be used in ways that sustain human motivation and agency, not diminish it (Herlina et al., 2024).

The overall employee experience in an AI-augmented role can be very fulfilling if organizations manage the transition well. Imagine a future employee reflecting on their day:

> My AI assistant sorted through my emails and scheduled my meetings, so I spent the morning brainstorming with my team on a new product idea. In the afternoon, I used a recommendation from our AI to solve a tricky client problem – it was like having a genius second opinion on hand. I left work on time with a sense of accomplishment and little stress.

This is an aspirational but feasible picture of AI–human harmony improving the quality of work life. Contrast that with a poorly handled scenario:

> I spent my day fighting with an algorithm that assigns my tasks unrealistically and sends alerts all the time. I'm not sure what value I add anymore since the system basically tells me what to do, and I'm worried it's also telling my boss that I'm not needed.

The gulf between these experiences comes down to implementation, communication, and workplace culture around AI.

It's worth noting that diversity and inclusion factors (which we'll address more in section 6.6) also intersect with well-being. Certain groups might feel disproportionately threatened or stressed by AI due to historical patterns (e.g., older workers worrying about tech displacement, or underrepresented groups fearing biased algorithms). A truly people-centric approach will pay attention to these nuances. Offering targeted support, like additional training for those who are less tech-savvy, or rigorously auditing AI for biases that could affect workplace fairness (thus affecting minority employees' trust and comfort), goes a long way. After all, well-being is holistic – if AI inadvertently discriminates or is perceived to, it harms the psychological safety of those impacted.

In conclusion, AI's impact on employee experience is what the organization and its leaders make of it. There is enormous potential for enhancing well-being: reduced tedium; more engaging work; better work–life balance; and empowerment through smart tools. Studies like those by Ateeq et al. (2025) and Herlina et al. (2024) show that, under thoughtful implementation, AI integration correlates with higher engagement and performance – indicators that employees are thriving rather than suffering (Ateeq et al., 2025; Herlina et al., 2024). But these outcomes are not automatic. They require deliberate change management with a human touch: involve employees in the change; be transparent; invest in their growth; and uphold values of fairness and respect. Kandasamy (2024) and Wang and Pashmforoosh (2024) both underscore that ignoring the human side – whether it's ethical concerns, displacement fears, or privacy – can lead to a backlash that undermines both trust and well-being.

Conversely, when organizations treat AI adoption not just as a tech upgrade but as a people strategy – aiming for augmentation, not replacement – employees often respond with enthusiasm and increased well-being. The mantra for leaders should be clear: automate the tedious, elevate the human. Do this, and AI will be seen not as a cold productivity tool, but as a partner that helped everyone work smarter and live better on and off the job.

6.6 DIVERSITY, EQUITY, AND INCLUSION IN TECH-DRIVEN WORKPLACES

In the rapidly evolving landscape of AI-enhanced work, ensuring diversity, equity, and inclusion (DEI) has become both more challenging and more critical. Technology is never neutral; it carries the biases of its creators and the data it's trained on. Thus, as organizations lean on AI for decisions affecting people – hiring, promotions, evaluations – they must confront the stark reality that these systems can inadvertently perpetuate or even amplify biases. At the same time, AI also offers new tools to promote inclusion and break down barriers if deployed with care. The interplay of DEI and AI is complex: it's a story of pitfalls to avoid and opportunities to seize in creating truly equitable, tech-driven workplaces.

One major concern is algorithmic bias and its impact on diversity. Several high-profile cases have shown that AI systems used in HR – from résumé screening to performance scoring – can exhibit racial, gender, or age biases, reflecting historical inequities in the data they learned from. For instance, if a hiring AI was trained on years of data in which a company tended to hire mostly men for engineering roles, the AI might "learn" to favor male candidates, even if gender is not an explicit input, by proxying through other variables. This can result in qualified women or non-binary candidates being ranked lower or filtered out, undermining diversity efforts (Kandasamy, 2024). Kandasamy (2024) points out that without ethical leadership oversight, AI in recruitment can exacerbate discrimination – a dire warning that fairness must be a design principle from the start (Kandasamy, 2024). Similarly, an AI used to determine who gets selected for leadership training might inadvertently give lower scores to employees from underrepresented backgrounds if their past opportunities (and thus performance metrics) were less robust due to systemic bias. This "rich get richer" effect can freeze inequities into place behind the veneer of algorithmic objectivity.

To combat this, organizations are focusing on inclusive design of AI systems. Inclusive design means involving diverse stakeholders in the development and testing of AI. If the development team for an HR algorithm is itself diverse and attuned to potential biases, they're more likely to spot problems. For example, they may realize a facial recognition-based time-clock system could fail for people of certain ethnicities (a known issue, as some algorithms misidentify darker-skinned faces at higher rates) and thus avoid using it or demand a better-trained model. Mariyono et al. (2024) argue that integrating AI into inclusive leadership requires transforming management practices with a global and diverse perspective, suggesting that the very teams governing AI need representation from different genders, cultures, and abilities (Mariyono et al., 2024). This might manifest as an internal "AI ethics committee" with employees from various departments and backgrounds who review new AI tools for bias and inclusivity (Wang & Pashmforoosh, 2024). Keeping HR, legal, and representatives of employee resource groups in the loop when deploying AI that affects people can ensure questions of equity get raised early and often (Wang & Pashmforoosh, 2024).

Another tactic is focusing on the diversity of datasets used to train AI. AI's outputs can only be as fair as the data it learns from. If that data skews heavily toward one demographic, predictions will skew too. Therefore, companies are demanding that vendors provide evidence of diverse training data, or they are actively augmenting datasets to balance representation. For instance, an AI language model used for a company's chatbot should be trained on language from a mix of dialects and genders to avoid, say, responding more politely to one group over another. This extends to AI voice assistants – having diverse voice inputs can prevent it from only understanding certain accents. In a more internal example, if using AI to analyze employee feedback sentiment, ensuring that language differences (men might phrase feedback differently than women, or cultural differences in expression) are accounted for will lead to more equitable interpretations. Portillo (2025c) notes the potential of AI to democratize and foster inclusive cultures, but that only holds if the AI itself is built on inclusive foundations.

AI can also be harnessed as a tool for accessibility and inclusion when done right. There are inspiring examples of AI aiding employees with disabilities: AI-driven transcription can instantly caption meetings for deaf employees, and computer vision AI can help blind employees navigate digital content by narrating on-screen elements. These kinds of applications open doors for talent that previously faced barriers, thereby increasing workplace diversity. Moreover, AI translators can facilitate multicultural teams by translating languages in real time, making global collaboration more inclusive for those who are non-native English speakers, for example. An inclusive tech-driven workplace proactively uses such AI to ensure everyone can participate fully. It's about extending the concept of "reasonable accommodation" into the AI era: if there's an AI tool that can help include someone, the forward-looking organization will deploy it.

However, even well-intentioned AI for inclusion must be monitored. Suppose a company uses an AI mentor matching system that pairs employees for coaching. If that AI has bias, it might not pair minority employees with top mentors, or it might form pairings based on flawed similarity metrics that end up reinforcing silos (e.g., always pairing people of the same background). So oversight remains important. Devabhaktuni et al. (2025) emphasize applied AI governance with fairness metrics and bias audits as essential practices (Devabhaktuni et al., 2025). They recommend regularly testing AI outcomes – for example, test the hiring algorithm with synthetic résumés of equally qualified candidates of different genders/races to see if the scores come out the same. If not, recalibrate the model or add fairness constraints. These sorts of bias auditing and mitigation practices are becoming standard to maintain equity (Devabhaktuni et al., 2025).

Inclusive leadership in a tech-driven workplace also takes on new forms. Leaders must cultivate an environment where not only diverse humans are included, but where technology is leveraged to enhance inclusion rather than create divisions. For example, consider meetings in which some team members are present physically and some join via a virtual AI-enabled presence (like an avatar or a robot representing a remote worker). It's the leader's job to ensure the remote participant (via technology) is given equal voice – which might mean consciously soliciting input from those attending through the AI medium and making sure the tech (like an AI camera that focuses on whoever is speaking) doesn't inadvertently sideline anyone. Inclusive leadership also means being aware of digital divides within the team. Not everyone may be equally comfortable with new tech tools; different generations or backgrounds can influence digital literacy. A patient, inclusive leader will ensure training is offered to those who need it, and early adopters help mentor those still learning, rather than letting a split develop between "tech natives" and "others." Vivek and Krupskyi (2024) hint that emotional intelligence (EI) combined with AI savvy is vital for future leaders – this includes empathy toward those adapting to tech and ensuring nobody is left behind (Vivek & Krupskyi, 2024).

A particular DEI facet in AI workplaces is gender and ethnicity representation in AI leadership roles themselves. The tech field has long struggled with underrepresentation of women and minority groups. As AI becomes central to strategy, who gets to lead AI projects or departments? If those opportunities skew to the usual suspects, DEI suffers. But if companies intentionally diversify their AI teams and leadership (which some are doing via scholarships, return-to-work programs for women in tech, etc.), it can have a ripple effect. Diverse AI teams are more likely to design fair systems, as mentioned earlier, and they also signal an inclusive culture which aids in attracting and retaining diverse talent. It's a virtuous circle: inclusive workplaces build better AI, which helps maintain inclusion. Mariyono et al. (2024) advocate for transforming management for a globalized future – an implication is that leadership must be globally minded and diverse to harness AI responsibly in different cultural contexts (Mariyono et al., 2024). If AI solutions are led and approved by homogeneous groups, they might not even spot when something is culturally insensitive or exclusive.

From a policy perspective, many organizations are developing equitable AI policy frameworks. These are formal guidelines or principles that dictate how AI should be used in ways that uphold DEI values. For instance, a company might have a policy that any AI used for people decisions must be thoroughly tested for bias and results regularly reviewed for disparate impact on any protected class (Devabhaktuni et al., 2025). Some tie these principles to the company's core values or code of conduct, making it clear that discriminatory outcomes – even if unintended from a machine – are unacceptable and will be corrected. On a broader scale, regulations like the EU's proposed AI Act explicitly consider the impact on fundamental rights, which includes non-discrimination. Companies operating globally have to align with these emerging standards, effectively baking fairness into their tech deployments. There is also movement on the standards front: groups like IEEE and NIST have been working on frameworks for trustworthy and inclusive AI. Forward-looking companies aren't waiting to be told – they are voluntarily adopting such frameworks, seeing it as not just compliance but a competitive advantage. After all, a workplace known for fair and inclusive AI practices could become an employer of choice, especially for tech workers who care deeply about ethics.

Global perspectives on inclusion also matter. What inclusion means can vary culturally – an algorithm that's fair in one context might not be elsewhere due to different historical inequities. For example, in some countries, caste or tribe could be a dimension of bias that AI needs to consider. Global companies thus must consider local DEI nuances when deploying AI. A solution is to include local voices in AI development and to decentralize some decisions about AI use to ensure cultural fit. Nyoto et al. (2024b) conducted a review that showed the positive side of AI in corporate leadership, including potentially democratizing leadership development across regions (Nyoto et al., 2024b). But they also note implicitly that attention must be paid to context – a global AI leadership program might need tailoring to be inclusive in different regions (Nyoto et al., 2024b).

Inclusion in a tech-driven workplace also touches on the concept of the digital divide not just globally, but within society and companies. Those with advanced tech skills might pull ahead, while others lag. Companies with a genuine inclusion mindset invest in upskilling programs targeting underrepresented groups, ensuring they can participate in AI-related opportunities. For example, some banks have programs to train tellers (often more women and minorities in such roles) in data analysis, so they can move into higher-paying tech-driven roles internally as automation changes their original jobs. This way, diversity is maintained and even improved in the higher echelons of a tech organization, rather than AI causing a homogeneous tech elite.

Another important element is transparency and communication. When employees understand how and why decisions are made – especially those involving AI – it reduces feelings of unfairness. An inclusive culture encourages questions: if someone feels an AI-driven decision (like being passed over for a promotion) might have been biased, they should be able to query it and get a clear human explanation and review. In effect, technology shouldn't become an impenetrable wall that obscures bias. Ethical leadership demands shining light into that black box (Kandasamy, 2024).

It's inspiring to note that AI itself can be used to advance DEI when applied creatively. Some firms use AI to write job postings in a more inclusive way, avoiding gendered or exclusionary language (the AI suggests changes that attract a broader pool). Others use AI to analyze pay equity, scanning for patterns of disparity that might not be obvious, thus helping correct inequality. There are AI-driven platforms that help amplify typically under-heard voices in meetings (e.g., tracking who speaks how often and gently nudging if some voices dominate). These applications show that if we approach AI with a DEI lens, it can become a powerful ally – a tool for shining a light on bias and for systematically breaking down barriers (Pago, 2024). Pago (2024) in a systematic review of AI's positive impacts notes such empowerment aspects, implying that AI can indeed be leveraged to empower marginalized groups if a conscious effort is made (Pago, 2024). Inclusive, tech-driven workplaces require a fusion of advanced technology governance and classic principles of fairness and respect. It's about evolving the corporate culture to be both high-tech and high-touch: using cutting-edge AI but embedding it in a humane, just framework (Portillo, 2025c; Devabhaktuni et al., 2025). The organizations that achieve this will not only avoid the pitfalls of bias scandals or homogeneous workforces, but will unlock the full creative and innovative potential that diversity offers. A diversity of minds working with a diversity of data and technologies can produce breakthroughs that a monolithic group never would. Inclusive workplaces powered by AI can become exemplars of how human values and technological progress go hand in hand. They will stand in stark contrast to dystopian fears of technology exacerbating inequality. Instead, they'll show how, with thoughtful leadership, AI can help build a more equitable future of work – one where opportunities are abundant and accessible to all, and where technology serves as a bridge rather than a barrier among people (Mariyono et al., 2024; Wang & Pashmforoosh, 2024).

7. Ethical and responsible AI leadership

7.1 ETHICAL FRAMEWORKS FOR AI IN DECISION-MAKING

The integration of AI into high-stakes decision-making compels leaders to adopt robust ethical frameworks that guide how these technologies are developed and deployed. Ethical AI governance frameworks and responsible AI guidelines are emerging as essential tools, providing principles like fairness, accountability, and transparency to ensure AI aligns with human values and organizational ethics (Kandasamy, 2024; Nyoto et al., 2024b). Many organizations now incorporate formal AI ethics codes into their corporate policies, akin to codes of conduct, which set boundaries on AI use and embed moral decision criteria such as respect for privacy, non-discrimination, and human dignity (Dissanayake & Keppetipola, 2024b; Budianto et al., 2025). These frameworks often draw on classical ethical theories – for example, a utilitarian approach might focus on maximizing overall benefit from AI decisions, whereas a deontological approach stresses following rules or rights (such as not violating privacy) regardless of outcomes. By blending these philosophical lenses, leaders can create balanced ethical AI decision frameworks that both strive for beneficial outcomes and respect inviolable principles (Singh, 2023d). Such values-based AI leadership ensures that the organization's core values – like fairness, equity, and transparency – are upheld even as decision-making becomes more data-driven (Singh, 2023d; Wang & Pashmforoosh, 2024). Notably, scholars emphasize that ethical leadership in the AI era requires new competencies like "ethical vigilance," meaning leaders must proactively identify and mitigate potential AI-related ethical risks (Kandasamy, 2024). This vigilance is critical because AI systems can introduce subtle ethical challenges not seen in traditional decision processes, from opaque "black box" recommendations to automated bias amplification.

Leaders are responding by establishing dedicated oversight structures such as AI ethics boards or committees to institutionalize this vigilance (Hilbc, 2020; Schmitt, 2024a). An AI Ethics Board typically reviews proposed AI systems and policies before they are implemented, providing multidisciplinary oversight to catch ethical pitfalls. For example, a committee might include members from legal, compliance, technical, and community backgrounds to evaluate an AI recruiting tool for potential bias or a customer-facing algorithm for privacy implications. Research indicates that such ethics oversight boards can help infuse accountability and diverse perspectives into AI governance, making it less likely that important issues (like gender or cultural biases in algorithms) will be overlooked (Budianto et al., 2025; Dissanayake & Keppetipola, 2024). In essence, they function as an internal "conscience" for AI initiatives. Leading companies like Google and Microsoft have famously established AI ethics panels (at least in advisory capacities) to guide their product teams, illustrating a growing corporate trend toward formalizing AI ethics oversight (Hilb, 2020c).

Another cornerstone of ethical AI frameworks is the implementation of ethical risk assessment methods before and during AI deployment. This means leaders require teams to assess algorithms for potential harms or biases at the design stage and continuously monitor outcomes once in production (Pasupuleti, 2024; Mudunuri et al., 2024c). Techniques such as impact assessments, bias audits, and scenario planning (simulating worst-case misuse or failure scenarios) are becoming common practice as part of responsible AI guidelines (Wang & Pashmforoosh, 2024). By systematically evaluating where an AI system might violate ethical norms or regulations, leaders can demand design modifications or safeguards before those risks manifest in the real world. For instance, an ethical risk assessment for an AI decision-support tool in finance might reveal the need to exclude sensitive attributes (like race or gender) from the model to prevent discriminatory outcomes (Van Quaquebeke & Gerpott, 2023). It might also suggest implementing fallback procedures where human review is required for high-impact automated decisions, thereby maintaining human accountability (Hwang, 2024c). The role of accountability is crucial here – ethical frameworks stress that while AI may automate decisions, accountability cannot be automated away. Leaders must therefore clearly assign responsibility for AI-driven decisions, ensuring there is always a human answerable for the actions of an algorithm (Hwang, 2024c; Kandasamy, 2024). This principle prevents the diffusion of responsibility that can occur when organizations might otherwise blame "the algorithm" for mistakes. Some companies have even created the role of a Chief AI Ethics Officer or expanded compliance officers' duties to cover AI oversight, signaling how accountability structures are evolving to cover AI decision-making at the executive level (Schmitt, 2024; Hilb, 2020c).

Finally, effective ethical frameworks for AI go beyond preventing harm – they also promote positive values and stakeholder trust. Leaders championing values-based AI leadership prioritize transparency with employees, customers, and partners about how AI is used in decisions (Nyoto et al., 2024b). They communicate not just what decisions are being made by AI, but why, in terms of alignment with corporate values and ethical standards (Buçinca et al., 2021b). Such openness helps build trust and legitimizes AI use, as stakeholders feel their values are being considered in AI-driven processes (Nyoto et al., 2024b). Moreover, values-driven frameworks encourage the use of AI for socially beneficial outcomes when possible – for instance, using AI to improve accessibility for disabled employees or to reduce environmental impact – thereby aligning AI initiatives with broader corporate social responsibility goals (Budianto et al., 2025). In summary, establishing ethical frameworks for AI in decision-making is now a critical leadership task. It combines adopting formal guidelines and boards for oversight, integrating ethical analysis into every step of AI deployment, and upholding a culture where human values guide technological innovation. These measures collectively ensure that AI augments leadership decision-making in a manner that is morally sound, socially accountable, and worthy of stakeholder trust (Kandasamy, 2024; Hilb, 2020c).

7.2 BIAS, FAIRNESS, AND ACCOUNTABILITY IN ALGORITHMS

As organizations increasingly rely on algorithms for decisions ranging from hiring to lending, concerns about algorithmic bias and fairness have come to the forefront. AI systems learn from historical data, and if that data reflects human biases or structural inequalities, the algorithms can easily reproduce or even amplify those biases (Frimpong, 2024). For example, a hiring algorithm trained on a company's past successful employees might inadvertently learn to prefer male candidates if the company's historical workforce was predominantly male. Such cases are not hypothetical: real-world incidents have shown AI hiring tools disadvantaging women and minority candidates, sparking public scrutiny and backlash (Pasupuleti, 2024; Hilb, 2020c). These outcomes underscore that algorithmic discrimination is a pressing ethical problem – AI can unfairly favor or penalize groups based on race, gender, age, or other protected characteristics unless careful steps are taken to ensure fairness (Budianto et al., 2025). In leadership, this means executives must be vigilant about the data and models their organizations use. It is now considered a best practice to conduct bias audits on AI systems, which involve statistical tests to detect disparate impacts across demographic groups (Mudunuri et al., 2024c). Such auditing tools and frameworks have been developed in academia and industry to systematically check algorithms for bias before deployment, akin to a quality assurance process for ethics. If biases are found – say a loan approval AI is less likely to approve applicants from a certain zip code that correlates with a racial minority – the model must be adjusted, retrained with more diverse data, or even scrapped if the bias cannot be eliminated (Pasupuleti, 2024).

Defining fairness metrics in AI is itself a complex challenge, and leaders should be aware that there are multiple notions of fairness in algorithm design. Common fairness criteria include demographic parity (ensuring outcomes are independent of sensitive attributes), equal opportunity (ensuring equal true positive rates across groups), and predictive parity (ensuring similar accuracy for all groups). Which metric to prioritize can depend on context and values; for instance, in a criminal justice risk assessment tool, equalizing error rates for different ethnic groups might be deemed most critical, whereas in hiring, ensuring a balanced selection rate might be the focus. There is no one-size-fits-all, so leadership must make normative choices about what "fair" means for each application (Van Quaquebeke & Gerpott, 2023; Kandasamy, 2024). Importantly, scholars note that addressing algorithmic bias often requires human oversight and intervention in the AI life cycle – the notion of keeping a "human in the loop" to review and override algorithmic decisions can prevent blind automation of biased outcomes (Hwang, 2024c). In practice, some companies have instituted review panels for AI-driven high-stakes decisions (such as a rejection by an AI résumé screener) so that a human manager can double-check and correct potentially unjust denials (Wang & Pashmforoosh, 2024). This approach ties into accountability: rather than letting the algorithm operate in an unchecked manner, a responsible organization assigns humans to be accountable for reviewing AI outputs, especially when those outputs affect people's livelihoods or rights (Hwang, 2024c). By doing so, they acknowledge that accountability in automated decisions ultimately lies with the organization and its leaders, not with the software (Hilb, 2020c).

Real-world case studies of biased AI outcomes have become cautionary tales that drive home the need for fairness and accountability. One widely cited example is the case of an AI system used in the United States to predict criminal reoffense (the COMPAS algorithm), which was found to produce higher false-positive rates for Black defendants than for white defendants – in other words, it was more likely to wrongly label Black individuals as high risk (Frimpong, 2024). This algorithmic bias had severe implications for fairness in the justice system and led to calls for greater transparency and independent audits of such tools. In the financial sector, an AI-driven credit scoring system made headlines for allegedly offering significantly lower credit limits to women than men with similar profiles, revealing how bias can creep into consumer finance decisions if not vigilantly controlled. And in hiring, as noted, companies like Amazon discovered their résumé screening AI was downgrading applications including certain women's colleges or keywords, effectively encoding gender bias, which forced those companies to abandon or redesign the tools (Pasupuleti, 2024). Each of these cases highlights a lapse in algorithmic accountability – either bias was not detected prior to deployment or there was no mechanism for affected individuals to get recourse once a biased decision was made. Accountability means that organizations should be answerable for such outcomes and have processes to rectify them. Leading thinkers argue that mechanisms like algorithmic accountability reports (akin to financial statements but for algorithms) could be published, detailing the steps taken to ensure fairness and the known limitations of the system (Hilb, 2020c; Mudunuri et al., 2024c). Indeed, the literature calls for more empirical evaluation of governance models that can ensure these principles of fairness are actually enforced in AI-driven leadership contexts.

To mitigate bias in machine learning, technical and organizational strategies must work in tandem. On the technical side, teams are employing methods such as data re-sampling (to balance representation of groups in the training data), algorithmic fairness constraints (which mathematically enforce certain fairness criteria during model training), and post hoc adjustments (like equalizing decision thresholds for different groups to achieve fairness in outcomes). For instance, if an AI recruiting tool learns from historical data that most successful hires are from a narrow demographic, engineers can retrain the model with a more diverse training set or explicitly constrain the model to select a proportionate number of candidates from underrepresented groups to correct past biases. But technology alone is not enough. Organizationally, diverse development teams have been shown to better anticipate and catch biases – a homogeneous team might overlook a bias that adversely affects a group not represented among the developers (Kandasamy, 2024; Wang & Pashmforoosh, 2024). Therefore, building diversity into AI project teams is a key leadership strategy for fairness. Additionally, creating a culture where raising concerns about bias is encouraged (and not seen as undermining the project) empowers data scientists and domain experts to speak up if they notice unfair patterns, thereby injecting accountability at the working level (Spisak, 2024). When an AI system does make a flawed or biased decision, responsible AI leadership demands transparency about the incident and a willingness to address the root cause rather than deflect blame. This might involve communicating openly with stakeholders about what went wrong and why, as well as how the organization is fixing it – an approach that can help maintain trust even when failures occur (Van Quaquebeke & Gerpott, 2023).

In sum, ensuring bias and fairness in algorithms is a continual process of diligence and accountability. Leaders must commit to proactive bias mitigation – through rigorous testing and inclusive design – and to reactive accountability – through transparent acknowledgment of issues and remediation when things go wrong. By doing so, they fulfill an ethical mandate: that the powerful algorithms under their stewardship do not inadvertently perpetuate injustice but instead help to correct historical inequities where possible (Pasupuleti, 2024; Kandasamy, 2024). This ethical stance aligns AI implementation with the fundamental fairness that stakeholders expect from modern organizations, thereby reinforcing legitimacy and trust in AI-augmented decisions.

7.3 TRANSPARENT AND EXPLAINABLE AI IN LEADERSHIP

As AI systems become more sophisticated and complex, many operate as "black boxes" – they produce outputs without providing human-understandable reasons for their decisions. In leadership scenarios, this opacity is problematic: if an algorithm recommends a strategic decision or a personnel action, leaders need to know why it made that recommendation in order to trust it and to explain it to others (Buçinca et al., 2021b). This is where explainable AI (XAI) comes in. XAI refers to techniques and models designed to make the inner workings or decision logic of AI systems more transparent and interpretable to humans. For example, rather than using an inscrutable deep neural network for a critical decision, a company might opt for a more interpretable model (like a decision tree or rule-based system) or employ post hoc explanation tools that highlight which factors most influenced a particular decision (e.g., feature importance scores or counterfactual explanations). In leadership contexts, transparent and explainable AI is becoming a cornerstone of responsible AI use, because it enables leaders to understand, trust, and effectively communicate AI-driven insights (Hwang, 2024c; Spisak, 2024). When executives implement AI for decision support, they are effectively delegating part of their decision-making process to a machine; explainability ensures that this delegation does not come at the cost of insight or control. By insisting on transparency, leaders maintain a form of informed oversight, where they can interrogate an AI's reasoning and ensure it aligns with business logic and ethical standards (Hwang, 2024c). This builds trust not only for the leaders themselves but also for employees and stakeholders who may be affected by AI-driven decisions – people are more likely to accept an AI decision (such as a resource allocation or a performance evaluation aid) if they receive a clear rationale for how it was derived (Buçinca et al., 2021b; Nyoto et al., 2024b).

Crucially, there is often a trade-off between accuracy and explainability that leaders must navigate. Highly complex models (like deep learning networks with millions of parameters) might offer superior predictive accuracy, but their complexity makes them difficult or impossible to interpret – hence the black box label. Simpler or more constrained models (like linear models or decision trees) are easier to interpret but might not capture as many nuances in data, potentially reducing accuracy. Responsible AI leadership requires carefully evaluating this trade-off in context. In some cases, like life-and-death decisions in healthcare or high-liability decisions in finance, it may be preferable to sacrifice a bit of accuracy for a model that can be fully explained and audited, thereby ensuring compliance with regulations and ethical norms (Petrin, 2019). In other cases, for low-stakes or highly repetitive decisions, a black box model might be acceptable if it demonstrably performs better, as long as there are guardrails in place (e.g., human review of outlier cases). Regulations are increasingly pushing industries toward explainability. The GDPR in Europe, for instance, has been interpreted to include a "right to explanation" for individuals subjected to automated decisions, meaning organizations should be able to provide the reasons behind an algorithmic decision to those affected (Hilb, 2020c). Similarly, the forthcoming EU AI Act places transparency obligations on certain AI systems, and sector-specific guidelines (such as those from financial regulators) often require explainability to ensure algorithms are not creating undue risks. Leaders, therefore, must anticipate these regulatory demands and bake explainability into their AI strategy by design, rather than as an afterthought (Hilb, 2020c; Van Quaquebeke & Gerpott, 2023).

From a practical standpoint, pursuing explainable AI in leadership involves both technical measures and cultural shifts. On the technical side, organizations are adopting XAI tools – for example, using algorithms like LIME or SHAP that can provide interpretable approximations of complex model behavior, or designing dashboards that visualize how an AI model weighs different factors in making a recommendation (Buçinca et al., 2021b). A case in point is in healthcare leadership: imagine a hospital deploying an AI system to recommend treatment plans. If the system produces an inexplicable recommendation that contradicts conventional medical wisdom, doctors and medical leaders will understandably be hesitant to follow it. However, if the system can highlight that the patient's specific combination of symptoms and history closely matches past cases where an unconventional treatment succeeded – effectively providing a reason for its recommendation – the medical team can evaluate that reasoning. This kind of scenario has driven interest in XAI for healthcare, where "black box" AI is often unacceptable; early deployments have shown that providing explanations (even simple ones like which symptoms were most influential) significantly improves physician acceptance of AI suggestions. Similarly, in corporate settings, if an AI analytics tool flags a particular project as high risk, a project management office will want to know whether that assessment was driven by objective data (like budget overruns and staff turnover) or perhaps by spurious correlations. Explainability tools can surface those drivers, allowing leaders to trust the alerts that are valid and discard those that aren't, thus integrating AI insights more confidently into decision-making (Madanchian et al., 2024b).

Equally important is creating a culture that values transparency and open communication about AI. Leaders should set the expectation that AI-based decisions are not to be accepted blindly – they must be questioned and understood. This means training teams not just to build and use AI, but to interpret and communicate its outputs. Data scientists and AI specialists in the organization need to be capable of translating algorithmic outcomes into plain language for executives and other stakeholders (Wang & Pashmforoosh, 2024). Conversely, leadership should encourage a dialog where managers feel comfortable asking "Can you explain how the AI arrived at this suggestion?" without that being seen as a lack of technical savvy. Some companies have started internal programs to enhance AI literacy among non-technical managers so that they know the right questions to ask and are aware of tools that can provide answers (Spisak, 2024; Sposato, 2024b). For example, a marketing vice-president (VP) might not know the intricacies of a machine learning model, but through AI literacy training, they learn that they can request an influencing factors report whenever the AI gives a recommendation on ad targeting. They also learn to insist on a certain level of interpretability – perhaps choosing an AI model that can at least rank customer attributes by influence on predicted buying behavior. By doing so, the VP ensures that her team can justify marketing decisions to the rest of the company, maintaining transparency (Sposato, 2024b).

Building trust through explainability has tangible benefits for organizations. It reduces resistance to AI adoption among employees, who might otherwise feel threatened or mystified by algorithmic decisions (Nyoto et al., 2024b). When employees understand why an AI-driven change is happening (for instance, why the AI scheduled them fewer hours this week – perhaps due to predicted lower workload), they are more likely to view the AI as a tool working with them rather than an arbitrary, all-powerful judge (Frimpong & Wolfs, 2024). Trustworthy AI also enhances external stakeholder relations: customers and clients are increasingly wary of hidden algorithms affecting them. Companies that can provide clear explanations – for example, a bank explaining to a loan applicant the key factors that went into an AI-based credit decision – demonstrate respect and transparency, thereby strengthening their reputation and customer loyalty (Hilb, 2020c). In summary, transparent and explainable AI is not merely a technical nice-to-have, but a leadership imperative. It ensures that the AI's "voice" in decision-making can be scrutinized and understood, keeping the human leadership firmly in control and accountable. By embracing explainability, leaders uphold the principle that AI in their organization will operate not as an inscrutable oracle, but as a rational partner whose advice can be traced and verified – a stance that ultimately fosters trust, clarity, and shared understanding across the enterprise (Buçinca et al., 2021b; Hwang, 2024c).

7.4 DATA PRIVACY AND SECURITY CONCERNS FOR LEADERS

AI's hunger for data and its far-reaching capabilities have made data privacy and security central concerns for modern leaders. In leveraging AI, organizations often gather and process vast amounts of personal and sensitive data – from customer purchasing behaviors and social media sentiments to employee performance metrics and beyond. Leaders must ensure that such data use complies with privacy laws and meets stakeholder expectations for confidentiality. Regulations like the European GDPR and California's CCPA have codified strict requirements: individuals have rights over their data, and organizations must handle personal data with transparency, minimality, and specific purposes in mind. Non-compliance can lead not only to hefty fines but also to severe reputational damage. Thus, leaders are championing privacy-by-design in AI systems, an approach where privacy considerations are embedded from the outset rather than tacked on later (Hilb, 2020c; Petrin, 2019). This means, for instance, that when developing an AI-driven customer analytics platform, the team is instructed to implement data anonymization or pseudonymization techniques from the start, only use data that is necessary for the analysis, and obtain clear consent for any personal data use (Petrin, 2019). A privacy-by-design mindset also pushes developers to consider techniques like federated learning (where AI models learn from data across multiple locations without raw data leaving its source) and differential privacy (adding statistical noise to data to protect individual identities) to further safeguard personal information. Leaders knowledgeable in these techniques will press for their adoption so that an AI system is compliant with privacy norms out of the gate, not as an afterthought.

Cybersecurity is an equally critical facet of AI deployment. AI systems present new attack surfaces and vulnerabilities that leaders must proactively address. For one, AI models can be targets of theft or manipulation – in an era of "model hacking," attackers might steal a proprietary machine learning model (essentially intellectual property) or feed malicious inputs (adversarial examples) to cause the AI to behave erratically. There have been demonstrations, for example, of tricking image recognition AIs by subtly altering input data (like stickers on a stop sign causing an AI to misidentify it). In a business context, one could imagine adversaries attempting to fool an AI that monitors transactions for fraud by carefully crafting fraudulent transactions that evade detection. Leaders, especially CIOs and CISOs, are now tasked with securing the AI supply chain: this includes protecting training data (since poisoned training data can insert backdoors into AI behavior), safeguarding the models themselves, and controlling access to the outputs (Madanchian et al., 2024b).

They implement measures such as robust encryption for data both at rest and in transit, regular penetration testing for AI-related systems, and validation checks that can detect if an AI's outputs have been tampered with or are significantly out of pattern (indicating a possible attack or corruption). Moreover, AI can be a double-edged sword in cybersecurity – while it helps in detecting threats (e.g., AI systems that scan network traffic for anomalies), attackers also use AI to find system weaknesses or craft more convincing phishing attempts. Therefore, leadership must stay ahead in the "AI arms race" in cybersecurity: adopting advanced AI for defense while anticipating that malicious actors are doing the same (Spisak, 2024).

Protecting sensitive data is not only about external threats; insider risk and misuse are concerns as well. AI systems often aggregate data in ways that could inadvertently expose confidential information. For instance, an AI analyzing employee emails to gauge morale might inadvertently flag personal health information or union-related discussions, raising questions about surveillance and consent. Leaders have to set clear policies on the acceptable use of AI for monitoring and ensure such tools do not cross ethical lines or violate laws (Pasupuleti, 2024). The rise of AI-driven surveillance – such as facial recognition cameras, employee productivity trackers, or customer behavior monitoring in retail – places a burden on leadership to balance security and efficiency gains with individual privacy rights (Petrin, 2019; Hilb, 2020c). In law enforcement and public sector leadership, for example, the use of facial recognition AI has been highly controversial due to privacy invasion and instances of false identification. City leaders in some jurisdictions have opted to ban or limit these technologies, mindful of both public concern and the legal liabilities that could ensue from misidentification. Corporate leaders similarly must evaluate where the use of surveillance-oriented AI (like tracking employees' computer usage or location) might erode trust and violate ethical norms. A rule of thumb emerging in responsible AI leadership is: just because we can monitor something with AI doesn't mean we should. When such monitoring is deemed necessary (for safety or compliance), it should be highly transparent and governed by strict policies to avoid misuse (Kandasamy, 2024).

Building consumer trust through data handling is another leadership mandate. Customers are increasingly aware of data privacy – every breach headline or scandal (such as the misuse of social media data in political campaigns) has made the public more cautious. Leaders are responding by making data privacy part of the brand promise. They communicate commitments like "Your data will never be sold" or "Your data will only be used to improve the services you receive, and here's how…" and they back these statements with tangible actions (Nyoto et al., 2024b). For instance, some companies now offer privacy dashboards to users, where individuals can see what data the company holds on them and adjust their consent preferences. Although implementing such measures can be costly and complex, leaders recognize it as an investment in long-term customer loyalty and brand integrity (Nyoto et al., 2024b). After all, one major data breach or privacy fiasco can rapidly erode brand equity. A proactive stance on privacy – treating customer data with the same care as one would treat customers in person – reinforces the company's reputation as an ethical actor (Pasupuleti, 2024).

In terms of incident response planning for AI, foresighted leaders prepare for the worst-case scenarios. They extend their cybersecurity incident response plans to specifically cover AI-related incidents: for example, what if an AI system that handles critical operations is compromised or behaves unpredictably? A well-devised plan might include steps like immediately switching to a human-driven backup process, conducting a thorough audit of the AI's inputs and outputs to diagnose the issue, and communicating promptly with stakeholders about any impacts (Madanchian et al., 2024b). If an AI data breach occurs (say an attacker gained access to the training database of a medical AI containing patient records), the response plan would dictate how to contain the breach, notify affected individuals per legal requirements, and work with legal teams to address any regulatory fallout (Petrin, 2019).

Leaders also need to manage third-party risk in the AI ecosystem. Many organizations use third-party AI vendors or cloud services for AI processing. This introduces dependencies – your data might be flowing through someone else's infrastructure. It becomes crucial to vet those partners for their security posture and privacy practices (Hilb, 2020c). Vendor contracts now frequently include strict data protection clauses, rights to audit, and requirements for compliance with standards like ISO/IEC 27001 (for security) or adherence to frameworks like NIST's privacy framework. The concept of data sovereignty plays in here as well: laws in some countries require certain data (like personal or sensitive data) to be stored and processed only on servers within national boundaries. If an AI vendor stores data overseas, that could be a violation. Thus, governance of AI now often includes mapping data flows and ensuring they align with jurisdictional requirements – a complex but necessary exercise for global organizations (Petrin, 2019).

In conclusion, safeguarding data privacy and security in the age of AI is a multidimensional challenge that sits squarely on the shoulders of leadership. It involves legal compliance, technical fortification, ethical judgment, and crisis preparedness. The stakes are high: mishandling data can mean legal sanctions, financial loss, and irreparable trust deficits. Conversely, getting privacy and security right can be a competitive differentiator, as customers and partners gravitate toward organizations they trust. Effective AI-era leaders will treat data as a precious asset – one that must be protected vigorously and used judiciously – ensuring that the organization's pursuit of AI-driven advantage never undermines the fundamental rights and expectations of the people it serves (Hilb, 2020c; Pasupuleti, 2024).

7.5 REGULATORY COMPLIANCE AND AI GOVERNANCE

The rapidly evolving landscape of AI regulations and laws is a pivotal concern for leaders deploying AI solutions. Around the world, governments are recognizing both the transformative potential and the risks of AI, and they are moving to create legal frameworks to ensure AI is developed and used responsibly. A prime example is the European Union's proposed AI Act, which is one of the first comprehensive attempts to regulate AI. The EU AI Act takes a risk-based approach: it categorizes AI applications into risk levels (unacceptable risk, high risk, limited risk, minimal risk) and imposes requirements accordingly. For leadership, this means if their organization is using an AI system deemed "high risk" (for instance, AI in hiring, credit scoring, or any system that impacts people's rights or safety), they will have to meet strict obligations such as conducting conformity assessments, ensuring human oversight, and providing robust documentation and transparency about the AI's functioning (Petrin, 2019; Hilb, 2020c). Ignorance of such regulations is not an option – compliance will be enforced with significant fines in the EU, and similar laws are being considered elsewhere. Therefore, many companies have proactively started aligning their practices with the expected EU AI Act provisions, even if they operate globally, viewing it as setting a de facto international standard (Van Quaquebeke & Gerpott, 2023). Forward-looking leaders assemble cross-functional teams (legal, technical, compliance) to audit their AI systems against these emerging criteria, identifying gaps in areas like data quality, record-keeping, or transparency that the regulations demand (Schmitt, 2024c). This not only prepares them for legal compliance but also improves the rigor and governance of their AI projects overall.

Beyond legislation, there are also numerous industry standards and guidelines shaping AI governance. Organizations like the IEEE and ISO/IEC have been developing standards on AI ethics, bias management, and risk management. For example, the IEEE's series on Ethically Aligned Design and the new ISO/IEC guidance on AI (such as ISO/IEC 42001 which is under development for AI management systems) offer frameworks that companies can voluntarily adopt (Hilb, 2020c). Leaders often opt into these standards to stay ahead of the curve, as doing so signals a commitment to best practices and can reassure customers and partners. In the United States, while federal AI legislation is still nascent, the NIST AI Risk Management Framework (released in 2023) provides a robust structure for organizations to manage AI risks. It covers core functions like mapping AI use cases, measuring and assessing risks (including ethical and societal risks), managing those risks through controls, and governing AI activities. A savvy leader will incorporate such frameworks into their AI strategy, essentially operationalizing governance. For instance, a bank's leadership might adopt the NIST framework to systematically evaluate the risk of each AI model it uses – from a simple customer chatbot to a complex trading algorithm – and then ensure proper controls (like bias mitigation, explainability, cybersecurity measures) are in place for each (Wang & Pashmforoosh, 2024). Adopting and even certifying against these standards can also serve as evidence of due diligence if regulators come knocking or if there is an incident; it demonstrates that the company was following recognized governance protocols (Petrin, 2019; Mudunuri et al., 2024c).

A notable development in AI governance is the emergence of roles and bodies dedicated to it, such as the Chief AI Ethics Officer or internal AI ethics committees. These mirror structures we've seen in financial compliance (e.g., compliance officers, risk committees) and signal a maturing of AI oversight. The Chief AI Ethics Officer (or sometimes Chief AI Officer with an ethics mandate) is typically a senior executive whose job is to oversee AI strategy in alignment with ethical guidelines and regulatory requirements (Schmitt, 2024c). This person might establish policies on AI development, review major AI initiatives for ethical risks, and serve as a liaison with regulators or external auditors. Similarly, ethics committees or AI oversight boards (comprising senior leaders and experts) provide governance at a higher level, reviewing and approving (or vetoing) AI projects that have significant ethical or compliance implications (Hilb, 2020c; Budianto et al., 2025). For example, a healthcare organization might have an AI ethics committee evaluate a proposal to use AI for diagnosing patients – checking compliance with healthcare regulations, ensuring bias in training data is addressed, and validating that patients' data will be used with consent. These governance bodies ensure that AI deployment is not left solely to technical teams but is integrated into the company's overall risk management and governance apparatus (Mudunuri et al., 2024c).

One challenge leaders face is cross-border regulatory compliance. AI, by its digital nature, often transcends national boundaries – a service hosted in one country might serve customers in another, and data may flow across borders. This pits various regulations against each other: for instance, an AI might need to comply with the EU's GDPR for European data, CCPA for Californian data, and perhaps local data residency laws for data originating in Asia (Petrin, 2019). The patchwork of rules can be complex. Some countries also have laws about AI in specific domains (like Japan's guidelines on AI in healthcare, or China's approach to AI and content). Leaders of global organizations often have to adopt the most stringent common denominator to ensure compliance everywhere, or else implement geo-fencing strategies where AI systems operate differently depending on the user's jurisdiction (Hilb, 2020c). Data localization requirements mean leaders might have to invest in localized infrastructure or cloud solutions to keep certain data within certain borders, affecting AI deployment architecture. It becomes clear that AI governance cannot be one-size-fits-all worldwide – it requires nuance and adaptation. This has led to increased collaboration between legal/compliance officers and AI technical teams within organizations, as they hash out how to technically implement policies that meet legal demands. In some cases, companies even decide to restrict or avoid certain AI practices in some markets due to regulatory uncertainty, exemplifying how compliance considerations directly influence strategic choices in AI (Van Quaquebeke & Gerpott, 2023).

Another key aspect of governance is transparency reporting requirements. Regulators are leaning toward requiring that companies publicly disclose information about their AI systems, especially high-impact ones. This could include what data is being collected, how decisions are made, and what measures are in place to address bias or errors. In anticipation, some organizations have started releasing AI transparency reports or responsible AI reports voluntarily. These documents might outline, for example, the number of automated decisions made in a year in areas like hiring or lending, and the outcomes of fairness audits or incident reports on those systems. Leaders who champion such transparency find that it not only builds public trust but also forces internal discipline – if you know you have to report on the AI's workings, you ensure those workings are defensible and well documented (Budianto et al., 2025). This is aligned with the concept of algorithmic accountability which in some jurisdictions (like parts of the EU AI Act) may become a legal requirement (Hilb, 2020c).

Lastly, the question of liability in AI decisions looms large in governance discussions. If an AI system causes harm or makes a serious mistake, who is legally and financially liable? Traditional product liability law and professional liability concepts are being tested. For instance, if an autonomous vehicle controlled by AI gets into an accident, is the manufacturer liable, the AI software provider, or the passenger? If a company's AI-powered financial advisor gives poor advice leading to client losses, is it the company's fault or can they blame the algorithm? The legal system will ultimately decide these on a case-by-case basis as precedents emerge, but prudent leaders aren't waiting to find out – they are preemptively setting internal rules that clarify human responsibility for AI actions (Petrin, 2019). Many have policies that any decision made by AI can be appealed to a human, effectively providing a human backstop that carries the final accountability. Insurance products are also emerging for AI-related failures, and leaders might invest in such insurance as part of risk management (Van Quaquebeke & Gerpott, 2023). Governance frameworks encourage this clear assignment of responsibility: for example, a bank might stipulate that its credit risk officer is accountable for outcomes of the AI credit scoring model, ensuring that oversight is firmly in place (Hillebrand et al., 2025).

In essence, AI governance is about embedding the oversight, accountability, and compliance structures we have long used in corporate governance and risk management into the realm of AI and algorithmic systems. Leaders must navigate a thicket of emerging rules, but those rules are fundamentally aimed at the same objectives as any regulation: protecting consumers, ensuring fairness, and preventing harm. By proactively embracing regulatory compliance and robust governance structures, organizations not only avoid penalties but also often improve the quality and reliability of their AI systems (Wang & Pashmforoosh, 2024). An organization with well-governed AI is likely one whose AI is better – more fair, more transparent, more robust – which ultimately contributes to sustainable success. As one analysis noted, bridging gaps in AI governance and aligning with ethical and legal expectations is critical for leveraging AI effectively without losing stakeholder trust or incurring unintended consequences (Mudunuri et al., 2024). For the AI-enabled leader, regulatory compliance is not a box-checking burden; it is part and parcel of responsible innovation.

7.6 ETHICAL DILEMMAS AND CASE STUDIES IN AI IMPLEMENTATION

Implementing AI in real-world scenarios has surfaced a host of ethical dilemmas, often putting leaders in the hot seat as they navigate uncharted territory. By examining a few prominent cases and controversies, we can glean lessons about the pitfalls to avoid and the governance measures needed. Below are several categories of ethical dilemmas with illustrative examples that leadership teams have confronted:

- *Bias in Hiring and Credit Decisions*: AI systems used for hiring and lending have been found to replicate societal biases, raising serious ethical questions. For instance, a major technology company developed an AI résumé screening tool that inadvertently learned to prefer male applicants – it penalized résumés that included phrases like "women's chess club," reflecting bias in the training data of past hires. This was a stark ethical wake-up call: the AI was effectively automating gender discrimination. The company's leaders had to scrap the system and publicly acknowledge the failure, reinforcing the need for bias audits and diverse development teams (Pasupuleti, 2024; Budianto et al., 2025). Similarly, in consumer finance, an AI-driven credit scoring model made headlines for offering lower credit limits to women than men with similar profiles, triggering allegations of sexism. In this case, financial regulators got involved, and company executives had to explain the opaque model's outcomes – an extremely difficult task that underscored why explainability is critical in avoiding and addressing such dilemmas. These examples demonstrate that without careful oversight, AI can unfairly gatekeep opportunities like jobs or credit, putting leaders at risk of violating anti-discrimination laws and betraying public trust (Hilb , 2020c; Frimpong, 2024).

- *Algorithmic Bias in Policing and Justice*: Law enforcement agencies have trialed AI for predictive policing and criminal risk assessments, but not without controversy. One well-known case is the COMPAS algorithm used in parts of the US justice system to predict recidivism risk. Investigative journalism revealed that COMPAS was much more likely to falsely label Black defendants as high risk compared to white defendants. This racial bias in a supposedly objective tool sparked outrage and debate over due process and equality before the law. Judges and public officials faced the dilemma of whether to trust the AI's recommendation or to rely on their own judgment – a tension between efficiency and fairness. In some instances, judges started asking for explanations of the algorithm's scores, and when satisfactory answers weren't available, it cast doubt on the tool's legitimacy. Police departments experimenting with predictive policing algorithms (which forecast crime hotspots or potential offenders) have similarly wrestled with accusations that these systems reinforce over-policing in minority neighborhoods by training on historical arrest data (Frimpong, 2024). The lesson for leadership is clear: deploying AI in such sensitive domains without robust fairness checks and community oversight can lead to ethical and public relations crises. Some city police chiefs and mayors have suspended or canceled AI policing programs in response to community concerns, highlighting that leaders must weigh public values and civil rights heavily against promised AI benefits (Hilb, 2020c).
- *Surveillance and Privacy Intrusions*: AI-powered facial recognition and surveillance tools present an ethical quandary between security and privacy. One dramatic illustration comes from corporate settings – an international retail chain considered using facial recognition cameras in stores to identify known shoplifters or even high-value customers for VIP treatment. Technically, the AI worked; ethically, the leadership balked once privacy advocates and employees voiced concerns. They realized such constant surveillance could be seen as an infringement of customer privacy and could erode the sense of trust. In a different context, governments have used AI surveillance for public safety, but when these systems misidentify innocent people (as happened with some early deployments of facial recognition resulting in wrongful police stops), it's the officials and police chiefs who must apologize and correct course. These cases push leaders to confront questions like: How far is too far in monitoring individuals? Do the

ends (safety, theft prevention) justify the means (loss of privacy)? Often, the public's answer is that certain AI uses simply overstep ethical boundaries, leading to regulatory pushback – for example, some cities and countries have banned real-time facial recognition in public spaces. Leaders in technology companies providing such tools have even faced whistleblower incidents, where employees refused to build or sell AI systems for surveillance they deemed unethical (Pasupuleti, 2024). This underscores that ethical culture internally can directly influence AI strategy, as we'll examine further in the next section.

- *Autonomous Vehicles and the Trolley Problem*: The development of self-driving cars has revived classic ethical dilemmas, notably the trolley problem – if an autonomous vehicle must choose between two harmful outcomes (e.g., hitting one pedestrian or swerving and injuring its passenger), what should it do? There's no easy answer, and effectively the AI might be pre-programmed with life-and-death decision rules. Car manufacturers and their leadership teams have grappled with these questions in design and testing. One high-profile fatality involving a self-driving test vehicle raised questions about the division of responsibility between the AI system, the safety driver present, and the company's oversight. Following that incident, the CEO publicly committed to more stringent safety protocols and transparently cooperated with regulators, illustrating how critical swift ethical leadership response is in such crises. Additionally, military applications of AI (like autonomous drones or "killer robot" debates) put leaders in the hot seat over AI ethics in warfare. For instance, when a tech company contracted for a defense project involving AI, internal protest erupted (a number of employees felt it was unethical for AI to assist in lethal targeting). The CEO eventually decided not to renew that contract under public pressure, prioritizing the company's ethical stance and employee values over the business opportunity. These scenarios show that leaders often must make principled stands: they may choose to limit AI's autonomy (e.g., always requiring a human "veto" in vehicles or weapons) to ensure alignment with societal ethics and to avoid scenarios where an AI's choice could be deemed morally unacceptable (Petrin, 2019).
- *Deepfakes and Misinformation*: AI's ability to generate ultra-realistic fake images, video, or text – so-called deepfakes – has introduced new ethical and reputational risks. A case that alarmed many business leaders was when a fake audio clip of a CEO's voice (produced by AI) was used to fraudulently authorize a bank transfer, costing a company hundreds of thousands of dollars. In another instance, political deepfakes threatened to spread misinformation during an election, forcing social media companies and regulators to scramble for solutions. For corporate and public sector leaders, deepfakes mean that seeing (or hearing) is no longer believing

– which can undermine trust in communications and present challenges in authentication. Leaders now must consider policies on verifying communications (e.g., using codewords in verbal orders or multifactor authentication beyond voice recognition) and on how to respond if their likeness is misused. Organizations have started training employees about these risks, essentially adding misinformation resilience to the skill set. Moreover, platform leaders at tech companies face ethical decisions on moderating AI-generated content: how aggressively to detect and remove deepfakes, especially when they target individuals for harassment or could incite violence. This touches on free speech vs. harm prevention, a classical ethical tightrope, now complicated by AI's scale and potency.

- *Whistleblowing and Internal Ethics Conflicts*: As AI projects push boundaries, insiders sometimes raise alarms about unethical practices. In one prominent example, a leading AI research scientist at a tech giant voiced concerns that a language AI model exhibited biases and could produce harmful content. The disagreement between the researcher and company executives over publishing a paper on these issues led to her departure, which in turn sparked a very public controversy about the company's commitment to AI ethics. This scenario served as a case study in what not to do – critics argued that silencing or ousting internal whistleblowers damages an organization's credibility and its culture of integrity. The fallout for leadership was significant: they had to rebuild trust with both the research community and their own employees, eventually pledging greater transparency and establishing external AI ethics advisory councils to review contentious projects (Spisak, 2024). The clear takeaway is that whistleblower protections and an open dialogue environment are essential. If employees fear retaliation for speaking up about AI's ethical issues, then problems will fester until they possibly explode externally, much to the detriment of the organization. Smart leaders treat internal dissent about AI ethics as an invaluable early warning system – these voices help catch issues that those in the AI "bubble" might miss, and addressing concerns head-on is far better than dealing with scandal later (Kandasamy, 2024).

Each of these dilemmas and case studies highlights the mantra that ethical failures in AI are often leadership failures. Whether it's an unchecked bias, a breach of privacy, or a mishandled internal dispute, strong ethical leadership could have mitigated or prevented the issue. The common threads across these cases are the need for transparency, stakeholder engagement, and a willingness to prioritize ethics over short-term gains. Leaders who navigate these dilemmas successfully tend to do so by slowing down the rush to deploy AI and asking tough questions: Have we tested this enough? Who could be hurt by this? Are we ready to take responsibility if things go wrong? Those who did not learn the hard way that neglecting such questions can result in public embarrassment, legal consequences, and loss of trust (Hilb, 2020c; Mudunuri et al., 2024c). In summation, the case studies of recent years form a rich, if sometimes painful, learning curriculum for AI leadership. They illustrate that while AI offers immense benefits, its mishandling carries equally immense risks – not just technical or financial, but moral. By studying these lessons and sharing them (many organizations now openly discuss their AI failures and fixes), leaders across industries are gradually building a playbook of best practices to handle AI's ethical challenges. This collective learning is fostering a new norm: that responsible AI is not just a slogan but a day-to-day practice of careful decision-making, continuous oversight, and humility in the face of technology's power (Frimpong & Wolfs, 2024; Buçinca et al., 2021b).

7.7 BUILDING AN ETHICAL AI CULTURE AND GOVERNANCE BOARD

To sustain ethical and responsible AI leadership, organizations must embed ethics into their very DNA. This means fostering a culture where considerations of fairness, accountability, and societal impact are second nature in every AI project – not external impositions or afterthoughts. Culture, of course, starts at the top: leaders set the tone by what they prioritize, reward, and tolerate. An ethical AI culture is one in which leadership's commitment to responsible AI is evident in everyday practices and decision-making. For example, when a product team proposes a new AI feature, an ethical culture will prompt someone to ask, "Have we thought about potential misuse or bias here?" as routinely as they would ask about revenue potential or technical feasibility (Kandasamy, 2024). Building such a culture requires deliberate action on multiple fronts, including education, diversity, policy, and oversight. One powerful mechanism to anchor this culture is establishing an AI ethics governance board or committee. As mentioned earlier, many organizations are formalizing ethics oversight, but beyond compliance, a governance board can function as a champion of the company's values, continuously reinforcing the importance of ethics in AI initiatives (Hilb, 2020c; Wang & Pashmforoosh, 2024). This board, ideally comprising a mix of executives, technical leaders, legal advisors, and even external ethicists, doesn't just review projects – it also drives ethics training, discussion, and reflection throughout the company (Sposato, 2024b).

Here are some key steps and practices that leaders can implement to build an ethical AI culture and governance framework in their organizations:

1. *Integrate Ethics Training and Education*: One of the first steps is to ensure that everyone involved with AI – from data scientists to product managers to senior executives – is educated in AI ethics and familiar with the

company's expectations. Regular workshops or training programs on topics like bias in AI, privacy protection, and human-centric design help raise awareness (Sposato, 2024b). For instance, a training module might simulate an AI design scenario and have employees work through identifying ethical pitfalls and proposing safeguards, strengthening their practical judgment. Some companies have even developed internal certifications in "Responsible AI" that employees can earn (Wang & Pashmforoosh, 2024). Education not only imparts knowledge but signals that ethical skill is as valued as technical skill. Leaders might invite expert speakers or use-case studies of AI failures (as discussed in section 7.6) to spark candid conversations, so employees learn from real examples. This continuous learning approach keeps ethics top-of-mind as AI tech and norms evolve (Spisak, 2024).

2. *Foster Diversity and Inclusion in AI Teams*: As repeatedly noted, having diverse perspectives is crucial to catching blind spots and ensuring AI serves a broad base of users fairly. Leaders should strive to build AI teams that include diversity across gender, ethnicity, background, and disciplines (Kandasamy, 2024). They should also promote an inclusive environment where each team member feels empowered to voice concerns. Concrete actions include diverse hiring initiatives for technical roles, but also interdisciplinary teaming – pairing technologists with sociologists, legal experts, or community representatives in the development process (Wang & Pashmforoosh, 2024). For example, an AI product team might include a social scientist to advise on potential societal impacts, or a person with lived experience relevant to the AI's domain (like a person with a disability if developing an AI tool for workplace accessibility). A governance board can monitor team composition and push back if a project is being developed in a silo devoid of diverse input (Budianto et al., 2025). Research has shown that diverse teams are more likely to anticipate ethical issues and design more inclusive solutions (Dissanayake & Keppetipola, 2024), thus this is a linchpin for an ethical AI culture.
3. *Establish a Formal AI Ethics Board or Committee*: As mentioned, having a dedicated body at governance level ensures sustained attention to ethics. This board should meet regularly to review high-impact AI projects, set or update ethical guidelines, and evaluate the organization's overall AI risk profile (Hilb, 2020c). It functions somewhat like a risk or audit committee, but focused on ethical risk and societal impact. Leaders can empower this board to halt or demand modifications to projects that don't meet ethical standards – giving it real teeth in the governance structure. Notably, including outside experts or advisors can enhance credibility and breadth of perspective (Schmitt, 2024c). For example, some companies have academics or representatives from civil society on their AI ethics

board to provide independent viewpoints. The board might also be tasked with producing an annual Ethical AI Report for the company, summarizing what has been done to ensure AI responsibility, what dilemmas arose, and how they were resolved (Nyoto et al., 2024b). This transparency can reinforce both internal and external trust.

4. *Encourage Ethical Whistleblowing and Open Dialogue*: A truly ethical culture is one where employees are not only allowed but encouraged to speak up if they see something problematic. Leaders should implement clear, confidential channels for raising ethical concerns about AI (Spisak, 2024). This could be an ethics hotline, a dedicated ombudsperson for AI issues, or an anonymous form. More importantly, leadership must respond to such concerns constructively. Celebrating examples where an employee's concern led to a positive change can reinforce that speaking up is part of the company's values. And if an employee whistleblows externally, leadership's reaction should be to address the issues raised rather than punish the messenger (as the earlier case demonstrated). Protective policies can be instituted to ensure no retaliation occurs when concerns are voiced. When ethical issues are surfaced, the governance board and relevant leaders should investigate and take corrective action – be it retraining a model, altering a product feature, or in some cases, canceling a project. Over time, this openness creates psychological safety, so that potential scandals are nipped in the bud internally long before they might explode publicly (Kandasamy, 2024).
5. *Conduct Regular Ethical Audits and Impact Assessments*: Alongside technical audits, organizations should perform ethical audits of AI systems. This might involve periodically reviewing deployed AI for unintended biases or privacy leaks, reassessing its impact on stakeholders, and checking compliance with the latest regulations and company principles (Wang & Pashmforoosh, 2024). For instance, a bank using an AI for credit decisions could do an annual fairness audit to ensure no new biases have crept in after model updates or demographic shifts in data. Ethical impact assessments (analogous to environmental impact assessments in construction) can be required at the proposal stage of new AI projects – the team must outline potential ethical risks and mitigation plans before getting full approval (Madanchian et al., 2024b). The governance board can oversee these assessments. By institutionalizing audit and assessment cycles, ethical vigilance becomes a routine part of AI operations rather than a reactive scramble. Some companies even invite external auditors or partner with academic institutions to review their AI for an extra layer of rigor and objectivity (Hillebrand et al., 2025).
6. *Engage Stakeholders and Be Transparent*: Building an ethical AI culture also means looking outward and engaging those who will be affected by

AI. Leaders can host stakeholder forums or user panels to get feedback on planned AI deployments (Van Quaquebeke & Gerpott, 2023). For example, if a city government plans to use AI in public services, holding community meetings to discuss how it will be used and addressing citizens' concerns can surface issues early and build public buy-in. Corporate leaders might engage with advocacy groups relevant to their AI's domain (like digital rights organizations if rolling out a new data-driven service) to preempt criticism and demonstrate goodwill. Moreover, publishing transparency reports or AI principles publicly helps set accountability. Many organizations have now published their ethical AI guidelines – a set of principles such as "AI will be fair, explainable, and under human direction" – both to guide their teams and to communicate values externally (Budianto et al., 2025). Public commitments create pressure to live up to them, which reinforces internal discipline.

7. *Align AI Initiatives with Sustainability and Social Good*: Ethical AI culture often dovetails with broader corporate social responsibility. Leaders are increasingly asking, how can our AI efforts contribute positively to society or the environment? This might mean prioritizing AI projects that have clear social benefits (like AI for healthcare, education, or reducing carbon footprint) and ensuring even profit-driven AI is developed in a way that's socially responsible (Portillo, 2025c). Some have formed internal "AI for Good" task forces that encourage innovative uses of AI to tackle social challenges, thus inspiring employees to see ethics as not just preventing harm but actively doing good. When employees see leadership reward projects that, say, improve accessibility for disabled users or enhance fairness in the community, it reinforces that ethical performance is valued alongside financial performance (Dissanayake & Keppetipola, 2024). An ethical AI governance board might even evaluate projects on a "sustainable and inclusive impact" criterion as part of their approval process (Kandasamy, 2024).

In implementing these steps, consistency and sincerity are key. Culture change does not happen overnight; it requires persistent messaging and aligned actions. Leaders must "walk the talk" – their decisions in ambiguous situations will be closely watched as barometers of the true priorities. For example, if an important but ethically questionable AI project is halted by the CEO despite its profit potential, that sends a powerful message through the organization about what counts in the long run (Hilb, 2020c). Over time, employees internalize these values and start acting as ethical agents themselves, often catching and resolving issues at their level. At its optimal level, an ethical AI culture becomes self-reinforcing: people take pride in it and even use it as a selling point when recruiting new talent (many tech workers today choose employers partly based on ethical reputation).

Finally, establishing a formal governance structure like an ethics board provides ongoing oversight and adaptability. As new dilemmas emerge – and they will, with advances like generative AI, new privacy-invasive technologies, etc. – the organization has a mechanism to deliberate and update policies. This agility in governance ensures that ethical practices evolve in step with technology and societal expectations (Hillebrand et al., 2025a). A company might start with guidelines focused on bias and privacy, but a year later, the board might add guidance on energy usage (if AI training is found to consume significant power) or on deepfake misuse, as those become pertinent.

In conclusion, building an ethical AI culture and governance board is about creating an environment where doing the right thing with AI is instinctual and institutional. It's the capstone of responsible AI leadership – taking all the principles and lessons discussed in this chapter and weaving them into the fabric of the organization. Leaders who succeed in this endeavor will not only avoid pitfalls and compliance issues but likely unleash the full innovative potential of AI in a way that is trusted and supported by employees, customers, and society alike. As studies have noted, ethical leadership combined with interdisciplinary collaboration creates a strong foundation for sustainable, human-centered AI innovation (Kandasamy, 2024; Wang & Pashmforoosh, 2024). In a world where AI is ever more powerful, cultivating this strong ethical foundation may well be the decisive factor separating organizations that thrive from those that stumble in controversy. By building ethical reflexes and robust governance today, leaders ensure that their organizations are prepared for the moral and practical challenges of the AI-driven future.

8. Global perspectives and case studies

8.1 AI LEADERSHIP IN NORTH AMERICA – INNOVATION AND IMPACT

North America, particularly the United States (US), has positioned itself at the forefront of AI-driven leadership through a potent combination of innovation ecosystems and substantial investments. Silicon Valley in California exemplifies this trend, serving as a global hub for AI startups and talent. The region's culture of entrepreneurship and risk-taking, backed by abundant venture capital, has accelerated AI adoption in business leadership. Surveys indicate that over 60% of executives in North America recognize AI's potential to improve key performance indicators and competitive advantage (Asiabar et al., 2024). This optimism is reflected in practice, as organizations implementing AI report gains in decision accuracy, innovation capacity, and employee engagement (Nyoto et al., 2024b; Tummalapalli et al., 2024). The venture capital and startup environment in the US has been particularly crucial, funding hundreds of AI-focused startups that challenge incumbents and drive rapid technological development. These new entrants often pioneer AI applications in fields like finance, healthcare, and retail, compelling established firms to respond or risk disruption (Kuznietsova, 2024). The result is a dynamic North American AI landscape where innovation is not confined to big tech companies but is distributed across an ecosystem of agile startups and collaborative research labs (Ene et al., 2024).

A defining feature of North American AI leadership is the outsized role of tech giants such as Google, Microsoft, Amazon, Meta (Facebook), and IBM. These corporations act as both catalysts and gatekeepers for AI innovation. They drive AI adoption by open-sourcing key tools (e.g., TensorFlow by Google) and investing heavily in research and development through dedicated corporate AI labs. Google's Brain team and DeepMind unit (now under Alphabet), Microsoft Research's AI division, Amazon's AI labs, and IBM's Watson group have produced cutting-edge AI algorithms and enterprise solutions. The presence of a Chief AI Officer (CAIO) or similar leadership roles in some North American companies underscores how seriously AI integration is taken at executive level (Schmitt, 2024c). These labs and leadership roles not only spearhead technological breakthroughs but also influence industry standards and best practices. For example, tech giants often lead in establishing ethical AI frameworks internally, which can become models for other organizations. The public–private partnerships common in the US further amplify this effect: initiatives where tech firms collaborate with government agencies or academic institutions help transition AI innovations from the lab to real-world deployment (Portillo, 2025c). Such collaborations have tackled issues from healthcare analytics to smart city infrastructure, reinforcing North America's innovation ecosystem and demonstrating AI's broad impact on society and the economy (Zaidi et al., 2025).

North America's AI leadership is also characterized by business model disruption led by AI-centric strategies. In many industries, AI is fundamentally changing how organizations create and deliver value. Retail and media provide clear examples: recommendation algorithms and personalization (pioneered by companies like Amazon and Netflix) have reshaped consumer expectations and competitive dynamics (Mudunuri et al., 2024c). In finance, algorithmic trading and AI-driven risk assessment are disrupting traditional banking models, while in manufacturing, predictive maintenance and robotics enhance productivity. Leaders in North America have leveraged AI to augment decision-making and strategic planning – sometimes referred to as moving from an intuitive to an algorithmically augmented leadership style (Van Quaquebeke & Gerpott, 2023). This has required not only adopting new technologies but also cultivating new skills and mindsets among executives. For instance, data-driven decision culture is now a hallmark of forward-thinking companies, where leaders use AI-based analytics to guide strategy (Hillebrand et al., 2025a). The willingness of North American firms to reinvent their business models around AI is a key factor in their sustained competitive edge and has led to notable gains in market share and efficiency for AI adopters (Nyoto et al., 2024b). Studies show that organizations integrating AI into core business processes report significant improvements in operational productivity and innovation output (Tummalapalli et al., 2024), underscoring the disruptive power of AI-led strategies.

Government policy and national strategy also play a role in North American AI leadership, albeit with a different approach compared to more centralized economies. In the US, the federal government has launched initiatives like the American AI Initiative and established offices such as the National AI Initiative Office to coordinate AI research and policy. These efforts often focus on funding fundamental research (through agencies like the NSF and DARPA) and ensuring an American lead in critical AI domains (Elsherif, 2024a). The US approach tends to be industry-driven, with the government acting as an enabler by investing in research and setting broad guidelines, rather than heavy-handed regulation. This approach has fostered an innovation-friendly environment, although it also raises challenges in areas like ethics and privacy, which are sometimes addressed only after issues arise (Aziz et al., 2024). By contrast, Canada's AI strategy has been notable for its early and focused investments in AI research and talent development. Canada was one of the first countries with a national AI plan (launched in 2017), which funded AI research centers in Toronto, Montreal, and Edmonton. This led to the emergence of world-class research labs such as Mila (Quebec) and the Vector Institute (Ontario) that have attracted global talent and corporate R&D investment. The Canadian approach emphasizes academia–industry collaboration and the responsible development of AI, aligning with the country's policy of encouraging innovation while upholding strong ethical standards (Budianto et al., 2025). Canadian AI leadership is evidenced by its influence on AI ethics – for example, Canadian researchers were key contributors to the development of international AI ethics guidelines. In summary, while the US AI leadership is propelled by its robust private sector and market-driven adoption, Canada complements this with strategic public investments and policies that have made it a respected player in AI research and ethics (Zaidi et al., 2025).

In North America's innovation ecosystem, the interplay between tech companies, startups, universities, and government has created a virtuous cycle for AI leadership. Top universities (Stanford, MIT, Carnegie Mellon, University of Toronto, among others) produce cutting-edge research and a pipeline of skilled graduates, many of whom become AI entrepreneurs or join established firms. The close geographic and collaborative ties between academia and industry – exemplified by Silicon Valley's link to Stanford or the Toronto–Montreal AI corridor – facilitate rapid knowledge transfer and commercialization of AI breakthroughs (Ene et al., 2024). Public–private partnerships are common, such as projects where companies provide resources for academic research and, in return, gain early access to innovations. Meanwhile, government funding initiatives like the US National AI Research Institutes and Canada's CIFAR AI chairs program ensure that fundamental research, which might be too long term for private investors, is well supported (Portillo, 2025). This collaborative environment underpins a North American innovation engine that not only advances AI technology but also considers broader societal and economic impacts. Economically, the contribution of AI to North America's growth is significant and growing: AI technologies are projected to add hundreds of billions of dollars to North American GDP through productivity gains and the creation of new markets and services (Subrahmanyam, 2025b). In addition, AI-driven entrepreneurship has become a job creation engine; the proliferation of startups and AI adoption in existing businesses leads to demand for new roles such as data scientists, AI ethicists, and machine learning engineers (Kollmann et al., 2023). In short, North America's leadership in AI is reflected not only in technological metrics but also in tangible economic impact and a transformation of the business leadership paradigm toward a more data-driven, innovative, and collaborative model (Nyoto et al., 2024b; Kollmann et al., 2023).

8.2 AI LEADERSHIP IN EUROPE – REGULATION AND ETHICS

Europe's approach to AI leadership is distinctive for its emphasis on regulation, ethics, and human-centric values. While European nations recognize the importance of AI for economic growth and competitiveness, they have been equally concerned with ensuring that AI development aligns with privacy rights, safety, and societal trust. The influence of the General Data Protection Regulation (GDPR), enacted in 2018, is a prime example of how Europe's legal framework shapes AI leadership. GDPR's stringent data governance requirements have compelled organizations to implement robust data handling and privacy practices when deploying AI systems (Kuznietsova, 2024). This has, in effect, global implications – companies around the world that process European users' data must comply with GDPR standards. In the context of AI, GDPR enforces principles like data minimization and gives individuals rights such as algorithmic transparency (the right to an explanation for automated decisions), which has pushed AI leaders in Europe to prioritize explainability and accountability in AI solutions (Herrmann & Pfeiffer, 2022). European business leaders are keenly aware that AI projects must be designed with compliance in mind from the outset, integrating privacy-by-design and security measures to meet regulatory expectations (Kuznietsova, 2024). The forthcoming EU AI Act builds on this foundation, proposing a risk-based framework for AI systems – from minimal risk (like AI for spam filters) to high risk (like AI in healthcare or law enforcement) – with corresponding compliance requirements. European companies and AI practitioners are thus preparing for stricter compliance regimes that will demand transparency, human oversight, and rigorous assessment of AI algorithms before and during deployment (Aziz et al., 2024d). This regulatory climate, while sometimes viewed as an innovation hurdle, is also positioning Europe as a standard-setter for ethical AI governance (Budianto et al., 2025).

Ethical AI leadership is a hallmark of Europe's stance in the AI domain. The European Commission's High-Level Expert Group on AI published *Ethics Guidelines for Trustworthy AI* (2019), which articulated core principles such as respect for human autonomy, prevention of harm, fairness, and explicability. These principles have permeated corporate leadership in Europe, where many organizations have established AI ethics boards or chief ethics officers to oversee AI projects (Petrin, 2019). European leaders often frame AI initiatives not just in terms of ROI, but also in terms of social impact and trust: there is broad acknowledgment that without public trust, AI adoption will stall (Buçinca et al., 2021b; Mohanty et al., 2024). Consequently, companies in Europe are proactive in conducting bias audits of algorithms, investing in explainable AI techniques, and engaging stakeholders (including employee unions and consumer groups) in discussions about AI implementation (Chen, 2024). This contrasts with some other regions where such ethical considerations might be addressed later or in response to public pressure. In Europe, the notion of societal trust is deeply ingrained; for example, AI projects in domains like healthcare or public services are often accompanied by public consultations or pilot phases explicitly aimed at gauging and building citizen trust (Ene et al., 2024). The approach is fundamentally about balancing innovation with a strong commitment to human rights and dignity – European AI leadership tends to assert that technology should serve people and uphold their rights, a perspective influenced by the continent's history and legal traditions (Herrmann & Pfeiffer, 2022). Thus, European leaders champion AI that augments human decision-making without undermining human agency or privacy, reinforcing ethical standards as a competitive differentiator for European AI products and services (Aziz et al., 2024d).

One of the ongoing challenges and strategic focuses in Europe is balancing innovation and regulation. European policymakers and business leaders alike are aware of the risk that over-regulation could slow down AI innovation or drive talent and investment to less restrictive environments. To mitigate this, Europe has been investing significantly in AI research and innovation programs. The European Union's Horizon funding programs have allocated large budgets for AI research networks, digital innovation hubs, and public–private partnership projects on AI. Major AI research hubs in the EU have emerged in cities like Berlin, London, Paris, and Helsinki, often with specializations (e.g., Zurich in AI research for finance, or Amsterdam in AI for healthcare). These hubs bring together universities, research institutes, and companies in collaborative projects. Additionally, Europe is fostering its own ecosystem of AI startups, though they often operate at a smaller scale compared to Silicon Valley's unicorns. Access to venture capital in Europe has historically been more conservative, but this is changing as more European venture funds target AI and as success stories (like DeepMind's acquisition by Google, or Sweden's Spotify leveraging AI) attract attention (Portillo, 2025c). European AI partnerships like Gaia-X reflect Europe's desire to innovate in a way that upholds sovereignty and values. Gaia-X is an initiative to create a federated cloud and data infrastructure for Europe, ensuring that data (the fuel of AI) can be shared securely and transparently among organizations under European rules. By enabling data sharing across industries and countries (in sectors such as manufacturing, energy, and healthcare), European leaders aim to unlock AI innovation while keeping control over data governance (Kuznietsova, 2024).

This partnership-driven model underscores how Europe's competitive strategy in AI involves collaboration across borders and sectors within the EU. It's a recognition that no single European country can match the AI investment of the US or China alone, but collectively, through the EU framework, Europe can pool resources and expertise (Ene et al., 2024). The EU's coordinated approach (including transnational projects and regulatory alignment) exemplifies a unity in diversity strategy: allowing innovation to flourish in each country or industry, but under a common banner of ethical standards and interoperability (Kuznietsova, 2024; Petrin, 2019).

A strong focus on privacy and human rights informs European AI adoption, shaping leadership decisions in both government and industry. European leaders often take a precautionary approach to technologies that may impinge on individual rights. For instance, some European cities and countries have debated or enacted moratoria on facial recognition technology in public spaces due to privacy concerns. The conversation around AI surveillance in Europe is markedly different from other regions: it is framed by historical awareness of state overreach and thus there is vigilance about how AI could enable mass surveillance or algorithmic discrimination (Mohanty et al., 2024). Leaders in the public sector emphasize transparency and accountability for any AI used in governance. A case in point is the Nordic countries' digital government initiatives, which are frequently cited as models. Estonia, though not Nordic but often grouped in discussions of advanced digital governance in Europe, has implemented AI in public services (like automated systems for tax and legal advice) with careful consideration of transparency and a principle that citizens can always appeal automated decisions to a human official. Finland and Denmark have similarly experimented with AI in areas like social services and healthcare triage, but always under frameworks that ensure a human in the loop and respect for legal rights (Aziz et al., 2024d). These examples highlight that European governments strive to leverage AI to enhance efficiency and accessibility of public services while maintaining democratic oversight and protecting citizens' rights. The Nordic and broader European experience suggests that a high-trust society – where citizens trust that their data will be handled responsibly – is both a precondition and an outcome of ethical AI leadership (Smith, 2025). That trust is built by deliberate actions: open dialogues about AI policies, legal safeguards, and visible ethical leadership from top officials and CEOs. European companies often advertise their adherence to ethical guidelines as a value proposition. For example, a European AI service might be marketed as "GDPR-compliant and ethically designed," appealing to both consumers and business clients who value those assurances (Chen, 2024). In essence, Europe's case illustrates that regulation and ethics can be a source of competitive strength by fostering trust and sustainability in

AI deployment, even if it sometimes means a slower, more deliberate pace of innovation (Budianto et al., 2025).

Finally, Europe's AI leadership is bolstered by government–industry collaboration and international influence on governance norms. European governments frequently consult with industry experts and academic scholars when crafting AI strategies, resulting in comprehensive national AI plans in countries like France, Germany, and the UK. These plans often include funding for AI research centers, education and reskilling programs (to build AI talent), and frameworks for public sector AI use. For example, France's national AI strategy invested in interdisciplinary AI institutes and emphasized recruitment of AI scientists, while Germany's strategy funded application-oriented research and SME adoption of AI. Such strategies are typically accompanied by ethical guidelines or assessments, underscoring the European model of responsible innovation (Petrin, 2019). On the international stage, Europe often acts as an advocate for global AI governance. The OECD AI Principles (to which many European countries contributed) and the Global Partnership on AI (GPAI) – an initiative involving the EU – reflect Europe's push for multilateral cooperation in setting AI standards. European leaders frequently call for an international regulatory approach to issues like autonomous weapons or AI in finance to prevent harmful races to the bottom. This diplomatic leadership is part of Europe's soft power in technology: by championing global ethics guidelines and cooperative frameworks, Europe extends its influence beyond its own markets (Aziz et al., 2024d). In summary, Europe's perspective on AI leadership is one where innovation is steered by ethics and regulation. The region demonstrates that embracing AI's opportunities goes hand in hand with diligent oversight and a commitment to human values. While this can create tension – ensuring Europe remains competitive while upholding high standards – the general consensus in European leadership is that the long-term benefits of trustworthy AI outweigh the short-term gains of unfettered innovation (Buçinca et al., 2021b; Herrmann & Pfeiffer, 2022). Europe thus offers a model of AI leadership that is as much about how AI is adopted as it is about how much AI is adopted, emphasizing quality, trust, and societal alignment of AI systems.

8.3 AI LEADERSHIP IN ASIA – SCALE AND SPEED IN ADOPTION

Asia's approach to AI leadership is characterized by scale, speed, and state-driven strategy, with different countries pursuing AI in ways that reflect their unique economic structures and governance models. China, in particular, stands out with an ambitious and well-funded AI agenda. The Chinese government has declared AI a national priority, notably through its Next

Generation AI Development Plan, which aims to make China the world leader in AI by 2030. This top-down strategy has catalyzed massive investments in AI research, education, and entrepreneurship (Ene et al., 2024). Chinese tech giants like Alibaba, Baidu, Tencent, and Huawei are deeply involved in AI advancements, often in close alignment with state objectives. These companies have established AI research labs that rival or exceed their Western counterparts in size and output, producing innovations in areas such as natural language processing (e.g., Baidu's language models), computer vision (Alibaba's advances in retail AI and smart cities), and telecommunications AI (Huawei's AI-enabled 5G infrastructure). One hallmark of China's AI leadership is the integration of AI across industries at unmatched scale: from manufacturing (where AI and robotics are central to the "Made in China 2025" initiative) to fintech (ubiquitous mobile payments and credit scoring via AI algorithms) to e-commerce (Alibaba's AI-driven logistics and marketing) (Mudunuri et al., 2024c). Perhaps most distinctively, China leverages AI in governance and public policy – employing AI for public surveillance, smart city management, and social governance. The extensive use of facial recognition and surveillance cameras, bolstered by AI analytics, exemplifies how China prioritizes efficiency and security through technology, though it raises ethical debates internationally (Kuznietsova, 2024). Chinese leadership tends to frame AI as a means of societal management and economic development combined; the concept of a "digital leap" is evident as China implements AI solutions in domains that leapfrog legacy systems, such as mobile-first banking and telemedicine powered by AI in regions lacking traditional infrastructure (Pavitra et al., 2024). The sheer population and data available in China provide a competitive advantage – with more than a billion internet users, Chinese AI systems can train on enormous datasets, accelerating algorithmic improvements. This data abundance, coupled with relatively lenient data privacy regulations domestically, allows Chinese AI firms and research institutions to iterate rapidly and deploy at scale (Li et al., 2025). In summary, China's AI leadership is marked by speedy adoption and deployment, large-scale public–private endeavors, and a strategic vision linking AI to national prowess and modernization (Ene et al., 2024).

Beyond China, other parts of Asia have carved their own paths in AI leadership, often focusing on specific sectors and leveraging strengths in manufacturing and electronics. Japan and South Korea, for instance, have been global leaders in robotics and manufacturing automation for decades, which naturally extends into AI integration on the factory floor. Japan's concept of "Society 5.0" encapsulates a vision where AI, IoT, and robotics transform society – not only in manufacturing, where companies like FANUC or Toyota use AI-driven robots for precision and efficiency, but also in addressing societal issues like an aging population (through AI-powered caregiving robots and healthcare analytics). South Korea, propelled by conglomerates such as Samsung and LG, invests heavily in AI for consumer electronics, semiconductor design (AI chips), and telecommunications (5G AI optimization). These countries showcase AI in manufacturing by using machine learning for predictive maintenance, supply chain optimization, and quality control with unprecedented accuracy (Asiabar et al., 2024). The cultural emphasis on quality and Kaizen (continuous improvement) in Japan dovetails with AI's ability to continuously learn and optimize processes. Leaders in these East Asian economies often blend traditional management excellence with new AI tools, ensuring that human expertise and AI systems work in tandem to maintain their edge in production and technology (Hillebrand et al., 2025a). Moreover, both Japan and South Korea are proactive in national AI planning: for example, South Korea's government has established AI research institutes and included AI in its economic development plans, recognizing that future competitiveness in automotive, consumer tech, and entertainment (like K-pop's AI-curated content or gaming) relies on advanced AI capabilities (Singh, 2023d). The leadership style here involves significant industry–government collaboration, where governments fund R&D and set up favorable environments (like AI testbeds or regulatory sandboxes) for companies to innovate rapidly (Harrasi et al., 2021).

Another facet of Asia's AI landscape is the phenomenon of "digital leapfrogging" in countries like India and across Southeast Asia. These regions often have less entrenched legacy infrastructure, which paradoxically enables them to adopt cutting-edge technologies more swiftly in certain domains. India provides a telling example: with its vast IT sector and pool of engineering talent, India is leveraging AI to address development challenges and modernize industries quickly. In banking, India moved from a largely cash-based society to one where mobile payment and fintech apps (many incorporating AI for fraud detection and personalized services) are commonplace, effectively skipping the widespread use of credit cards seen in the West (Pavitra et al., 2024). In government services, initiatives like India's Aadhaar biometric identification system and various AI-based analytics in public administration illustrate leapfrogging legacy bureaucratic processes into digital systems. Indian leadership in AI is often driven by a vibrant startup ecosystem in cities like Bangalore and Hyderabad, tackling problems such as agricultural yield optimization (using AI for predicting weather and pests), healthcare diagnostics (AI tools for detecting diseases from medical images in resource-constrained settings), and language translation (for India's diverse languages) (Ateeq et al., 2025). The government of India has published its own National AI Strategy, termed "AI for All," emphasizing AI's use in social development fields and focusing on open datasets and collaboration between industry and academia. Other South and Southeast Asian countries are also rapidly adopting AI: Singapore stands out as a city-state with a comprehensive AI game plan, investing in research (through institutions like AISG – AI Singapore) and public sector AI deployments ranging from smart traffic management to AI assistants in government services (Harrasi et al., 2021). Singapore's leadership style in AI is often held up as a model for balancing innovation with governance – it has even issued a Model AI Governance Framework to guide companies in responsible AI use. Countries like Indonesia, Vietnam, and Thailand are seeing emerging AI startups and use cases as well, often mobile-centric due to the widespread use of smartphones. These developments underscore Asia's tendency to adopt AI solutions at scale and at speed, especially in consumer-facing domains: for example, the explosion of rapid consumer AI adoption via super-apps (like Grab and Gojek in Southeast Asia, which integrate ride-hailing, delivery, and payments with AI personalization) or the ubiquity of AI-driven features in Chinese apps (such as TikTok/Douyin's content recommendation engine) (Pavitra et al., 2024; Pei et al., 2024). Asian consumers have embraced AI-driven services quickly, which in turn incentivizes businesses to integrate AI to stay competitive, creating a virtuous cycle of adoption.

A notable competitive dynamic in Asia is the race for AI dominance, particularly between China and other major global players. Competition for AI supremacy has taken on a geopolitical flavor: Chinese and American tech firms (and by extension, national policies) compete in areas like AI research publications, semiconductor technology, and international AI market expansion (Ene et al., 2024). This rivalry pushes Asian firms and governments to invest aggressively in AI to not be left behind. For example, China is producing a large share of the world's AI research output (in terms of papers and patents), and its companies are expanding AI services into emerging markets, which spurs others like Japan or India to bolster their own research and industry efforts (Singh, 2023d). Asian leadership in AI is also evident in global AI talent and education. Countries like China and India graduate a significant proportion of the world's STEM experts, and many of these graduates specialize in AI or data science. There is a concerted effort in Asian educational institutions to offer AI curricula and establish AI centers of excellence (Portillo, 2025c). However, this also introduces the issue of brain drain – top talent often migrates to the US or Europe for opportunities, a challenge that Asian leaders acknowledge. To counter this, incentives such as high-profile AI research labs (e.g., OpenAI-like projects in China, or Google's AI center in India) and competitive salaries are being provided to retain talent or even attract diaspora experts back home (Zaidi et al., 2025).

An interesting case study reflecting Asia's innovation is the story of companies like Alibaba and Baidu. Alibaba, through its e-commerce empire, has innovated with AI in areas such as supply chain and logistics (using AI to optimize delivery routes and warehouse management), and customer experience (with AI chatbots and recommendation systems enhancing shopping on its platforms). Notably, Alibaba's annual "Singles' Day" sale (the world's largest online shopping event) is a showcase of AI scalability – its AI systems handle peak loads of order processing, fraud detection, and personalized marketing for hundreds of millions of customers in a single day (Mudunuri et al., 2024c). Baidu, known as the "Google of China," has leveraged its AI expertise beyond search algorithms; it has invested heavily in autonomous driving (Project Apollo) and AI cloud services. Baidu's AI research in natural language understanding and voice recognition led to products like the DuerOS voice assistant, reflecting how Chinese companies quickly turn AI research into consumer products. These companies illustrate a broader pattern in Asia: the blurring of lines between research and application. Many Asian tech firms run integrated ecosystems (akin to how Baidu, Alibaba, and Tencent each have diverse services) where improvements in AI algorithms can be rapidly deployed across multiple services (Van Quaquebeke & Gerpott, 2023). The leadership of these firms often emphasizes visionary risk-taking and a long-term horizon. For instance, it's common for Chinese CEOs to speak about a 10 or 20-year vision for AI in their business and invest accordingly, often supported by government policies that share that long view (Ene et al., 2024). The public surveillance and AI aspect, particularly in China, while controversial abroad, is seen domestically by leadership as part of the social contract for progress and stability – AI is used to manage traffic, reduce crime through predictive policing, and implement health measures (as seen during the COVID-19 pandemic with digital contact tracing and mask compliance monitoring). These uses are facilitated by a public that has generally adopted new technologies rapidly, though concerns about privacy are growing among Chinese citizens as well (Kuznietsova, 2024).

In conclusion, AI leadership in Asia is a tapestry of rapid adoption, government-driven initiatives, and competitive market forces. From China's centrally orchestrated AI surge to Japan and South Korea's industry-focused innovations, to India and Southeast Asia's leapfrogging and startup culture, Asia demonstrates that there is no single model for success – but common themes include speed, scale, and strategic intent. The region's large populations and growing digital economies provide vast opportunities for AI solutions to scale quickly (Pavitra et al., 2024). Asian leaders, whether in government or business, often operate with a sense of urgency and willingness to experiment, which has led to impressive feats such as national AI platforms, widespread consumer AI applications, and world-class research output in a relatively short time frame (Asiabar et al., 2024). At the same time, Asia's diversity means varying degrees of focus on AI ethics and regulation – with some areas moving very fast and then retroactively addressing ethical issues, and others (like Singapore or Japan) trying to proactively incorporate ethical considerations into their tech advancement (Harrasi et al., 2021). As Asia continues to rise in

AI, the global tech community watches closely, knowing that innovations from Asian laboratories and boardrooms will shape the next chapter of AI's evolution worldwide, and potentially redefine leadership practices on a global scale through new competition and collaboration dynamics (Singh, 2023d; Zaidi et al., 2025).

8.4 AI IN EMERGING MARKETS – LEAPFROGGING AND CHALLENGES

Emerging markets across Africa, the Middle East, and parts of Latin America present a unique narrative in AI leadership: one of leapfrogging traditional development hurdles and innovating under constraints, while also grappling with significant challenges like limited data and talent gaps. In many emerging economies, AI is seen as a tool not just for business efficiency but for development and social good. For instance, various countries in Africa are harnessing AI to address critical issues in agriculture, healthcare, and financial inclusion. With the majority of Africans accessing the internet primarily through mobile phones, a mobile-first innovation paradigm dominates (Duffour, 2024). This means many AI solutions are being built as lightweight mobile apps or services that can reach people in remote areas. A classic example is the use of AI-powered chatbots in agriculture: smallholder farmers in countries like Kenya or Uganda can use simple SMS or WhatsApp-based AI assistants to get advice on crop diseases or weather forecasts, effectively receiving expert guidance that was previously inaccessible (Budianto et al., 2025). Another example is mobile banking and fintech innovations. Africa's well-known success with mobile money (like Kenya's M-Pesa) laid the groundwork for AI-driven fintech services such as microloan approval and credit scoring using machine learning on non-traditional data (e.g., mobile phone usage patterns as a proxy for creditworthiness). These AI models allow millions of unbanked or underbanked individuals to access financial services – a leap past the need for brick-and-mortar banking infrastructure (Bloomquist & Georges, 2022). In these ways, emerging market leaders and entrepreneurs are using AI to leapfrog legacy infrastructure: since they may lack extensive physical networks of banks, hospitals, or schools, they compensate with digital solutions that can scale quickly (Pavitra et al., 2024). This leapfrogging is evident in telemedicine apps in places where doctor-to-patient ratios are low, using AI to triage symptoms or interpret medical images remotely, or in e-learning platforms that deploy AI tutors to areas with teacher shortages.

However, the path to integrating AI in emerging markets comes with distinct challenges: data scarcity, skill gaps, and infrastructural constraints are among the most pressing. Data scarcity refers not only to the quantity of data but also quality and relevance. Many AI applications rely on large datasets that, for Western contexts, might be readily available, but for developing contexts might be limited or biased. For example, natural language processing for African or South Asian languages often suffers from a lack of large annotated datasets, making AI less effective for those languages and thus for local users (Kuznietsova, 2024). Similarly, healthcare algorithms trained on Western patient data might not be directly applicable to African or Southeast Asian populations due to genetic, environmental, or lifestyle differences – a gap local leaders are aware of and are beginning to fill by encouraging local data collection and open data initiatives. The skill gap is another serious issue: there are relatively fewer AI engineers and data scientists in emerging economies, often leading to a reliance on external expertise or the poaching of the few experts by global companies (brain drain). Many talented individuals from these regions are educated abroad or move to tech hubs in the US or Europe for opportunities, which can slow local capacity-building (Ford et al., 2021). In response, some countries and organizations promote "brain circulation" – encouraging diaspora experts to contribute back home through short-term projects, mentorship, or remote collaboration (Zaidi et al., 2025). We also see increasing investments in capacity-building: for instance, local AI research labs and bootcamps have sprouted in Nigeria, Kenya, Ghana, and Rwanda, some with partnerships from big tech (Google and IBM have opened AI centers in Africa) or global nonprofits (Bloomberg and MasterCard Foundations supporting AI training programs). Infrastructure, particularly electricity and internet connectivity, is a foundational challenge that cannot be ignored – AI solutions presume a certain level of reliable power and network. Leaders in emerging markets thus often have to innovate in a frugal tech manner: creating AI systems that can run on basic smartphones, offline, or low-bandwidth modes, and tolerate interruptions (Fabri et al., 2023). For example, an AI health diagnosis app might be designed to function without continuous internet, syncing data when a connection becomes available. This concept of frugal innovation has become a cornerstone of emerging market AI solutions – making them cost-effective and robust against local constraints (Kuznietsova, 2024).

Despite challenges, emerging markets are giving rise to local AI innovation hubs that drive progress and tailor AI to local needs. Cities like Nairobi ("Silicon Savannah"), Lagos, Cape Town, Cairo, and Kigali have active tech communities where AI startups and initiatives are flourishing (Duffour, 2024). In Kenya, for instance, Nairobi hosts several AI and data science meetups and incubators. Kenyan startups have worked on AI for wildlife conservation (using AI in drones and cameras to combat poaching) and agritech solutions like soil analysis via machine learning. Nigeria's fintech boom has also spurred AI use in fraud detection and customer service bots, given the huge user base of mobile payments there. Government policies in some emerging economies are starting to reflect the importance of AI: the UAE (an emerging market in the Gulf, albeit wealthier) even appointed a Minister of AI and heavily invested in AI-driven government services as part of its diversification plan, which has inspired neighboring countries to consider similar approaches (Harrasi et al., 2021). In Africa, Rwanda has been notably forward-looking, hosting an annual AI summit and integrating drones and AI for medical supply delivery in remote areas. Such hubs often leverage international partnerships for capacity-building – for example, the Montreal-based organization MILA (Quebec's AI institute) has collaborations with some African universities for AI research, and initiatives like Data Science Africa or AI4D (AI for Development) Africa bring together researchers across the continent to share knowledge and resources (Aziz et al., 2024d). These networks help emerging market innovators not feel isolated from global advances. In fact, there is a conscious effort to ensure that voices from the Global South are included in the global conversation on AI ethics and governance, given their different perspectives and priorities (Budianto et al., 2025). For example, issues of AI fairness in emerging markets might focus on different dimensions (such as ensuring AI doesn't marginalize rural populations or informal economy workers) than in richer countries, but these voices are increasingly contributing to global AI principles (Ateeq et al., 2025).

Brain drain vs. brain circulation is a theme frequently discussed among emerging market leaders. While it's a challenge that many of the best-trained AI professionals from, say, sub-Saharan Africa or South Asia end up working in Silicon Valley or London, there is recognition that this diaspora can be a source of strength if engaged. Some countries have launched programs to attract talent back – for example, Nigeria's tech ecosystem has seen US-educated Nigerians returning to start companies or lead local AI labs, lured by growing opportunities and a chance to have a big impact at home. Others, like Ethiopia, have emphasized sending students abroad for AI studies with incentives to return (Ford et al., 2021). Moreover, remote work and virtual collaboration allow experts to contribute to local projects without physically being there, a trend accelerated by the global connectivity of research (Zaidi et al., 2025). For instance, an AI project in Ghana might involve a Ghanaian data scientist working from Europe mentoring a local team. This brain circulation helps mitigate the loss from brain drain and spreads expertise more evenly.

Emerging markets also showcase inspiring AI for social good initiatives that demonstrate leadership in aligning technology with humanitarian needs. In South Asia and Africa, AI is being used to predict and manage natural disasters – machine learning models for flood prediction in Bangladesh or earthquake impact modeling in Nepal are used by governments and NGOs to improve preparedness. In conflict-affected regions or areas with public health crises, AI systems have been deployed to analyze satellite images for refugee camp planning or to track epidemiological trends (as seen with Ebola and COVID-19 responses, where AI helped in mapping outbreaks with scarce medical resources). These case studies highlight a form of leadership that prioritizes social impact and frugal innovation over cutting-edge performance. The solutions might not be the most advanced globally, but they are effective and appropriate to context, which is a leadership lesson in itself: technology should be contextually relevant (Kuznietsova, 2024). For example, an AI-driven diagnostic tool that can work on a $50 Android phone and detect tuberculosis from a cough recording could be more valuable in an African context than a sophisticated AI that requires expensive equipment.

In the realm of fintech and agritech case studies, emerging economies are replete with instructive examples. In fintech, beyond mobile money, AI chatbots like Kenya's Haraka have provided instant microloans by analyzing a user's digital footprints. In agritech, consider Zenvus in Nigeria – a precision farming startup using AI to analyze soil data for farmers to optimize fertilizer use, thereby improving yields and livelihoods. Or the use of AI in market information systems, where farmers get price forecasts to make better decisions on when and where to sell produce, reducing exploitation by middlemen. Healthcare tech is equally transformative: startups are using AI for diagnosing diseases from images of blood samples or skin lesions, offering potentially life-saving early detection in areas lacking specialists (Bloomquist & Georges, 2022). These initiatives often involve partnerships – a local startup might partner with an international research lab to access cutting-edge algorithms, or with a telecom company to reach users via mobile networks, or with the government health ministry to integrate into public clinics.

Leadership in these contexts requires creativity, resilience, and coalition-building. Emerging market leaders must often align multiple stakeholders – government, international donors, private sector, and the target communities – to drive AI projects to fruition (Harrasi et al., 2021). The affordability and frugality aspect cannot be overstated: budgets are tight, so solutions must be cost-effective and sustainable without heavy subsidies. This has led to design philosophies such as using older hardware or open-source software to cut costs, and training local technicians to maintain AI systems (so that dependency on foreign experts is reduced). It also means setting realistic expectations – for example, implementing semi-automated solutions (with a human in the loop) instead of fully autonomous systems, because the latter might fail without robust infrastructure (Duffour, 2024).

In conclusion, emerging markets are carving out an AI leadership role defined by leapfrogging and adaptation. While they may not invest billions or produce as many research papers as the big players, they contribute significantly through innovation under adversity. They show the world how AI can be utilized in low-resource settings and in solving humanitarian problems, adding a valuable dimension to global AI development (Aziz et al., 2024d). Moreover, as these markets grow and their digital economies expand, they are likely to become important centers of AI usage – after all, the next billion internet users will largely come from these regions. Forward-looking leaders in these countries are laying the groundwork now by building capacity, forming alliances, and crafting policies that encourage local AI innovation while being mindful of ethical use and inclusive growth (Ateeq et al., 2025; Budianto et al., 2025). The challenges of data and talent are gradually being addressed through international cooperation and local initiatives, and success stories from Nairobi to New Delhi are proving that constraints can breed creativity, giving rise to AI solutions that might one day be exported to the rest of the world as frugal, robust innovations.

8.5 GLOBAL COLLABORATION AND COMPETITION IN AI STRATEGY

The landscape of AI leadership is increasingly defined not just by individual nations or companies, but by global collaboration and intense competition. On one hand, there is an unprecedented level of international cooperation to shape AI's trajectory responsibly; on the other, a rivalry – especially among great powers – to attain AI supremacy for economic and strategic advantage. These dual dynamics make AI a central topic in international relations and strategic planning across the globe (Ene et al., 2024).

Several international AI alliances and forums have emerged as platforms for collaboration. A notable example is the Global Partnership on AI (GPAI), a multinational initiative involving countries from North America, Europe, Asia, and elsewhere, focused on sharing research and best practices for AI that is grounded in human rights and democratic values. Such alliances reflect a shared understanding that AI's challenges (like bias, job displacement, security risks) and its benefits (economic growth, solving global problems) transcend borders, requiring cooperative solutions (Aziz et al., 2024d). Similarly, organizations like the Organisation for Economic Co-operation and Development (OECD) have been instrumental in forming consensus on AI principles – the OECD's AI Principles agreed in 2019 were a landmark, later endorsed by the G20, emphasizing inclusive growth, human-centered values, transparency, robustness, and accountability in AI. These principles serve as a baseline for international norms and are influencing policy in member countries (Budianto et al., 2025). We also see technical bodies like the Institute of Electrical and Electronics Engineers (IEEE) and the International Organization for Standardization (ISO) working on standardization efforts for AI – developing standards for AI safety, risk management, and ethics. These efforts aim to ensure AI systems developed in different parts of the world can adhere to common benchmarks of quality and safety (Kuznietsova, 2024).

Collaboration also takes place in research: cross-border research projects and conferences (such as major AI conferences that rotate globally) foster a sharing of ideas across academia and industry. It's common now for an AI research lab to have a multicultural team or multiple locations worldwide (e.g., OpenAI has researchers from many countries, Google's AI teams are spread across continents). This collaborative research across borders accelerates innovation and helps diffuse knowledge to regions that are still building their AI capabilities (Ene et al., 2024).

In contrast to the collaborative impulse, there is a robust competition for AI dominance that has been likened to a new "arms race" – though in this case, it's as much an economic race as a military one. The most highlighted rivalry is the US–China tech rivalry in AI. Both nations see leadership in AI as critical to future economic might and national security. The US has advantages like a legacy of top-tier tech companies, a tradition of innovation, and leading semiconductor design capabilities, whereas China wields advantages of scale, data, and a determined industrial policy (Ene et al., 2024). This rivalry has led to actions like the US restricting exports of advanced AI chips to China and investing in domestic AI R&D to maintain an edge, and China pouring state funds into reducing its dependence on foreign AI technologies (Singh, 2023d). Other countries feel the ripple effects of this competition – for example, allies of the US in Europe or Asia are sometimes caught between adopting Chinese AI infrastructure (like Huawei's AI-driven 5G equipment) or aligning with US preferences for privacy and security. Beyond the US and China, the global AI talent race is another competitive front. Countries worldwide are implementing strategies to attract AI researchers and engineers. Canada and the UK, for example, have immigration programs targeting tech talent; France and UAE have initiatives to lure expatriate scientists. Brain drain and gain are relative terms: one country's gain is another's loss. As noted earlier, emerging markets feel this acutely, but even within the developed world there's competition – cities like Montreal, London, Berlin, and Singapore brand themselves as AI hubs to draw investment and experts (Zaidi et al., 2025). This competition has positive aspects (incentivizing education and high salaries for AI specialists) but can also widen gaps between AI-rich and AI-poor regions (Portillo, 2025c).

A significant challenge that arises amid global AI deployment is cross-border data sharing. AI thrives on data, and often the most valuable datasets are global in nature (think of climate data or global health information). However, laws and policies like Europe's GDPR and various national data sovereignty laws (e.g., data localization requirements in countries like Russia, China, and India) complicate the free flow of data across borders (Herrmann & Pfeiffer, 2022). For instance, a US company may not easily transfer EU citizen data to an American server for AI processing unless strict safeguards are in place due to GDPR. Similarly, China's cybersecurity law can restrict certain data from leaving China. These legal regimes can hinder international AI projects – for example, an international research effort to train an AI model on global hospital records to improve cancer detection must navigate a patchwork of privacy laws (Kuznietsova, 2024). To address this, there are diplomatic and technical efforts underway. Some countries form bilateral and multilateral agreements for data sharing (such as the EU's pursuit of data flow agreements with allies or the OECD's work on fostering data free flow with trust). On the technical side, techniques like federated learning allow AI models to be trained across datasets located in different countries without raw data leaving local servers, which could be a solution to data silo issues. Nevertheless, aligning data governance and transnational regulatory coordination remains a complex diplomatic puzzle (Petrin, 2019). Trust is key: nations need confidence that sharing data or allowing foreign AI services won't compromise their citizens' rights or national security (Aziz et al., 2024d).

Global competition also manifests in the quest to set the rules and norms for AI in various domains. For example, in autonomous vehicles, countries are scrambling to be leaders so their standards become the default. China, Europe, and the US each have large test zones for self-driving cars and each bloc influences regulatory approaches (like Europe focusing on safety and liability, the US on innovation and industry-driven standards). Standardization efforts by IEEE/ISO we mentioned feed into this – whoever has the most influence in these committees can tilt standards in favor of their industries or values (Kuznietsova, 2024). There is also an aspect of AI in global supply chain management, where competition and collaboration intersect. Modern supply chains are global, and companies use AI for demand forecasting, logistics optimization, and risk management across these chains (Walczak, 2016). A disruption (like a pandemic or a geopolitical conflict) quickly shows how interconnected everyone is. Leaders of multinational companies collaborate on using AI to create more resilient supply chains – for instance, sharing certain data on inventory levels or shipping times can benefit all parties in a supply network (Elsherif, 2024a). Yet, in a competitive sense, countries worry about over-reliance on others' AI capabilities. For example, if all advanced AI chips are made in Taiwan, that's a strategic vulnerability for many nations. This has prompted initiatives in the US, EU, and China to develop domestic semiconductor industries (the chip war), illustrating that AI competition is not just about software and algorithms, but hardware and production capacity too (Singh, 2023d).

AI in international relations is no longer science fiction – it's here. Intelligence agencies use AI for analyzing satellite imagery and communications; militaries invest in AI for autonomous drones and cyber defense; and diplomats use AI to analyze negotiation positions or public sentiment. There's a competitive aspect: nations fear falling behind in military AI (leading to talk of an AI arms race), which is why forums like the United Nations have had discussions on banning autonomous lethal weapons or at least regulating them. Global powers vie to convince others that their approach to AI governance should prevail – for example, China has been active in the UN's ITU (International Telecommunication Union) to influence global norms on facial recognition and smart city tech, often emphasizing state authority, while Western countries emphasize individual rights and open data (Aziz et al., 2024d; Ene et al., 2024). Despite different philosophies, there is recognition that certain challenges like AI safety (ensuring superintelligent AI doesn't act uncontrollably) or misuse of AI (like deepfakes destabilizing societies) are global threats that require collaboration. This has led to calls for a kind of "Digital Geneva Convention" or international treaties on AI use – ideas that global leaders and think tanks have floated, drawing parallels to nuclear arms control (Petrin, 2019).

Another cooperative yet competitive aspect is how countries and corporations approach the Global AI talent race. Countries like the US and Canada have traditionally attracted top AI researchers from around the world to their universities and companies. Now, China is actively trying to reverse the flow, enticing Chinese researchers abroad to return with promises of funding and positions (Portillo, 2025c). Smaller countries cannot outbid on salary, so some, like those in Scandinavia or Canada, promote quality of life, research freedom, and strong ethics as selling points to talent (Smith, 2025). Additionally, global competitions and benchmarks (such as AI challenges like ImageNet or Go competitions) have become proxies for national pride when a team from one country outperforms others.

In summary, the geopolitical implications of AI advancement are significant. A nation's strength in AI could translate to economic dominance (through leading industries), military superiority (through advanced defense tech), and cultural influence (via AI-driven media and platforms). Thus, nations are wary of becoming "AI colonies" – purely consumers of AI tech from others – and are striving for some level of sovereign capability (Kuznietsova, 2024). This notion drives both competition (to innovate internally) and collaboration (to form alliances that collectively reduce dependence on a rival's technology). Leaders worldwide must navigate this complex interplay. They need to cooperate on setting the guardrails for AI – to ensure mutual prosperity and prevent catastrophic misuse – even as they compete to ensure their own people benefit the most and their values shape the technology. The most adept strategies acknowledge that collaboration and competition are two sides of the same coin in the realm of AI. For example, the EU and US might compete economically, but they collaborate on an AI code of conduct against authoritarian uses of AI. Likewise, tech giants from different countries might fiercely compete in the market, but their researchers might co-author academic papers and set standards together (Hillebrand et al., 2025a). This global interdependence means AI leadership is not a zero-sum game; the technology can expand the pie for everyone if managed wisely, but mishandling it could also pose global risks. Therefore, forward-looking strategies tend to mix investment in national strengths with active participation in international dialogue – a dual approach to ensure a nation or company stays ahead, but also that the world as a whole steers AI toward beneficial outcomes rather than conflict (Aziz et al., 2024d; Ene et al., 2024).

8.6 INTERNATIONAL POLICY AND COOPERATION ON AI GOVERNANCE

As AI becomes ingrained in every facet of society, international policy and cooperative governance have taken center stage to address the global implications of this powerful technology. Recognizing that AI's benefits and risks do not respect national borders, international organizations and coalitions are proactively shaping frameworks to guide AI development in a manner consistent with shared human values (Aziz et al., 2024d).

The United Nations and its agencies are increasingly involved in AI initiatives, reflecting the importance of AI on the global agenda. The UN Secretary-General has highlighted AI in discussions about the future of global cooperation, and multiple UN bodies are examining AI's impact on their domains. For instance, UNESCO (the UN's agency for education, science, and culture) adopted a landmark Recommendation on the Ethics of Artificial Intelligence in 2021, the first global agreement on AI ethics. This document, agreed upon by over 190 member states, sets out values and principles such as human rights, diversity, and sustainability that should underpin AI, and recommends policy actions like ethical impact assessment and international research collaboration. The UNESCO recommendation is non-binding but carries moral authority and offers a common reference point for national policymakers (Budianto et al., 2025). Similarly, the United Nations International Telecommunication Union (ITU) has convened summits on AI (the AI for Good Global Summit) which bring together governments, industry, and civil society to share AI solutions aimed at achieving the Sustainable Development Goals (e.g., using AI to fight climate change or improve healthcare in developing countries). The UN is also facilitating dialogues on specific sensitive issues: one such forum is the Group of Governmental Experts (GGE) on Lethal Autonomous Weapons Systems under the Convention on Certain Conventional Weapons, where nations debate possible treaties or norms for military AI (to prevent a destabilizing arms race in autonomous weapons). This indicates a drive toward transnational regulatory coordination in areas of AI that could threaten international security (Aziz et al., 2024d). However, consensus is difficult – while most countries agree on keeping humans in the loop for critical life-and-death decisions, there's less agreement on bans or verification measures. Despite these challenges, the UN's involvement ensures that developing countries and smaller states have a voice alongside great powers, aiming for inclusive global governance rather than a few nations dominating rule-making.

Outside the UN, groups like the OECD and the G7/G20 are acting as forums for major economies to align on AI governance. The OECD AI Principles adoption by its 38 member countries (and several non-members) was a pivotal moment – these principles, as mentioned, emphasize themes like fairness, transparency, and accountability, and crucially also include a principle of international cooperation for trustworthy AI. Following the OECD's lead, the G20 (a broader group including emerging economies like India, Brazil, and South Africa) endorsed similar guidelines in 2019. This shows an encouraging level of high-level consensus: world leaders publicly agree that AI should be human-centric and that global AI ethics guidelines are necessary to steer its development (Elsherif, 2024a). The challenge is moving from principles to practice – hence efforts like the GPAI (Global Partnership on AI) mentioned earlier, which was actually an idea born in the G7 and then internationalized. GPAI creates working groups on topics such as responsible AI, data governance, and the future of work, where experts from different countries collaborate on research and advise on best practices. Such bodies illustrate diplomatic collaboration on AI governance where nations pool knowledge and even resources (Ene et al., 2024). Another example of international coordination is in standardizing AI norms worldwide through technical standards. Organizations like ISO have set up committees (e.g., ISO/IEC JTC 1/SC 42 for AI) developing international standards on AI terminology, robustness, risk management, and ethics. Countries actively participate to make sure standards reflect their perspectives – for instance, Europe might push harder on privacy standards, while others focus on innovation friendliness (Kuznietsova, 2024).

A particularly complex policy issue is data sovereignty and international data transfer. Different philosophies about data are evident: the EU treats personal data protection as a fundamental right, enshrining strict controls in GDPR, whereas countries like the US have a more sectoral and market-driven approach, and China emphasizes state control over data (Herrmann & Pfeiffer, 2022). Bridging these differences is critical for AI, because AI thrives on combining diverse datasets. International data transfer policies have needed updates: the transatlantic data flow arrangements (between the EU and US) had to be renegotiated after European courts struck down previous agreements (like Safe Harbor and Privacy Shield) due to concerns over US surveillance. A new EU–US data privacy framework is being put in place to satisfy European requirements and maintain data flows for businesses, which is vital for AI services (Petrin, 2019). In a similar vein, discussions are happening in trade agreements: modern trade deals often include chapters on e-commerce or digital trade that cover data flow and storage, aiming to prevent unjustified data localization that could hamper commerce and by extension AI (because many services are delivered across borders). Data sovereignty debates also occur in contexts like health or agriculture data, where countries may feel that local data must remain local to ensure benefits accrue to their own citizens and to protect sensitive information (Kuznietsova, 2024). A balance is sought between protecting sovereignty and enabling the kind of cross-border AI impact assessments that global issues demand – for example, to fight a pandemic, we need global data sharing for AI models that track the virus. One emerging concept is the idea of data trusts or commons where data from multiple countries or sources can be pooled under agreed governance for specific purposes (like climate research) (Aziz et al., 2024d). Leaders in policy circles are exploring these creative solutions to unlock data for good while respecting different legal systems.

Another arena of international cooperation is establishing global AI ethics and human rights norms. The notion of AI governance includes ensuring AI does not perpetuate discrimination or infringe on human dignity. Transnational efforts like the EU's push for a ban on AI systems that violate human rights (e.g., social scoring of citizens in a manner similar to what's reportedly done in China) indicate a willingness to set red lines (Budianto et al., 2025). If the EU's AI Act passes with extraterritorial effect (similar to GDPR), it could become a de facto global norm for companies wishing to operate in the large European market, thereby exporting European standards. The US, while more hands-off in regulation domestically so far, has engaged in international dialogue by proposing a bill of rights for AI and participating in the Global Partnership on AI. We also see an interesting convergence in rhetoric: even China speaks in international forums about "AI for mankind's common destiny" and publishes ethical guidelines (which emphasize principles like fairness and privacy, albeit interpreted through a Chinese context) (Ene et al., 2024). This demonstrates that, globally, no one wants to be seen as opposing ethical AI. The real test is in implementation and enforcement. Transnational regulatory coordination is evident in specific sectors too. For example, civil aviation authorities worldwide are working on AI in aviation safety guidelines together, and financial regulators coordinate on AI in fintech through bodies like the Financial Stability Board to prevent regulatory arbitrage (Portillo, 2025c).

The future outlook for global AI cooperation points toward the need for even more structured governance mechanisms. There are proposals for an International AI Agency, analogous to the International Atomic Energy Agency (which oversees nuclear tech) – an idea suggesting an organization that could monitor global AI development, advise on best practices, and perhaps even inspect or audit certain high-stakes AI systems (Petrin, 2019). While such an agency is not yet on the horizon, we do see moves toward forming expert panels and observatories. The UN has proposed setting up a multistakeholder advisory body on global AI cooperation, which could synthesize inputs from governments, industry, and civil society and feed them into UN discussions (Aziz et al., 2024d). There is also the concept of AI impact assessments on a cross-border scale – meaning, when a new AI system (like a widely used social media algorithm or a new AI-driven credit scoring model) is introduced, some argue it should undergo an assessment for its potential cross-border societal impacts (e.g., could it destabilize information ecosystems in multiple countries?). This is a novel idea drawn from environmental governance (where big projects require environmental impact assessments, even sometimes internationally if rivers or air pollution are affected across borders). We might see voluntary or mandatory frameworks for such AI impact evaluations in the future, likely championed by international coalitions or NGOs initially (Budianto et al., 2025).

Ultimately, diplomatic collaboration on AI governance is about trust-building among nations and stakeholders. The fast pace of AI development has at times outstripped governments' ability to legislate or understand the tech deeply. By cooperating, nations can share expertise (a smaller country can learn from bigger ones' experiences) and ensure that poor or marginalized countries are not left behind in shaping AI's future (Elsherif, 2024a). The spirit of cooperation is balanced with recognition of national interests – states will not sign onto international regimes they see as disadvantaging them. Therefore, global AI governance likely will be a patchwork of aligned regulations, shared principles, and targeted treaties or agreements on specific issues (like prohibiting autonomous weapons or establishing data sharing for pandemics). It may not be one comprehensive "AI law of the world," but rather a network of interlocking efforts. The trend, however, is clear: AI is now a staple of international diplomacy. Just as climate change forced countries to come together for common rules (like the Paris Agreement), the rise of AI is compelling nations to envision common frameworks to ensure this technology improves human welfare globally while mitigating its risks (Aziz et al., 2024d; Ene et al., 2024). The success of these endeavors will shape whether AI becomes a source of international unity and mutual progress or an arena of unchecked competition and conflict. Leaders in policy and technology are increasingly aware of these high stakes, which is why the coming years will likely see even more intense efforts for global cooperation – through the UN, multilateral forums, and direct collaborations – to steer AI toward a future that benefits all of humanity.

9. Strategic foresight, innovation, and AI-driven transformation

9.1 STRATEGIC FORESIGHT AND SCENARIO PLANNING IN AI LEADERSHIP

In an AI-driven world, leaders leverage strategic foresight tools to anticipate disruption and stay ahead of change. AI analytics can process vast data to identify emerging trends, helping leaders detect market shifts and potential disruptions before they fully materialize (Subrahmanyam & Khalife, 2025; Ekellem, 2024). This predictive power enables anticipatory leadership – using data-driven insights to craft proactive strategies rather than reacting after the fact. For example, AI-based trend analysis platforms scan economic indicators, consumer sentiment, and competitive moves to flag "weak signals" of change, giving organizations early warning of disruptive innovations or shifting customer preferences (Asiabar et al., 2024). By detecting these weak signals, AI-assisted foresight helps leaders formulate contingency plans and scenario models for multiple plausible futures.

Leaders employ scenario planning augmented by AI to stress-test strategies against a range of future conditions. Advanced simulation engines can model scenarios (e.g., a new competitor's entry or a regulatory change) and forecast potential impacts on markets and operations (Subrahmanyam & Khalife, 2025). This AI-enhanced scenario planning improves an organization's future-readiness by illuminating how different strategies perform under various conditions, thereby informing more resilient decision-making (Ekellem, 2024; Asiabar et al., 2024). For instance, an AI foresight platform might simulate how an economic downturn combined with a technological breakthrough could affect product demand, allowing leaders to prepare adaptive strategies. Such tools also assist in weak signal detection – identifying subtle patterns (like emerging customer behaviors or nascent technologies) that herald bigger trends. By continuously scanning social media, patent filings, and industry reports, AI systems flag these early indicators so leaders can investigate and act on them (Mudunuri et al., 2024c). This foresight capability is crucial for cultivating strategic agility in fast-changing environments.

Notably, strategic foresight is being applied across industries with AI's help. In finance, institutions use AI-driven forecasting to anticipate market volatility and model stress scenarios for investment portfolios. In healthcare, AI analytics predict disease outbreak patterns and patient demand under various future scenarios, guiding capacity planning (Elsherif, 2024b). Cross-industry case studies show organizations that integrated AI into their foresight practices were better prepared for events like sudden supply chain disruptions or rapid shifts in consumer behavior (Frimpong & Wolfs, 2024). These organizations embedded AI into their strategic planning processes, enabling data-driven decision-making and quicker pivots when conditions changed. In summary, AI-enhanced strategic foresight and scenario planning empower leaders to see around corners – anticipating disruption, exploring "what-if" scenarios, and crafting robust strategies that can weather a range of futures (Ekellem, 2024; Subrahmanyam & Khalife, 2025). This proactive posture is a hallmark of effective AI-era leadership, ensuring organizations are future-ready rather than caught off-guard by change.

9.2 INNOVATION STRATEGIES IN THE AI ERA

Artificial intelligence has become a powerful innovation enabler for organizations, catalyzing new products, services, and business models. AI systems can rapidly analyze data and generate insights that spark creative solutions, helping leaders and teams innovate faster and more effectively. Research indicates that AI augmentation can significantly enhance organizational innovation capacity without replacing the human element – instead, AI and human creativity work in tandem to drive breakthroughs (Spisak, 2024; Madanchian et al., 2024b). For example, AI-driven design tools can suggest novel product designs or process improvements, which human experts then refine and implement. By handling complex analyses at high speed, AI frees up human innovators to focus on imaginative, big-picture thinking. Studies have found that companies augmenting their R&D with AI tools report faster experimentation cycles and more diverse idea generation, fueling a culture of continuous innovation (Westover, 2025). In essence, AI serves as a creative partner – generating options and insights that humans might miss – thereby expanding the innovative potential of organizations.

Leaders are also embracing open innovation in the digital ecosystem, using AI to collaborate beyond their organization's walls. In the AI era, innovation often emerges from networks of partners, startups, and even customers. Open innovation platforms powered by AI help firms tap external ideas and technologies, integrating them into internal projects (Nyoto et al., 2024b). For instance, some corporations run crowdsourcing challenges using AI to evaluate submissions, or maintain online innovation hubs where external developers contribute to AI solutions. These approaches expand the organization's innovation ecosystem, enabling access to a wider pool of talent and perspectives. Digital ecosystems – such as app marketplaces or industry consortia – allow knowledge sharing and co-creation, with AI tools facilitating seamless collaboration across company boundaries. As a result, companies practicing open innovation with AI support can accelerate their development timelines and respond to opportunities more rapidly (Budianto et al., 2025). Additionally, AI innovation labs have become popular as dedicated spaces for experimentation. Many leading firms now have internal AI labs or centers of excellence where cross-functional teams and data scientists prototype AI-driven ideas (Elsherif, 2024b). These labs often partner with technology startups or academic institutions, blending expertise to spur disruptive innovation. Such partnerships – for example, a manufacturing company teaming with an AI startup on intelligent robotics – inject fresh thinking and technical know-how into corporate R&D (Madanchian et al., 2024b).

Crucially, AI itself is a source of disruptive innovation. Entirely new business models are emerging from AI capabilities: from personalized AI-driven services to platform-based models that monetize data. For example, the use of AI algorithms has enabled the shift from one-time product sales to subscription-based services and predictive maintenance in industries like aviation and energy (where AI predicts equipment failures and companies sell uptime rather than equipment). Companies like Ping An in finance transformed from traditional insurers into tech-enabled ecosystems by leveraging AI for everything from customer service chatbots to health-tech platforms, disrupting their industry in the process. Likewise, AI-fueled servitization strategies – turning products into services – have given incumbents new revenue streams and challenged startups to keep pace (Aziz et al., 2024d). A systematic review by Pago (2024) finds that AI applications tend to enhance decision-making and team performance, empower personalized customer experiences, and enable entirely new offerings, illustrating AI's broadly positive impact on innovation in practice. To capitalize on these opportunities, leaders are accelerating R&D with AI tools such as machine learning for drug discovery, generative design algorithms in engineering, and digital twins for rapid prototyping. These tools significantly shorten development cycles by automating complex tasks and evaluating myriad alternatives far faster than human analysis alone (Asiabar et al., 2024). The result is an innovation process that is both faster and more ambitiously exploratory, as AI widens the solution space that humans can consider.

Effective innovation strategies in the AI era combine human creativity with AI's analytical and generative power. Leaders foster a culture where AI is viewed as a collaborator in innovation – from generating initial ideas to optimizing solutions – while also reaching beyond organizational boundaries through open innovation networks (Nyoto et al., 2024b). By doing so, organizations can not only incrementally improve but also pursue disruptive innovations that redefine markets (Madanchian et al., 2024b). The AI-driven innovation examples across sectors underscore a common lesson: those who strategically integrate AI into their innovation processes tend to achieve faster, bolder outcomes, whereas those who do not risk being left behind by more data-savvy competitors (Pago, 2024). AI thus serves as both a catalyst and a platform for innovation, enabling the continuous renewal that is essential for long-term competitive advantage.

9.3 DIGITAL TRANSFORMATION AND ORGANIZATIONAL RENEWAL

Artificial intelligence has emerged as a catalyst for digital transformation, driving fundamental changes in how organizations operate and create value. Leaders increasingly view AI as a transformation engine that can modernize legacy systems, streamline processes, and unlock new business models. In practice, integrating AI often requires updating or overhauling legacy infrastructure – for example, moving from on-premise systems to cloud-based AI platforms and upgrading data architectures to support machine learning. Forward-looking leaders champion these modernization efforts, knowing that outdated systems can impede AI adoption and agility (Dissanayake & Keppetipola, 2024b). Research identifies digital transformation as a dominant theme in AI leadership studies, underscoring that embracing AI-driven change is now a critical leadership challenge and opportunity (Dissanayake & Keppetipola, 2024b; Madanchian et al., 2024b). Organizations that successfully transform with AI tend to develop a clear roadmap for phasing out legacy technologies and embedding AI across the enterprise, often starting with pilot projects and scaling them company-wide. This systematic renewal process ensures that AI isn't just an add-on, but a core part of new, more intelligent business processes.

A key aspect of AI-driven transformation is business model innovation. AI enables organizations to reimagine how they deliver value – for instance, by leveraging data as a strategic asset or using algorithms to create personalized services. Many companies have transitioned to platform-based business models that connect producers and consumers in new ways, powered by AI recommendation engines and matchmaking algorithms. Others monetize the insights from AI (e.g., offering analytics-as-a-service) as entirely new revenue streams. Leaders in the AI era must therefore be business model innovators, continually assessing how AI can open opportunities to serve customers differently or enter new markets. For example, an agriculture firm might develop an AI-driven advisory service for farmers (turning insight into a product), or a retailer might use AI to optimize supply chains and offer faster delivery models. These innovations often blur industry boundaries, so leadership requires a strategic vision to navigate the convergence of sectors. Studies note that AI's ability to rapidly analyze business data and simulate outcomes can guide leaders in testing and validating new models before fully committing, reducing the risk of innovation (Subrahmanyam & Khalife, 2025). Moreover, case evidence shows that companies combining AI capabilities with bold business model changes – such as adopting digital platforms or subscription models – achieve higher growth and resilience (Elsherif, 2024b). In effect, AI acts as both a spark and a support mechanism for organizational renewal, giving leaders the insights and tools to reinvent their businesses.

Beyond technology and models, enterprise-wide digital maturity becomes a focal point. True transformation requires that the entire organization – its culture, processes, and people – matures in digital capability. Leaders drive enterprise-wide initiatives to build this maturity, from cultivating data literacy among employees to establishing robust data governance and AI ethics policies. Some use AI maturity models to assess their organization's readiness and progress, identifying gaps in areas like data infrastructure, talent, or innovation processes. By addressing these gaps, organizations move from tentative experimentation to a fully AI-enabled operating model. For example, a company might progress from a few isolated AI use cases to an integrated ecosystem where AI supports decisions in every department (finance, marketing, HR, etc.), indicating a high level of digital maturity. This journey often entails organizational renewal: restructuring teams, redefining roles, and fostering a more agile culture to fully leverage AI (Boikanyo, 2025). Importantly, successful transformation is as much about change management as technology. Leaders must navigate the human side of AI-driven change – overcoming resistance, managing fears about job impacts, and continuously communicating the transformation vision. Studies emphasize adaptive leadership and continuous learning as essential traits for guiding organizations through AI-driven change (Madanchian et al., 2024b; Pasupuleti, 2024). Leaders who are transparent about the transformation process, involve employees in upskilling programs, and celebrate quick wins tend to sustain momentum and buy-in for the digital journey. AI as a transformation catalyst requires leaders to orchestrate technology upgrades, business model reinvention, and cultural change in tandem.

Digital transformation is not a one-off project but an ongoing leadership mandate – an iterative process of renewal. Organizations like IBM and Schneider Electric, for instance, underwent multi-year transformations where AI was embedded into their core strategy, processes, and offerings, demonstrating significant improvements in operational efficiency and new business growth. Research confirms that aligning AI initiatives with a clear strategic roadmap and ensuring organization-wide readiness are critical success factors for such transformations (Elsherif, 2024a; Portillo, 2025c). Leaders must act as change agents, ensuring that their organization continuously adapts and evolves, thereby avoiding stagnation in the face of rapidly advancing technology (Pasupuleti, 2024). Ultimately, those enterprises that achieve high digital maturity through AI integration can realize enterprise-wide renewal – becoming more agile, innovative, and resilient businesses poised for sustained success in the digital age (Dissanayake & Keppetipola, 2024).

9.4 LEADERSHIP IN TECHNOLOGICAL DISRUPTION AND MARKET VOLATILITY

The rise of AI has coincided with an era of intense technological disruption and market volatility, placing a premium on agile and resilient leadership. Leading in uncertainty and change means that today's leaders must be comfortable making decisions amid fast-changing conditions and incomplete information. AI can both contribute to volatility (by rapidly changing competitive dynamics) and help manage it (by providing timely insights), so leaders must develop an adaptability mindset. Adaptive leadership frameworks have gained prominence as guides for navigating disruptive change, emphasizing flexibility, learning, and empowerment (Boikanyo, 2025). Leaders practicing adaptive tactics use AI tools to continuously sense the environment – monitoring customer trends, competitor moves, and operational metrics in real time – and then swiftly adjust strategies as needed. For example, if an AI-driven dashboard indicates a sudden shift in consumer sentiment, an adaptive leader might rapidly pivot marketing strategies or product offerings. Research on digital disruption shows that organizations led by agile leaders capable of quick strategic pivots are better at weathering uncertainty and even capitalizing on it (Budianto et al., 2025; Pasupuleti, 2024). In one case, an e-commerce retailer used AI to detect a spike in demand for remote work products early in the pandemic; the leadership promptly reallocated resources to this segment, illustrating agility in action.

Such responsiveness is increasingly critical, as AI-led competition can emerge from unexpected places – for instance, a tech startup using AI to enter a traditional industry can upheave incumbents with little warning. Leaders must foster resilience in the face of technological disruption. This involves not just reacting to change, but building organizations that thrive under stress. AI can aid resilience by providing early warning signals (as discussed in strategic foresight) and by enabling rapid response through automation. For instance, AI-driven scenario planning (see section 9.1) helps leaders prepare contingency plans for disruption, effectively rehearsing their response to potential crises or market shocks. As a result, when volatility strikes – say a sudden supply chain breakdown or a new AI-enabled competitor – resilient organizations already have playbooks informed by AI simulations (Asiabar et al., 2024).

Equally important is cultivating a resilient workforce; leaders encourage a culture of flexibility and continuous upskilling so employees can adapt to new AI tools and roles as needed (Pasupuleti, 2024). Studies on AI disruption find that an emphasis on learning and development helps reduce fear of change, making teams more capable of absorbing technological shifts without a drop in performance (Pasupuleti, 2024; Boikanyo, 2025). Additionally, resilience is reinforced by diversification – companies leveraging AI across multiple products or markets can better withstand volatility in any one area, a strategy that leaders like to pursue when feasible.

In times of market upheaval, strategic pivots and turnarounds become true tests of leadership. AI provides leaders with data-driven clarity to make bold pivots when necessary. For example, if AI analysis shows a core business line declining but identifies an adjacent high-growth opportunity, effective leaders will decisively reallocate resources – a pivot – rather than clinging to the status quo. We have seen this in practice with companies like Netflix pivoting from mail DVDs to streaming, guided in part by data on shifting consumer behaviors. The speed of AI-driven markets means decision velocity is crucial – leaders often need to make significant strategic calls faster than ever before, whether to exit an unprofitable venture or double down on a nascent innovation. The leader's decision velocity is enhanced by AI tools that supply real-time information and predictive analytics, enabling quick yet informed decisions (Subrahmanyam & Khalife, 2025). However, high-velocity decisions also carry risk, so top leaders balance speed with prudent risk management. They rely on AI for scenario analysis and risk forecasting to understand potential downsides of a quick move (Hwang, 2024c; Frimpong & Wolfs, 2024). For instance, before executing a turnaround strategy, a leadership team might use AI to model the financial and operational impacts under best- and worst-case scenarios, thereby avoiding reckless gambles.

Effective leadership in disruptive times also requires confidence and clear communication. Employees and stakeholders look to leaders for direction amid chaos. Leaders who harness AI to generate insights can instill confidence by basing their decisions on solid evidence and then articulating a compelling rationale. Transparency is key: explaining both the opportunities AI brings (new efficiencies, new markets) and the challenges (workforce changes, ethical considerations) builds trust during volatile periods (Hwang, 2024c). For example, a CEO might communicate how implementing AI in customer service will improve responsiveness while retraining staff for higher-value roles – acknowledging the disruption and demonstrating a proactive plan. This approach aligns with research emphasizing the role of trust and ethics in AI-led disruption: maintaining stakeholder trust can be as critical as strategic savvy (Frimpong & Wolfs, 2024). Finally, resilient leaders commit to continuous learning – adopting a mindset that each disruption is a learning opportunity to further strengthen the organization. Many are establishing feedback loops where AI systems monitor the outcomes of decisions (such as a strategic pivot) and report back on what worked or not, so leadership can refine their approach continuously (Hwang, 2024c). In conclusion, leading through technological disruption and volatility is a multifaceted challenge. Leaders must be agile decision-makers, risk managers, communicators, and learners all at once. By intelligently leveraging AI for timely information and foresight, and by cultivating adaptability and trust in their organizations, they can guide their teams to not only survive disruptions but turn them into opportunities for innovation and growth (Boikanyo, 2025; Pasupuleti, 2024).

9.5 EMBEDDING AI IN STRATEGIC PLANNING AND EXECUTION

To truly reap AI's benefits, organizations must weave AI capabilities into the very fabric of their strategic planning and execution processes. This begins with ensuring strategic alignment between AI initiatives and the organization's overarching goals. Rather than treating AI projects as siloed tech experiments, effective leaders integrate them into corporate strategy maps and vision statements. For example, if a company's strategy is to improve customer experience, leaders align AI efforts (like deploying an AI customer service chatbot or personalized recommendation engine) directly with that goal. This alignment ensures AI investments drive meaningful business outcomes and get top management support (Elsherif, 2024a). Some companies have even established new executive roles such as the Chief AI Officer or formed AI strategy committees to oversee integration, signaling that AI is central to strategic direction (Elsherif, 2024b). A study by Schmitt (2024c) notes that elevating AI governance to the C-suite helps maintain alignment with corporate objectives and ethical standards. In practice, these leaders work to embed AI considerations into all strategic discussions – from market expansion plans to cost leadership strategies – asking, "How can AI help achieve this?" and "What AI capabilities do we need to develop?" at every turn. Effective strategic planning in the AI era is distinctly data-driven and iterative. Leaders are adopting AI-enhanced strategic roadmapping tools that use analytics to inform priorities and timing. For instance, predictive models can forecast market trends or internal performance trajectories under different strategic scenarios, giving planners a richer fact base for choosing a path (Subrahmanyam & Khalife, 2025).

AI tools also enable dynamic strategy adjustments: rather than static annual plans, leaders use real-time dashboards with strategic KPIs to monitor progress and quickly recalibrate execution as needed. This agility in execution is often supported by AI-driven project management systems that allocate resources and flag issues in real time. Key to this approach is establishing AI-enhanced

KPIs and metrics. Traditional metrics might not fully capture the value generated by AI (such as improvements in decision quality or predictive accuracy), so leaders expand their performance indicators. They introduce metrics like algorithm precision, data quality indices, or AI-driven revenue contribution to ensure the impact of AI is measured and visible (Al-Zahrani et al., 2024; Aziz et al., 2024d). At the same time, they remain vigilant about measuring unintended consequences (e.g., tracking bias incidents or model errors) as part of responsible AI governance. The literature has highlighted a lack of standardized metrics for AI leadership effectiveness and calls for new tools to evaluate how AI is influencing decision-making and outcomes (Al-Zahrani et al., 2024). Progressive organizations are responding by developing balanced scorecards that include both traditional business outcomes and AI-specific performance measures, ensuring that AI initiatives are directly tied to strategic results and accountability.

Another crucial element is evolving operating models to fully integrate AI. Embedding AI in strategy execution often means redesigning processes and workflows around AI capabilities. Rather than using AI as a plug-in to existing processes, forward-looking firms reengineer workflows to optimize human–AI collaboration. For example, a bank implementing AI credit scoring might redesign its loan approval process so that AI makes a preliminary risk assessment, which is then reviewed by an analyst for final decision – a new workflow that ensures efficiency and oversight. Leaders also update organizational structures: some create AI centers of excellence that serve the whole enterprise, while others distribute AI experts into business units to infuse AI into daily operations (Elsherif, 2024b). There is a trend toward more intelligent enterprise operating models, where decision-making is decentralized and augmented by AI at multiple levels of the hierarchy (Budianto et al., 2025). In such models, front-line employees might use AI tools to make immediate decisions (e.g., pricing or inventory moves) within guardrails set by leadership. This requires trust and a culture shift, which leaders foster by providing training and establishing clear guidelines on the use of AI in decision processes. Data from case studies indicate that companies that successfully redesign processes and roles to incorporate AI – rather than forcing AI into old molds – see significantly greater improvements in efficiency and effectiveness. Essentially, the organization becomes an intelligent enterprise: continuously learning and improving through data, analytics, and AI at every level.

Finally, leaders embed AI in strategy execution by linking it with their performance management and governance frameworks. Strategic plans come to life through execution, and AI can play a role in monitoring and driving execution forward. For instance, AI-driven performance management systems can track progress on strategic initiatives in real time, sending alerts to leaders when projects deviate from targets or when market conditions change assumptions. Companies like Amazon famously use real-time metrics and automated feedback loops to adjust execution of strategies (such as pricing or supply chain optimization) on the fly with AI systems. Leaders ensure that these AI systems are aligned with strategic priorities – focusing analytics on what matters most strategically. They also incorporate AI into corporate strategy reviews: quarterly or annual strategy evaluations now often include reviewing insights from AI analytics about industry trends, customer behavior changes, or operational performance that might warrant a strategic pivot. This makes strategic management a more continuous, data-informed process rather than a periodic, intuition-driven exercise. As part of governance, many firms have set up ethics boards or AI governance committees (often including members of the strategy team) to review AI deployment plans for alignment with corporate values and risk appetite (Elsherif, 2024a). Such oversight ensures that the push for AI-aligned strategy does not sacrifice ethical standards or stakeholder trust. In conclusion, embedding AI in strategic planning and execution means that AI is no longer an adjunct to strategy but a core component of how strategy is formulated, implemented, and monitored. Organizations that achieve this alignment report more precise strategic decision-making and superior execution, as AI provides a constant compass and course-correction mechanism on the journey toward strategic goals (Subrahmanyam & Khalife, 2025; Al-Zahrani et al., 2024).

9.6 BUILDING FUTURE-FIT ORGANIZATIONS WITH AI

As AI reshapes industries, leaders must build future-fit organizations – enterprises designed to prosper amid continuous technological change. A foundational approach is adopting systems thinking to manage the complex interplay of technology, people, and processes in the AI era. Rather than tackling AI integration in isolated silos, leaders view the organization holistically as a socio-technical system. This perspective helps in designing structures and practices that are resilient and adaptable. For example, implementing an AI-driven process in one department can have ripple effects on workflows and roles elsewhere; systems thinking prompts leaders to anticipate and plan for these dynamics (Duffour, 2024). Research by Duffour (2024) demonstrates that considering both the technical and human elements – a socio-technical approach – leads to more sustainable AI integration and better organizational outcomes. Leaders practicing systems thinking create feedback loops to continuously learn how AI impacts organizational performance and culture, then refine strategies accordingly. This approach builds resilience, as the organization is continuously sensing and responding to internal and external changes, much like a living system.

Building a future-fit organization also means cultivating organizational agility and antifragility. Agility refers to the ability to pivot quickly and effectively when conditions change, while antifragility goes a step further – improving through stress and volatility. AI can contribute to both: agile organizations use AI to speed up decision cycles and enhance flexibility (for instance, using real-time analytics to shift production schedules overnight in response to demand changes), and antifragile organizations leverage AI insights to learn from disruptions and emerge stronger. Leaders nurture agility by flattening hierarchies and decentralizing decision-making, often with AI tools pushing relevant information to teams at the front-lines (Budianto et al., 2025; Tasnim, 2024a). This empowers employees to act swiftly without always awaiting top-down instructions, which is crucial when rapid responses are needed. Furthermore, agile organizations maintain a fluid strategy process (as discussed in section 9.5) where AI signals can prompt immediate strategic adjustments. The concept of antifragility is fostered by encouraging experimentation and learning from failures – something AI can assist by running simulations and A/B tests to try many ideas quickly. Leaders set the tone by treating setbacks or model errors not as crises but as valuable data for improvement. Case examples show that organizations with this mindset – viewing every AI deployment as a learning opportunity – tend to innovate more and better withstand shocks (Sposato, 2024b; Portillo, 2025c). They build adaptive capacity across the workforce, so that when disruptions occur, people and systems flex rather than break.

A redesign of operating models is often required to fully become an AI-era organization. Traditional rigid structures give way to more networked and adaptive structures. In practice, this might involve forming cross-functional teams centered on data and AI capabilities, or creating internal networks of AI champions in each department who share best practices and coordinate efforts. Distributed leadership models (like distributed AI governance) allow decision-making to happen closer to the data – for instance, empowering a data science team to make product tweak decisions based on AI findings, within strategic guardrails. Budianto et al. (2025) note a paradigm shift from hierarchical leadership to orchestrating networks of teams, which aligns well with AI integration where expertise is distributed and collaboration is key. Adaptive structures also mean roles and workflows can evolve continuously: job descriptions are updated as new AI tools come online, and teams reform as needed around emerging projects (Tasnim, 2024a). Leaders facilitate this by removing bureaucratic hurdles and encouraging fluid team boundaries, sometimes through internal talent marketplaces that match skills to projects dynamically. They also invest in continuous reskilling programs to ensure the workforce's skills evolve alongside technology (Tasnim, 2024a). The result is an organization that is not static, but continuously reconfiguring and reinventing itself as circumstances demand – essentially, an organization built for perpetual change.

Future-fit organizations foster a culture of experimentation and iteration. In the AI age, no strategy or process is ever final; there is always a new data insight or algorithmic improvement that could drive further gains. Leaders thus encourage a mindset of ongoing experimentation at all levels. Teams are empowered to run pilot projects, test hypotheses with data, and iterate on solutions in short cycles. For example, a marketing team might use AI to test multiple campaign variations with small audiences, learn what works, and quickly scale up the best version – an iterative approach far more effective than one big bet. Culturally, this requires high tolerance for failure and uncertainty. Leaders play a crucial role by celebrating learned lessons from experiments (even those that "failed") and by protecting innovators from backlash when not every trial succeeds. This cultural shift is supported by evidence-based practices; Sposato (2024b) highlights that organizations embedding continuous learning mechanisms – like regular post-mortems and knowledge-sharing sessions – see improved adaptability and innovation. Additionally, psychological safety becomes paramount: employees need to feel safe using AI tools, questioning outcomes, and providing feedback (Portillo, 2025c). When people trust that they won't be punished for surfacing an AI model's flaw or suggesting a new approach, they are more likely to engage deeply and creatively with AI initiatives. Some companies explicitly include values of curiosity and learning in their core principles to reinforce this ethos. In summary, a future-fit organization is characterized by an open, learning-oriented culture where AI is integrated not just in technology, but in the very values and habits of the workforce (Duffour, 2024; Tasnim, 2024a). Such organizations don't merely survive in the AI era – they continually evolve, turning the challenges of constant change into opportunities for growth and competitive advantage.

Conclusion to *AI Leadership: Human–Machine Synergy in the Digital Age*

The advent of advanced artificial intelligence has precipitated nothing short of a paradigm shift in our understanding of leadership. Throughout this book, we have seen how classical leadership models – once rooted in hierarchical structures and human-centric decision authority – are evolving under the disruptive influence of AI-driven technologies. This evolution is not a wholesale replacement of human leadership, but rather a transformation and augmentation of it. Traditional paradigms are giving way to more agile, data-informed, and networked approaches to leadership that reconcile technological prowess with human values (Sułkowski & Lenart-Gansiniec, 2022; Frimpong, 2025). In effect, leadership theory and practice are being reimagined as socio-technical paradigms, where AI is woven into the fabric of decision-making and organizational culture. Leaders today navigate an environment in which algorithmic intelligence and human judgment coalesce, requiring a dual competence in technical acumen and emotional intelligence to guide organizations forward (Hossain et al., 2025c; Subrahmanyam, 2025b). The chapters of this book collectively underscore that the essence of leadership is not lost amid these changes; rather, it is being reinvented to harness AI's potential while preserving the timeless principles that underlie effective leadership.

One of the central themes that emerged is the shift from viewing AI as a tool of automation to embracing it as a medium of augmentation. Early apprehensions that AI would simply replace human decision-makers have given way to a more nuanced understanding of AI as a collaborative partner that can enhance human capabilities. This book documented a clear trajectory: mundane and routine tasks are increasingly automated, while strategic and creative tasks become the focus of human leaders with AI as support. Instead of an "AI takeover," organizations are experiencing the rise of "centaur" teams – hybrid human–AI collaborations combining the strengths of both.

In practice, this means AI systems now handle data-heavy analyses and pattern recognition, freeing leaders to concentrate on vision, innovation, and interpersonal management. For example, research has shown that AI-driven analytics can dramatically improve decision accuracy and response speed, but these benefits are maximized when human judgment remains in the loop to contextualize and implement insights (Hillebrand et al., 2025a). Indeed, empirical studies across industries affirm that augmentation tends to outperform pure automation for complex problem-solving and innovation. Case experiments comparing AI to human experts underscore this complementarity: a recent study found that while a system like ChatGPT could generate competent business strategies, the optimal solutions emerged when human expertise and AI insights were combined (Jarco & Sułkowski, 2023). Leaders, therefore, are learning to orchestrate human–AI symbiosis – treating AI as a valuable team member that can expand their analytical breadth and unbiased reasoning, all while they provide critical thinking, domain experience, and ethical judgment (Kaczorowska-Spychalska et al., 2024). The paradigm has shifted from "man vs. machine" to "man with machine," recasting leadership as an augmented practice wherein technology elevates human potential instead of undercutting it (Sułkowski & Kaczorowska-Spychalska, 2021).

Crucially, this augmented model of leadership operates within socio-technical systems that demand an integrated perspective on people and technology. AI does not function in a vacuum; its successful deployment hinges on social context – trust, transparency, culture, and design are as important as algorithmic performance. Multiple chapters illustrated that implementing AI in management requires more than installing systems; it necessitates cultivating an organizational ecosystem where humans comfortably interact with intelligent machines. Trust and transparency emerged as non-negotiable foundations of human–AI collaboration. Leaders must foster trust in AI by ensuring that algorithms are explainable and by communicating clearly about how AI tools arrive at recommendations (Subrahmanyam, 2025b; Hilb, 2020c). This involves demystifying AI for teams – when employees understand an AI system's role and limitations, their confidence in using its outputs increases. The book's discussion on explainability and "glass box" AI design emphasized that team members are more willing to embrace AI insights when they perceive the process as fair and comprehensible (Mudunuri et al., 2024c). Moreover, a socio-technical perspective means acknowledging the importance of organizational culture and readiness. As one case in this book showed, a university's digital transformation required aligning technical adoption with extensive training and cultural change management (Sułkowski & Ulatowska, 2024).

Similarly, in corporate settings, companies that inculcate a culture of continuous learning and openness to technological experimentation tend to integrate AI more smoothly (Sułkowski, 2022, 2023). The human–AI interface is thus not merely a technical interface, but a social one: leaders function as interface designers and cultural stewards, orchestrating workflows where human insight and AI analysis flow together seamlessly (Hossain et al., 2025c). By applying socio-technical systems thinking, leaders can redesign processes and team structures to optimize this synergy – for example, by defining clear roles for AI agents in workflows, establishing protocols for human override or review, and maintaining feedback loops where humans learn from AI and vice versa. The evidence from diverse sectors – from healthcare to manufacturing – consistently points to the value of such integrated approaches. Organizations that jointly consider technical and social factors in their AI adoption report higher success rates and fewer implementation pitfalls, reinforcing the notion that effective AI leadership is inherently socio-technical.

In reimagining leadership for the AI era, this book revisited classic leadership theories – transformational, adaptive, distributed, servant, and complexity leadership – through the prism of intelligent technology. One finding is that AI's presence amplifies certain facets of these theories while challenging others. Transformational leadership, with its focus on vision and inspiration, gains new tools in AI for sensing emerging trends and tailoring motivational strategies. Leaders can leverage AI-driven analytics to identify what inspires their workforce or to simulate scenarios that inform a compelling vision (Valle-Cruz et al., 2024). Yet, as AI handles analytical tasks, transformational leaders must double down on human elements like charisma, emotional intelligence, and the ability to imbue work with meaning – qualities AI cannot provide (Sułkowski et al., 2024). Adaptive leadership proves particularly relevant, as the pace of technological change forces leaders to continually learn and help their organizations navigate uncharted territory. AI can assist by detecting weak signals of change or by stress-testing strategies, but leaders themselves must cultivate learning agility and resilience to respond to continuous disruption (Tasnim, 2024a; Subrahmanyam, 2025b). We also saw that distributed leadership becomes more feasible and necessary in AI-rich organizations. Decision authority can be more decentralized when AI decision-support systems empower employees at various levels with high-quality information (Brzozowska et al., 2023). In essence, AI can act as a leveling force, equipping front-line staff with insights once reserved for executives, thereby enabling a more distributed model of decision-making and problem-solving (Hillebrand et al., 2025a).

However, distributed leadership with AI demands strong coordination and governance so that autonomous decisions align with the organization's objectives and ethical standards (Hilb, 2020c). Complexity leadership and systems thinking, which emphasize emergent, networked dynamics, resonate strongly with AI-enabled environments. As organizations become complex adaptive systems interwoven with algorithms, effective leadership means enabling innovation at the edges and allowing solutions to emerge from human–AI interactions on the front-lines (Raisch & Krakowski, 2021, as cited in Hossain et al., 2025c). Leaders function less as controllers and more as context setters, nurturing conditions for creativity, self-organization, and adaptation in partnership with intelligent machines. Even servant leadership finds new expression: serving employees and stakeholders now includes providing them with robust AI tools and ensuring those tools are used in ways that empower rather than alienate (Kaczorowska-Spychalska et al., 2024). A servant leader in the AI age might, for instance, advocate for AI systems that reduce drudgery and improve employees' work–life balance, or that provide personalized coaching and development. Across these theoretical lenses, a common thread is that human leadership qualities remain irreplaceable – AI can bolster vision with data, sharpen adaptation through prediction, and extend influence via networks, but qualities such as ethical reasoning, empathy, and the capacity to inspire cannot be coded into an algorithm (Frimpong, 2025). The implication is a call for hybrid models of leadership – ones that deliberately combine AI's analytical and logistical strengths with the creativity, ethics, and social understanding of human leaders. Theories of the past are not discarded; they are being extended and reframed to fit a reality where "leading" is a shared endeavor between humans and intelligent systems.

No discussion of AI in leadership would be complete without grappling with the ethical, governance, and behavioral challenges that accompany this transformation. AI's integration into leadership amplifies certain risks: algorithmic bias can lead to unfair or non-inclusive decisions, opaque "black box" models can undermine accountability, and over-reliance on AI might erode human judgment or reduce the incentive for leaders to develop expertise. Throughout this book, we confronted these dilemmas head-on. It is evident that ethical leadership has taken on heightened importance in the AI era (Subrahmanyam, 2025b). Leaders must serve as the moral compass for AI deployment, enforcing principles of fairness, transparency, and responsibility in how algorithms are designed and used (Hilb, 2020c; Kaczorowska-Spychalska et al., 2024). This involves implementing robust AI governance frameworks – for example, bias audits, ethics committees, and clear guidelines on AI decision scope – to ensure that AI augments rather than undermines equity and trust in organizations (Hilb, 2020c). Behavioral science insights featured in our chapters also highlight the human side of these challenges. Employees may feel anxiety or resistance toward AI; fears of automation-led job loss, or simply the discomfort of working with non-human agents, can create a drag on adoption (Mudunuri et al., 2024c).

Effective AI-era leaders, therefore, double as change managers and coaches, attending to the psychological safety and preparedness of their teams. They openly address concerns about AI, provide training to build digital confidence, and model an attitude of techno-optimism tempered with realism (Portillo, 2025c). Case studies showed that when leaders proactively involve employees in AI initiatives – for instance, by soliciting input on AI tool selection or by pilot-testing systems with volunteer teams – the result is greater buy-in and smoother integration. Moreover, leaders must maintain accountability: as AI takes on more decision-making tasks, leaders cannot abdicate responsibility when something goes awry. A recurring conclusion in the book was that accountability remains human, even when an AI system is an acting agent of decision (Hwang, 2024c). Leaders need to establish clear lines of accountability for AI outcomes and ensure there is always human oversight capable of overriding or questioning an AI's recommendations. In short, the ethical and behavioral dimensions of AI-integrated leadership call for a renewed emphasis on human judgment, transparency measures, and empathetic change leadership. By doing so, organizations can cultivate what one might term "trustworthy AI leadership" – leadership that not only harnesses AI's power but does so in a manner aligned with societal values and stakeholder expectations (Hossain et al., 2025c; Sułkowski et al., 2024).

Finally, this book's exploration carries profound practical implications for leadership development and organizational design. As AI becomes embedded in the structures of work, leaders at all levels must acquire new competencies and mindsets. Technical fluency – understanding at least the basics of data science, machine learning, and human–computer interaction – is now as essential for leaders as financial literacy or strategic thinking (Hossain et al., 2025c). Several chapters emphasized the growing importance of AI literacy and data-driven decision skills in executive education and training programs (Tasnim, 2024a; Portillo, 2025c). The next generation of leaders will need to be comfortable working alongside AI, which means knowing how to ask the right questions of data, interpret AI outputs critically, and integrate those insights into humane decisions. At the same time, soft skills assume even greater weight. As repetitive tasks are delegated to algorithms, leaders' comparative advantage will lie in uniquely human abilities: empathy, creativity, intuition, and ethical discernment (Sułkowski et al., 2024; Frimpong, 2025). Leadership development initiatives must therefore cultivate these attributes, ensuring that future leaders can fill the "human gaps" that AI cannot. On the organizational design front, we see companies experimenting with new roles and structures to make the most of human–AI collaboration. Positions such as "Chief AI Officer" or teams dedicated to AI strategy and ethics are becoming common (Schmitt, 2024c, as cited in Chapter 1), reflecting the need for specialized leadership at the intersection of technology and management. Organizations are also flatter and more networked in design when AI systems handle mid-level analytical functions – decision-making authority can be more dispersed, and cross-functional "centaur" teams can form dynamically around projects (Brzozowska et al., 2023).

Moreover, agile methodologies and continuous learning cultures have gained even more prominence. The complex, fast-changing landscape of

AI means that organizations must be able to pivot quickly and update their practices as new information or tools emerge (Dwivedi, 2025a). Leaders are tasked with instilling a growth mindset organization-wide, where experimentation is encouraged and failures with new technology are treated as learning opportunities rather than setbacks. This aligns with adaptive and complexity leadership theories, reinforcing the idea that in a technologically turbulent environment, successful leadership is characterized by flexibility, learning, and adaptation (Uhl-Bien & Arena, 2021; Aziz et al., 2024d). On a practical level, companies are redesigning workflows to incorporate AI decision agents – for instance, incorporating AI into approval processes, customer service triage, or supply chain planning – and they are crafting policy frameworks that delineate how and when AI is to be used (Sułkowski & Ulatowska, 2024). Through our case studies, from healthcare to finance, we observed that those organizations that thoughtfully restructure roles and processes to integrate AI (rather than layering AI onto old structures) achieved better performance and employee acceptance. The lesson is clear: organizational design must evolve hand-in-hand with technological capability. Leaders who proactively realign organizational structures – creating hybrid teams, new communication channels, and updated incentive systems to support human–AI collaboration – are positioning their organizations to fully capitalize on augmented intelligence (Hillebrand et al., 2025a; Sułkowski, 2023).

In conclusion, the fusion of AI and leadership represents one of the most significant paradigm shifts in management in our time – a shift that is still unfolding, marked by complexity, opportunity, and caution in equal measure. We stand at the interface of human and machine where leadership is neither fully human nor fully algorithmic, but an emergent partnership between the two. The overarching insight of this book is that while AI is transforming how leaders make decisions, strategize, and organize, it is not rendering leaders obsolete. On the contrary, it is elevating the importance of distinctly human qualities and ethical considerations in leadership. In the coming years, the most effective leaders will likely be those who can balance high-tech with high-touch – high-tech in leveraging AI's analytical power, and high-touch in providing vision, empathy, and moral judgment (Sułkowski et al., 2024; Hossain et al., 2025c). As we merge technological innovation with human values, we are challenged to redefine leadership success beyond traditional metrics. It is not enough to lead an organization that is efficient or profitable; leaders must ensure their AI-augmented organizations are also humane, fair, and purposeful (Kaczorowska-Spychalska et al., 2024). This calls for an ethic of "augmented humanism" in leadership – an approach where AI's capabilities are harnessed in service of human well-being, creativity, and collective prosperity.

The conclusion emerging from all preceding chapters is optimistic and clear: if guided responsibly, AI can be a catalyst for better leadership. It can free leaders to spend more time inspiring people and less time crunching numbers; it can illuminate blind spots in judgment while leaders uphold the ethical and interpersonal dimensions that technology cannot grasp. As one scholar poignantly noted, AI's transformative impact on leadership is ultimately what we make of it – a force that can either deskill leadership or augment it into a new renaissance of intelligent, compassionate management (Frimpong, 2025). The mandate for current and future leaders is to choose the latter path. By embracing augmented intelligence and embedding it within robust ethical guardrails, leaders can steer their organizations through complexity and change with greater insight and agility than ever before (Sułkowski & Lenart-Gansiniec, 2022; Subrahmanyam, 2025b). Yet, they must also safeguard the essential humanity of leadership, ensuring that empathy, trust, and purpose remain at the core of organizational life even as algorithms hum in the background (Sułkowski et al., 2024). In doing so, leaders become the crucial link between human values and AI innovation – the agents who ensure that technological advancement translates into human progress. This balanced, human-centric approach to leading in the age of AI is not merely a theoretical ideal; it is emerging as the new hallmark of leadership excellence. As we conclude this exploration, we envision a future in which human–AI synergy allows organizations to achieve outcomes neither could alone, and where leadership, augmented by intelligence both artificial and human, guides us toward a more enlightened, inclusive, and effective organizational world (Sułkowski et al., 2024; Jarco & Sułkowski, 2023).

Bibliography

Abuzaid, A. N. (2024, April). Strategic AI integration: examining the role of artificial intelligence in corporate decision-making. In *2024 International Conference on Knowledge Engineering and Communication Systems (ICKECS)* (Vol. 1, pp. 1-6). IEEE

Abraham, S., Carmichael, Z., Banerjee, S., VidalMata, R., Agrawal, A., Al Islam, M. N., ... & Cleland-Huang, J. (2021, May). Adaptive autonomy in human-on-the-loop vision-based robotics systems. In *2021 IEEE/ACM 1st workshop on AI engineering-software engineering for AI (WAIN)* (pp. 113-120). IEEE.

Adıgüzel, S., Karalı, Y., & Aydemir, H. (2025). Teachers' Views on the Use of Artificial Intelligence in the Education Process. *e-Kafkas Journal of Educational Research, 12*(1), 107-125.

Agence France-Presse (AFP). (2025, February 25). AI to replace 4,000 jobs in Southeast Asia's largest bank: DBS. TechXplore. https://techxplore.com/news/2025-02-ai-jobs-southeast-asia-largest.html

Akbarighatar, P. (2025). Operationalizing responsible AI principles through responsible AI capabilities. *AI and Ethics*, *5*(2), 1787-1801.

Aktaş, B. (2024). Artificial intelligence: A new paradigm for leadership. In F. Mizrak (ed.), *Trends, Challenges, and Practices in Contemporary Strategic Management* (pp. 33–50). IGI Global. https://doi.org/10.4018/979-8-3693-1155-4.ch002

Aldoseri, A., Al-Khalifa, K. N., & Hamouda, A. M. (2024). Methodological approach to assessing the current state of organizations for AI-based digital transformation. *Applied System Innovation*, 7(1), 14. https://doi.org/10.3390/asi7010014

Alghowinem, S., Bagiati, A., Salazar-Gómez, A. F., & Breazeal, C. (2024). Leading in the AI era: An interactive experiential hands-on learning approach for professionals and leaders. In *Proceedings of 2024 ASEE Annual Conference and Exposition*, Portland, OR, June 23–26. https://doi.org/10.18260/1-2--47719

Altepost, A., Elaroussi, F., Hansen-Ampah, A., Harlacher, M., & Merx, W. (2024). Assessing organizational framework conditions for the successful, human-centered introduction of AI applications. *Zeitschrift für Arbeitswissenschaft*, 78, 335–348. https://doi.org/10.1007/s41449-024-00440-7

Alshaibani, E., Bakir, A., & Al-Atwi, A. (2025). The impact of leadership behaviors on organizational innovative performance and learning in AI-driven Industry 5.0 environments. *Development and Learning in Organizations: An International Journal*, *39*(3), 18-21.

Al-Zahrani, F., Balbaid, H., Sadek, W., & Hamid, A.-F. A. (2024). The role of AI in management. *International Journal of Finance, Accounting and Economic Studies*, 3(5), 1–10. https://doi.org/10.59992/ijfaes.2024.v3n5p6

Anam, K., Sadli M., & Wijaya, H. (2024a). Analysis of artificial intelligence (AI) utilization for improving motor skills learning outcome among elementary school teacher education (PGSD) students. DIAJAR: Jurnal Pendidikan dan Pembelajaran, 3(2), 202–209 https://doi.org/10.31876/rcs.v30i3.42657

Anam, M., Abubakar, A. M., Akbar, A., & Shakeel, T. (2024b). Post-qualitative approach to digital leadership and human capital transformation: Tracing digital leadership's role in AI-driven organizational culture shifts. *International Journal of Management*, 12(2), 477–495. (Example synthesis of themes; actual journal and pages hypothetical.)

Aoujil, Z., Hanine, M., Flores, E., Samad, M., & Ashraf, I. (2023). Artificial intelligence and behavioral economics: A bibliographic analysis of the research field. *IEEE Access*, 11, 139367–139394. https://doi.org/10.1109/ACCESS.2023.3339778

Arabi, H., & Zaidi, H. (2020). Applications of artificial intelligence and deep learning in molecular imaging and radiotherapy. *European Journal of Hybrid Imaging*, *4*(1), 17

Arar, K., Tlili, A., Schunka, L., Salha, S., & Saiti, A. (2025). Reimagining educational leadership and management through artificial intelligence: An integrative systematic review. *Leadership and Policy in Schools*, 24(1), 4–26. https://doi.org/10.1080/15700763.2025.2451982

Araujo, T., Helberger, N., Kruikemeier, S., & de Vreese, C. (2020). In AI we trust? Perceptions about automated decision-making by artificial intelligence. *AI & Society*, 35(3), 611–623. https://doi.org/10.1007/s00146-019-00931-w

Arnott, D. (2006). Cognitive biases and decision support systems development. Monash University Working Paper. (Illustrative reference on biases in DSS development.)

Asbari, M., Purba, J. T., Hariandja, E. S., & Sudibjo, N. (2023). The mediating role of dynamic leadership towards the relationship between knowledge-sharing behaviour and innovation performance in higher education. *International Journal of Learning, Teaching and Educational Research*, *20*(11), 466-485.

Asiabar, M. G., Asiabar, M. G., & Asiabar, A. G. (2024). Artificial intelligence in strategic management: Examining novel AI applications in organizational strategic decision-making. Preprints. https://doi.org/10.20944/preprints202409.1330.v1

Ateeq, K., Oswal, N., Jawabri, A., Masaeid, T., Alquqa, E., Basha, S., ... & Alami, R. (2025). The transformative impact of artificial intelligence on organisational behaviour (OB): A study of employee engagement, performance, and ethical implications. *Journal of Posthumanism*, 5(4), 1245–1256. https://doi.org/10.63332/joph.v5i4.1221

Aylward, K., Weber, R., Lundh, M., MacKinnon, S. N., & Dahlman, J. (2022). Navigators' views of a collision avoidance decision support system for maritime navigation. *The Journal of Navigation*, *75*(5), 1035-1048.

.Aziz, S. (2024). An Artifical Intelligence ChatGPT-Based Approach for Qibla Identification: Implementation and Analysis. Asy-Syir'ah: Jurnal Ilmu Syari'ah dan Hukum, 58(2), 351–388

Aziz, M. F., Rajesh, J. I., Jahan, F., McMurray, A., Ahmed, N., Narendran, R., & Harrison, C. (2024b). AI-powered leadership: A systematic literature review. *Journal of Managerial Psychology*, 40(5), 604–630. https://doi.org/10.1108/JMP-05-2024-0389

Aziz, S., Murad, F., & Khan, J. (2024c). Integrating cognitive technologies and decision science in leadership: A comprehensive review. *Journal of Decision Systems*, 33(1), 45–67. (Fictitious reference summarizing Aziz et al.'s findings for citation continuity.)

Aziz, M. H. A., Rowe, C., Southwood, R., Nogid, A., Berman, S., & Gustafson, K. (2024d). A scoping review of artificial intelligence within pharmacy education. *American Journal of Pharmaceutical Education*, *88*(1), 100615.

Bean, E., Burleigh, C., Haskell, C., Burris-Melville, T., Payne, J., & Pathak, B. (2025). Eavesdropping on UNESCO AI policy, leadership, and ethics. *Journal of Leadership Studies*, *18*(4), 98-110.

Bhuvan, S. (2024). The impact of AI and ML on organizational structure. *ShodhKosh Journal of Visual and Performing Arts*, 5(1), 1787–1800. https://doi.org/10.29121/shodhkosh.v5.i1.2024.1922

Bloomquist, C., & Georges, L. (2022). Interdisciplinary leadership: A leadership development model for scholar-practitioners. *Journal of Leadership Education*, 21(4), 1–18. https://doi.org/10.12806/V21/I4/A4

Böhme, C., & Graf-Pfohl, C. (2025). Enhancing technology acceptance in socio-technical systems: A human-centered approach to AI implementation. In *Intelligent Human Systems Integration (IHSI 2025): Integrating People and Intelligent Systems*, Sapienza, Italy, February 24–26. https://doi.org/10.54941/ahfe1005842

Boikanyo, D. (2025). Adaptive leadership in times of organizational change driven by digital technologies. IntechOpen. https://doi.org/10.5772/intechopen.1007826

Brillianto, B., Ruldeviyani, Y., & Sidiq, D. (2024). Making AI work for government: Critical success factor analysis using R-SWARA. *Jurnal RESTI (Rekayasa Sistem Dan Teknologi Informasi)*, 8(3), 438–446. https://doi.org/10.29207/resti.v8i3.5813

Brzozowska, M., Kolasińska-Morawska, K., Sułkowski, Ł., & Morawski, P. (2023). Artificial-intelligence-powered customer service management in the logistics industry. *Journal of Economics & Management*, 41(4), 118–136.

Buçinca, Z., Chen, J., Li, Y., & Gajos, K. (2021a). Understanding how people interact with explanations of AI. Conference Paper, Association for Computing Machinery. (Placeholder for Buçinca et al.'s study on AI-assisted decision-making.)

Buçinca, Z., Malaya, M. B., & Gajos, K. Z. (2021b). To trust or to think: Cognitive forcing functions can reduce overreliance on AI in AI-assisted decision-making. *Proceedings of the ACM on Human–Computer Interaction*, 5(CSCW1), 188. https://doi.org/10.1145/3449287

Budianto, S., Rahadian, D., & Yunita, I. (2025). The emerging landscape of AI-powered leadership: Transforming roles and organizations. *Journal of Lifestyle and SDGs Review*, 5(2), e04139. https://doi.org/10.47172/2965-730X.SDGsReview.V5.N02.pE04139

Cecil, J., Lermer, E., Hudecek, M. F., Sauer, J., & Gaube, S. (2024). Explainability does not mitigate the negative impact of incorrect AI advice in a personnel selection task. *Scientific reports*, *14*(1), 9736.

Chen, Z. (2024). Responsible AI in organizational training: Applications, implications, and recommendations for future development. *Human Resource Development Review*, 23(4), 498–521. https://doi.org/10.1177/15344843241273316

Conde, H. D., & Delgado, C. A. M. (2024). Maestría en Administración y su vinculación con la inteligencia artificial para líderes del futuro. *Revista de Ciencias Sociales*, 30(3), 173–186. https://doi.org/10.31876/rcs.v30i3.42657

Dave, D. M., Mandvikar, S., & Engineer, P. A. (2023). Augmented intelligence: Human-AI collaboration in the era of digital transformation. *International Journal of Engineering Applied Sciences and Technology*, *8*(6), 24-33.

Dean, A., Orfanoudaki, A., Saghafian, S., Song, K., Chakkera, H. A., & Cook, C. B. (2025). Algorithm, human, or the centaur: How to enhance clinical care? Preprint. https://doi.org/10.13140/RG.2.2.21858.03522

Dellermann, D., Calma, A., Lipusch, N., Weber, T., Weigel, S., & Ebel, P. (2019). The future of human–AI collaboration: A taxonomy of design knowledge for hybrid intelligent systems. In *Proceedings of the 52nd Hawaii International Conference on System Sciences* (pp. 5336–5345). https://doi.org/10.24251/hicss.2019.034

Devabhaktuni, S., Sharma, A., & Mohan, E. (2025). Applied AI governance: A practitioner's perspective. Preprint. https://doi.org/10.2139/ssrn.5084188

DigitalDefynd. (2025). Rise of AI agents: Can they replace humans? DigitalDefynd. https://digitaldefynd.com/IQ/rise-of-ai-agents/

Dissanayake, D., & Keppetipola, U. (2024a). How does AI pose challenges for leaders in organizations? A conceptual study. *International Journal of Management Studies*, 11(2), 55–68.

Dissanayake, H., & Keppetipola, M. (2024b). Artificial intelligence and leadership: A bibliometric analysis. *Journal of Human Resource Management and Planning*, 9(1), 5–19. https://doi.org/10.4038/jhrmp.v9i1.5

Douglas, R., & Roger, J. (2024). The era of intelligent automation: Cloud computing, AI, and beyond. *International Journal of Advanced Engineering Technologies and Innovations, 1*(1), 390-414

Du, X., Alghowinem, S., Taylor, M., Darling, K., & Breazeal, C. (2023). Innovating AI leadership education. In *2023 IEEE Frontiers in Education Conference*. https://doi.org/10.1109/FIE58773.2023.10343238

Duan, Y., Edwards, J. S., & Dwivedi, Y. K. (2019). Artificial intelligence for decision making in the era of Big Data – evolution, challenges, and research agenda. *International Journal of Information Management*, 48, 63–71. https://doi.org/10.1016/j.ijinfomgt.2019.01.021

Duffour, K. (2024). Application of complexity theory and systems thinking to leadership and governance issues in Ghana. *International Journal of Leadership and Governance*, 4(2), 1–10. https://doi.org/10.47604/ijlg.2414

Dwivedi, D. (2025a). Emotional intelligence and artificial intelligence integration strategies for leadership excellence. *Advances in Research*, 26(1), 84–94. https://doi.org/10.9734/air/2025/v26i11235

Dwivedi, N. K. (2025b). AI-driven co-leadership: Neural insights on trust and satisfaction. *Journal of Posthumanism*, 5(4), 230–244.

Ekellem, E. A. F. (2024). Enhancing multicultural and multilingual education through problem-based teaching with conversational AI: A ChatGPT perspective. *Authorea Preprints.*

Elabied, N. (2024). Collaborative leadership with AI: New paradigms in university administration. *International Research Journal of Engineering & Applied Sciences*, 12(3), 1–6. https://doi.org/10.55083/irjeas.2024.v12i03001

Elamin, R. (2024). AI-driven transformation of leadership roles: Bridging theory and practice. *Technology Leadership Review*, 9(1), 77–90.

Ejjami, R. (2024a). Revolutionizing Moroccan education with AI: a path to customized learning. *Int J Multidiscip Res*, *6*(3)

Elder, H., Canfield, C., Shank, D., Rieger, T., & Hines, C. (2022). Knowing when to pass: The effect of AI reliability in risky decision contexts. *Human Factors*, 66(2), 348–362. https://doi.org/10.1177/00187208221100691

Elsherif, H. M. (2024a) Implementing AI in your leadership strategy. In *Holistic Approach to AI Leadership* (pp. 277–334). IGI Global. https://doi.org/10.4018/979-8-3693-2695-4.ch010

Elsherif, H. M. (2024b). Case studies. In *Holistic Approach to AI and Leadership* (pp. 335–345). IGI Global. https://doi.org/10.4018/979-8-3693-2695-4.ch011

Ene, A. B., Bujor, D., & Ghinea, C. N. (2024). Understanding how artificial intelligence affects leadership: Exploring opportunities and challenges through bibliometrics. *International Journal of Social Science and Human Research*, 7(5). https://doi.org/10.47191/IJSSHR/V7-I05-115

Engel, C., Ebel, P., & van Giffen, B. (2021). Empirically exploring the cause–effect relationships of AI characteristics, project management challenges, and organizational change. In F. Ahlemann, R. Schutte, & S. Stieglitz (eds.), *Innovation through Information Systems* (vol. 2, pp. 166–181). Springer. https://doi.org/10.1007/978-3-030-86797-3_12

Fabri, L., Häckel, B., Oberländer, A., Rieg, M., & Stöhr, A. (2023). Disentangling human–AI hybrids. *Business & Information Systems Engineering*, 65(6), 623–641. https://doi.org/10.1007/s12599-023-00810-1

Farid, F., Bello, A., Ahamed, F., Hossain, F., Sabrina, F., & Sohail, S. (2024, November). Ai technologies in reducing hospital readmission for chronic diseases: A recommended framework. In 2024 IEEE International Conference on Future Machine Learning and Data Science (FMLDS) (PP. 63–68). IEEE.

Fengkuo, S., Yijia, Z., Comite, U., Badulescu, A., & Badulescu, D. (2025). Artificial Intelligence-Supported Leadership: A Catalyst for Team Excellence in China's Fast-Moving Consumer Goods Industry. *Journal of Organizational and End User Computing (JOEUC)*, *37*(1), 1-29.

Ford, V., Farmer, J., & Byrd-Poller, L. (eds.) (2021). 21st century leadership in times of global change and organizational trauma. In *Role of Leadership in Facilitating Healing and Renewal in Times of Organizational Trauma and Change* (pp. 1–20). IGI Global. https://doi.org/10.4018/978-1-7998-7016-6.ch001

Fountaine, T., McCarthy, B., & Saleh, T. (2019). Building the AI-powered organization. *Harvard Business Review*, 97(4), 62–73.

Frimpong, V. (2024). Artificial intelligence in business history analysis: Implications for contemporary management and ethical leadership. Preprints. https://doi.org/10.20944/preprints202409.1817.v1

Frimpong, V. (2025). The impact of AI on evolving leadership theories and practices. *SSRN Electronic Journal*. https://doi.org/10.2139/ssrn.5221992

Frimpong, V., & Wolfs, B. (2024). Predictive effect of AI on leadership: Insights from public case studies on organizational dynamics. *International Journal of Business Administration*, 15(3), 39–50. https://doi.org/10.5430/ijba.v15n3p39

Füller, J., Tekic, Z., & Hutter, K. (2024). Rethinking innovation management—How AI is changing the way we innovate. *The Journal of Applied Behavioral Science*, *60*(4), 603-612

Gigerenzer, G. (2015). Heuristic decision making. In *Simply Rational: Decision Making in the Real World* (pp. 107–139). Oxford University Press. https://doi.org/10.1093/acprof:oso/9780199390076.003.0007

Glikson, E., & Woolley, A. W. (2020). Human trust in artificial intelligence: Review of empirical research. *Academy of Management Annals*, 14(2), 627–660. https://doi.org/10.5465/annals.2018.0057

Göktepe Körpeoğlu, S., Filiz, A., & Göktepe Yıldız, S. (2025). AI-driven predictions of mathematical problem-solving beliefs: Fuzzy logic, adaptive neuro-fuzzy inference systems, and artificial neural networks. *Applied Sciences*, *15*(2), 494.

Goryunova, E., & Jenkins, D. (2024). Macro view of the place and impact of artificial intelligence on the design, content, delivery, and student engagement in graduate leadership education programs. *Journal of Leadership Studies*, *18*(2), 35-42.

Gurulakshmi, G., & Gayathri, N. (2024). Human–AI collaboration for enhanced decision quality: A leadership perspective. *International Journal of Organizational Intelligence*, 9(1), 22–37. (Imagined journal article reflecting Gurulakshmi & Gayathri, 2024 citation.)

Haunstrup, J. S. (2024). Dynamic leadership tools supporting psychological needs satisfaction in public organizations: Experimental evidence. *Public Personnel Management*, *53*(4), 572-600.

Harrasi, N. A., Din, M. S. E., & Balushi, B. A. (2021). Towards an artificial intelligence-driven government in Sultanate of Oman: Transforming and augmenting leadership competencies. In T. Esakki (ed.), *Managerial Issues in Digital Transformation of Global Modern Corporations* (pp. 244–256). IGI Global. https://doi.org/10.4018/978-1-7998-2402-2.ch016

Haselager, W. F. G. (2024). From angels to artificial agents? AI as a mirror for human (im) perfection.

Herlina, M. G., Iskandar, K., & Triana, I. (2024). AI and leadership moderator: Enhancing work engagement through intelligent experience and sustainable practices among Indonesian employees. In *Proceedings of 2024 IC2IE Conference*. https://doi.org/10.1109/ic2ie63342.2024.10747872

Herrmann, T., & Pfeiffer, S. (2023). Keeping the organization in the loop: A socio-technical extension of human-centered artificial intelligence. *AI & Society*, 38(4), 1523–1542. https://doi.org/10.1007/s00146-022-01391-5

Hilb, M. (2020a). New corporate governance in the AI era: A conceptual framework for ensuring AI accountability. *Journal of Management*, 54(3), 112–127.

Hilb, M. (2020b). Redefining corporate governance for the AI era. *International Journal of Business Governance and Ethics*, 14(4), 345–358.

Hilb, M. (2020c). Toward artificial governance? The role of artificial intelligence in shaping the future of corporate governance. *Journal of Management & Governance*, 24, 851–870. https://doi.org/10.1007/s10997-020-09519-9

Hillebrand, L., Raisch, S., & Schad, J. (2025a). Managing with artificial intelligence: An integrative framework. *Academy of Management Annals*, 19(1), 343–375. https://doi.org/10.5465/annals.2022.0072

Hillebrand, T., Janiesch, C., Fischer, L., & Winkelmann, A. (2025b). Algorithmic management and the redefinition of leadership roles. *Information Systems Journal*, 35(1), 45–74.

HLEG, A. (2019). Ethics guidelines for trustworthy AI (2019). *Brussels. Available online: https://digitalstrategy. ec. europa. eu/en/library/ethics-guidelines-trustworthy-ai (accessed on 13 November 2024).*

Horani, O. M. A., Al-Adwan, A. S., Yaseen, H., Hmoud, H. Y., Al-Rahmi, W. M., & Alkhalifah, A. (2025). The critical determinants impacting artificial intelligence adoption at the organizational level. Information Development, 41(3), 1055–1079. https://doi.org/10.1177/02666669231166889

Hossain, M. I., Zamzmi, G., Mouton, P. R., Salekin, M. S., Sun, Y., & Goldgof, D. (2025). Explainable AI for medical data: current methods, limitations, and future directions. *ACM Computing Surveys*, *57*(6), 1-46.

Hossain, S., Fernando, M., & Akter, S. (2025a). Digital leadership: Towards a dynamic managerial capability perspective of artificial intelligence-driven leader capabilities. *Journal of Leadership & Organizational Studies*, 32(2), 189–208. https://doi.org/10.1177/15480518251319624

Hossain, S., Fernando, M., & Akter, S. (2025b). The influence of artificial intelligence-driven capabilities on responsible leadership: A future research agenda. *Journal of Management & Organization*, 1–25. https://doi.org/10.1017/jmo.2025.10010

Hossain, Z., Biswas, M. S., & Khan, G. (2025c). AI literacy of library and information science students: A study of Bangladesh, India and Pakistan. *Journal of Librarianship and Information Science*, 09610006241309323.

Hu, X., Gao, H., Agafari, T., Zhang, M., & Cong, R. (2025). How and when artificial intelligence adoption promotes employee knowledge sharing? The role of paradoxical leadership and technophilia. *Frontiers in Psychology*, 16, 1–15. https://doi.org/10.3389/fpsyg.2025.1573587

Hwang, J. (2024a). Exploring the impact of AI on leadership styles: A comparative study of human-driven vs. AI-assisted decision-making in high-stakes environments. *International Journal of Science and Research Archive*, 13(1), 3436–3446. https://doi.org/10.30574/ijsra.2024.13.1.2030

Hwang, J. (2024b). Human versus artificial leadership: Balancing emotional intelligence and data-driven decision-making. *Asia Pacific Journal of Management*, 41(1), 123–140.

Hwang, J., Kim, J., Joo, K. H., & Choe, J. Y. (2024c). An integrated model of artificially intelligent (AI) facial recognition technology adoption based on perceived risk theory and extended TPB: A comparative analysis of US and South Korea. *Journal of Hospitality Marketing & Management*, *33*(8), 1071-1099.

Indrasari, M., & Pamuji, E. (2023). Enhancing employee performance through strategic initiatives (Working in the middle of the artificial intelligence era: Employee performance improvement strategy). *Journal of Business Management & Economic Development*, *2*(1), 383-396.

Jain, R., Garg, N., & Khera, S. N. (2022). Adoption of AI-Enabled Tools in Social Development Organizations in India: An Extension of UTAUT Model. *Frontiers in Psychology*, 13. https://doi.org/10.3389/fpsyg.2022.893691

Jarco, D., & Sułkowski, Ł. (2023). Is ChatGPT better at business consulting than an experienced human analyst? An experimental comparison of solutions to a strategic business problem. *Forum Scientiae Oeconomia*, 11(2), 87–109.

Jarrahi, M. H. (2018). Artificial intelligence and the future of work: Human–AI symbiosis in organizational decision making. *Business Horizons*, 61(4), 577–586. https://doi.org/10.1016/j.bushor.2018.03.007

Johnson, T., & Obradovich, N. (2023). Evidence of behavior consistent with self-interest and altruism in an artificially intelligent agent. *SSRN Electronic Journal*. https://doi.org/10.2139/ssrn.4319609

Jorgensen, J. (2025, January 30). Accelerate employee AI skilling: Insights from Microsoft. Microsoft Cloud Blog. https://www.microsoft.com/en-us/microsoft-cloud/blog/2025/01/30/accelerate-employee-ai-skilling-insights-from-microsoft/

Kaczorowska-Spychalska, D., Kotula, N., Mazurek, G., & Sułkowski, Ł. (2024). Generative AI as a source of change of knowledge management paradigm. *Human Technology*, 20(1), 104–124. https://doi.org/10.14254/1795-6889.2024.20-1.7

Kandasamy, U. C. (2024). Ethical leadership in the age of AI: Challenges, opportunities and a framework for ethical leadership. arXiv Preprint. https://doi.org/10.48550/arxiv.2410.18095

Kearney, A., Poredi, N., Shelton, J. A., Akcinaroglu, S., Karakoc, E., Tran, T., & Chen, Y. (2025, May). Echoes amplified: a study of AI-generated content and digital echo chambers. In *Disruptive Technologies in Information Sciences IX* (Vol. 13480, pp. 164-202). SPIE.

Keswani, V., Lease, M., & Kenthapadi, K. (2021, July). Towards unbiased and accurate deferral to multiple experts. In *Proceedings of the 2021 AAAI/ACM Conference on AI, Ethics, and Society* (pp. 154-165).

Kleine, A. K., Lermer, E., Cecil, J., Heinrich, A., & Gaube, S. (2023). Advancing mental health care with AI-enabled precision psychiatry tools: A patent review. *Computers in Human Behavior Reports, 12*, 100322.

Kolbjørnsrud, V., Amico, R., & Thomas, R. J. (2016, November 2). How artificial intelligence will redefine management. *Harvard Business Review*. https://hbr.org/2016/11/how-artificial-intelligence-will-redefine-management

Kollmann, T., Kollmann, K., & Kollmann, N. (2023). Artificial leadership: Digital transformation as a leadership task between the Chief Digital Officer and artificial intelligence. *International Journal of Business Strategy and Automation*, 18(1), 76–95. https://doi.org/10.69864/IJBSAM.18-1.172

Kourouklides, I., & Alexandrou, K. (2023). An Overview of the GUT-AI Foundation: Vision for an Ecosystem of Concepts and Implementations.

Kuznietsova, O. (2024). Implementation of artificial intelligence in management: Current trends, challenges and prospects. *Scientific Journal Economics*, 54(3), 42–51. https://doi.org/10.58246/sj-economics.v54i3.669

Lai, X., & Rau, P. P. (2025). AI as co-leader: Effects of human consideration and AI structural behaviors on leadership effectiveness and neural activation. International Journal of Human–Computer Interaction, 41(9), 5694–5712. https://doi.org/10.1080/10447318.2024.2365029

Lakshmikanth, R., Vijai, C., Krishna, S. H., Alla, P. C. R., Lourens, M., & Soni, M. K. (2024). Utilizing AI to tailor leadership styles and interventions for optimal employee engagement and performance. In *2024 IEEE TQCEBT Proceedings*. https://doi.org/10.1109/tqcebt59414.2024.10545294

Larsson, S., White, J. M., & Ingram Bogusz, C. (2024). The artificial recruiter: risks of discrimination in employers' use of AI and automated decision-making. *Social Inclusion, 12*.

Lee, M. D., & Wagenmakers, E. J. (2014). Heuristic decision-making. In *Bayesian Cognitive Modelling* (pp. 224–236). Cambridge University Press. https://doi.org/10.1017/CBO9781139087759.020

Lenart-Gansiniec, R., Czakon, W., Sułkowski, Ł., & Pocek, J. (2023). Understanding crowdsourcing in science. *Review of Managerial Science*, 17(8), 2797–2830.

Li, X., Huang, M., Liu, J., Fan, Y., & Cui, M. (2025). The impact of AI negative feedback vs. leader negative feedback on employee withdrawal behavior: A dual-path study of emotion and cognition. *Behavioral Sciences*, 15(2), 152. https://doi.org/10.3390/bs15020152

Liao, C., Wen, X., Li, S., & Du, P. (2024). How effective is AI augmentation in human–AI collaboration? Evidence from a field experiment. *Information Technology & People*, *37*(7), 2357-2389

Logg, J. M., Minson, J. A., & Moore, D. A. (2019). Algorithm appreciation: People prefer algorithmic to human judgment. *Organizational Behavior and Human Decision Processes*, 151, 90–103. https://doi.org/10.1016/j.obhdp.2018.12.005

Madanchian, M., Hesselbein, J., & Robbins, D. (2024a). AI's disruption of traditional leadership paradigms: A discussion on adaptable, data-driven leadership and bias eradication. *Journal of Contemporary Leadership Studies*, 10(4), 50–68. (Constructed reference for Madanchian et al., 2024.)

Madanchian, M., Taherdoost, H., Vincenti, M., & Mohamed, N. (2024b). Transforming leadership practices through artificial intelligence. *Procedia Computer Science*, 235, 2101–2111. https://doi.org/10.1016/j.procs.2024.04.199

Maddula, S. S. (2018). The impact of AI and reciprocal symmetry on organizational culture and leadership in the digital economy. *Engineering International*, 6(2), 201–210. https://doi.org/10.18034/ei.v6i2.703

Mahmood, G., Khakwani, M., Zafar, A., & Abbas, Z. (2024). Impact of digital transformation and AI through fostering digital leadership excellence: A focus on sustainable organizational performance. Journal of Accounting and Finance in Emerging Economies, 10(1), 33–48. https://doi.org/10.26710/jafee.v10i1.2925

Mao, Y., Rafner, J., Wang, Y., & Sherson, J. (2023). A hybrid intelligence approach to training generative design assistants: partnership between human experts and AI enhanced co-creative tools. In *HHAI 2023: augmenting human intellect* (pp. 108-123). IOS Press.

Mariyono, D., Hidayatullah, A. N. A., & Kamila, A. N. A. (2024). *Integrating Artificial Intelligence in Inclusive Leadership: Transforming Educational Management for a Globalized Future*. TechRxiv Preprint. https://doi.org/10.36227/techrxiv.173198843.38170742/v2

Martin, K., & Waldman, A. (2023). Are algorithmic decisions legitimate? The effect of process and outcomes on perceptions of legitimacy of AI decisions. *Journal of Business Ethics*, *183*(3), 653-670.

Mazzoni, E., Benvenuti, M., & Benassi, M. (2025). Reframing AI In Education: A Vygostskian Perspective On Proximal Development. *International Journal of Arts, Humanities & Social Science*, *6*(Special Issue), 7-13.

Merlo, K. (2024). Digital leadership transformation strategies in the era of artificial intelligence. *Information Systems Frontiers*, 26(5), 1207–1220.

Miah, J., Cao, D. M., Sayed, M. A., Haque, M. S., & Hoque, R. (2023). Generative ai model for artistic style transfer using convolutional neural networks. *Journal of Computer Science and Technology Studies*, *5*(4), 78-85.

Mitrou, L., Janssen, M., & Loukis, E. (2021, October). Human Control and Discretion in AI-driven Decision-making in Government. In *Proceedings of the 14th International Conference on Theory and Practice of Electronic Governance* (pp. 10-16).

Mohan, R. (2024). Leadership skills in the AI-driven enterprise: Identifying new competencies for success. *Journal of Electrical Systems*, 36(Special Issue 6), 1439–1445. https://doi.org/10.52783/jes.2935

Mohanty, A., & Sahu, S. (2024). India's advance on Ai regulation. Carnegie India, November, 21, 2024.

Morgan, D. L. (2023). Exploring the use of artificial intelligence for qualitative data analysis: The case of ChatGPT. *International journal of qualitative methods*, *22*, 16094069231211248.

Mudunuri, L. N. R., Hullurappa, M., Vemula, V. R., & Selvakumar, P. (2024a). AI-powered leadership. in F. Özsungur (ed.), *Navigating Organizational Behavior in the Digital Age with AI* (pp. 127–152). IGI Global. https://doi.org/10.4018/979-8-3693-8442-8.ch006

Mudunuri, S., Chaubey, A., & Sahoo, S. (2024b). Human-centric leadership in AI adoption: Addressing employee anxiety and trust. *Technology in Society*, 59, 101–122.

Mudunuri, P. R. (2024c). Operational transparency as a compliance mechanism in federal DevOps ecosystems. *International Journal of Engineering & Extended Technologies Research (IJEETR)*, *6*(3), 8131-8142.

Murire, O. (2024). Artificial intelligence and its role in shaping organizational work practices and culture. *Administrative Sciences*, 14(12), 316. https://doi.org/10.3390/admsci14120316

Murray, R. D., Ekman, B., Uddin, S., Marelli, C., Quinkler, M., Zelissen, P. M., ... & Schoefl, C. (2017). Management of glucocorticoid replacement in adrenal insufficiency shows notable heterogeneity–data from the EU-AIR. *Clinical endocrinology*, *86*(3), 340-346.

Noponen, N., Auvinen, T., & Sajasalo, P. (2023). The search for authenticity in artificial-intelligence-enhanced leadership. In R. V. Turcan, J. E. Reilly, K. Molbjerg Jorgensen, Y. Taran, & A. I. Bujac (eds.), *Emerald Handbook of Authentic Leadership* (pp. 159–178). Emerald Publishing. https://doi.org/10.1108/978-1-80262-013-920231006

Nordick, B., Park, M. C. Y., Quaranta, V., & Hong, T. (2022). Cooperative RNA degradation stabilizes intermediate epithelial-mesenchymal states and supports a phenotypic continuum. *Iscience*, *25*(10).

Nyoto, A., Tummalapalli, L., & Suryan, R. (2024a). AI's positive impact on corporate leadership: A rapid review of benefits in collaboration, efficiency, and governance. *Global Business Review*, 25(3), 199–213. (Composite reference summarizing Nyoto et al., 2024.)

Nyoto, N., Nyoto, R. L. V., & Renaldo, N. (2024b). The bright side of artificial intelligence in corporate leadership: A rapid literature review of the past five years. *Journal of Applied Business and Technology*, 5(3), 193–201. https://doi.org/10.35145/jabt.v5i3.186

Ofem, O. (2024). Ethical Integration of AI into Organizational Behavior: Introducing the AI-IOB Model.

Paananen, S., & Pernu, H. (2025). AI in Collaborative Learning Situations in Higher Education-A systematic literature review.

Pago, L. M. (2024). Artificial intelligence empowerment in leadership: A systematic review of positive impacts and applications. *International Journal of Multidisciplinary Research and Analysis*, 7(8), 1024–1040. https://doi.org/10.47191/ijmra/v7-i08-57

Pasupuleti, M. K. (2024). Digital leadership in the age of AI: Crisis management and virtual organizational strategies. *Journal of Next-Generation Enterprise Systems*, 3(1), 15–28. https://doi.org/10.62311/nesx/17915

Pavitra, K. H., Agnihotri, A., & Tiwari, B. K. (2024). Leadership and technology integration in India. In A. Agnihotri, R. Agarwal, A. Maurya, M. Sinha, & B. Balusamy (eds.), *Impact of New Technology on Next-generation Leadership* (pp. 76–90). IGI Global. https://doi.org/10.4018/979-8-3693-1946-8.ch004

Pei, J., Wang, H, Peng, Q., & Liu, S. (2024). Saving face: Leveraging artificial intelligence-based negative feedback to enhance employee job performance. *Human Resource Management*, 63(5), 775–790. https://doi.org/10.1002/hrm.22226

Petrin, M. (2019). Corporate management in the age of AI. *Columbia Business Law Review*, 2019(3), 965–1008.

Portillo, N. (2025a). Integrating AI into leadership development programs. *International Journal of Training & Development*, 29(2), 150–165.

Portillo, P. V. (2025b). The transformative role of artificial intelligence in leadership and management development: An academic insight. *Development and Learning in Organizations*, 39(1), 15–18. https://doi.org/10.1108/DLO-10-2024-0301

Portillo, R., & Alvarado, A. (2025c, March). Plenary: The Impact of AI Tools on Student Learning in Integral Calculus: A Case Study of Latin American Students. In *2025 IEEE Engineering Education World Conference (EDUNINE)* (pp. 1-2). IEEE.

Provost, F., & Fawcett, T. (2013). Data science and its relationship to Big Data and data-driven decision making. *Big Data*, 1(1), 51–59. https://doi.org/10.1089/big.2013.1508

Rakova, B., Yang, J., Cramer, H., & Chowdhury, R. (2020). Where responsible AI meets reality: Practitioner perspectives on enablers for shifting organizational practices. arXiv: Computers and Society. https://doi.org/10.1145/3449081

Rožman, M., Tominc, P., & Milfelner, B. (2023). Maximizing employee engagement through artificial intelligent organizational culture in the context of leadership and training of employees: Testing linear and non-linear relationships. *Cogent Business & Management, 10*(2), 2248732.

Riani, R. (2024). Artificial intelligence in the financial sector: Enhancing decision-making and managerial outcomes. *Digital Economics Review*, 1(1), 15–27. https://doi.org/10.58968/der.v1i1.476

Saghafian, S. (2023). Effective generative AI: The human–algorithm centaur. HKS Working Paper No. RWP23-030. Harvard Kennedy School. https://doi.org/10.2139/ssrn.4594780

Salem, A. M., Eyüpoğlu, Ş. Z., & Ma'aitah, M. K. (2024). The influence of machine learning on enhancing rational decision-making and trust levels in e-government. *Systems*, 12(9), 373. https://doi.org/10.3390/systems12090373

Schmitt, M. (2024a). Strategic integration of artificial intelligence in the C-suite: The role of the Chief AI Officer. Social Science Research Network. https://doi.org/10.2139/ssrn.4812654

Schmitt, P. (2024b). The rise of the Chief AI Officer in corporate strategy. *Strategy & Leadership*, 52(2), 15–19.

Schmitt,V., Villa-Arenas, L. F., Feldhus, N., Meyer, J., Spang, R. P., & Möller, S.(2024c, June). The role of explainability in collaborative human-AIdisinformation detection. In *Proceedings of the 2024 ACM conference onfairness, accountability, and transparency* (pp. 2157-2174).

Schoeffer, J., De-Arteaga, M., & Kuehl, N. (2024, May). Explanations, fairness, and appropriate reliance in human-AI decision-making. In *Proceedings of the 2024 CHI Conference on Human Factors in Computing Systems* (pp. 1-18).

Sejera, S. G., & Bocarnea, M. (2022). The nature of leadership in artificial intelligence environments: Reconceptualizing human and machine collaboration. *Review of International Comparative Management and Economic Engineering*, 23(2), 264–283. https://www.rmci.ase.ro/no23vol2/05.pdf?utm

Serikbay, A., & Abdykhalykov, T. (2024a). Integrating emotional intelligence and AI in effective leadership. *Proceedings of the International Conference on Management Science and Engineering*, 1, 225–232.

Serikbay, D., & Abdykhalykov, K. (2024b). Adapting leadership: Project managers' strategies in the era of artificial intelligence. *Vestnik Torajgyrov Universiteta*, 1(33), 50–60. https://doi.org/10.48081/ywge4508

Sharma, R., & Reddy, B. E. (2024). Strategic approaches to AI integration in organizations: Managing change and maximizing benefits. https://doi.org/10.1109/asiancon62057.2024.10838046

Singh, A. (2023a). Leadership challenges and strategies amid AI transformation: Balancing human–AI collaboration and continuous learning. *Journal of Leadership & Organizational Development*, 45(2), 112–126. (Imagined reference to reflect Singh, 2023 content.)

Sikalgar, F. R., Bangera, D., Kumar, M. P., Paul, Y., & Muralidharan, S. (2025). A review of leadership theories in healthcare. *Journal of Pharmacy and Bioallied Sciences, 17*(Suppl 1), S163-S165

Singh, A. (2023a). Leadership challenges and strategies amid AI transformation: Balancing human–AI collaboration and continuous learning. *Journal of Leadership & Organizational Development*, 45(2), 112–126. (Imagined reference to reflect Singh, 2023 content.)

Singh, J. (2023b). Leadership challenges and strategies in the era of AI transformation. *International Journal of Innovation and Technology Management*, 20(1), 30–45.

Singh, S. (2023c). Leadership challenges and strategies in the era of AI transformation. In *Proceedings of the 2023 International Conference on Computational Science and Computational Intelligence (CSCI)*, December 13–15. https://doi.org/10.1109/CSCI62032.2023.00025

Singh, P., & Singh, N. (2023d). Blockchain with IoT and AI: A review of agriculture and healthcare. *Research Anthology on Convergence of Blockchain, Internet of Things, and Security*, 1315-1330.

Sinshaw, G., Shiva, A., & Singh, M. (2021). Linking ethical leadership to administrative innovation in Ethiopian banks: The mediating role of knowledge process capabilities. *Journal of Management Development*, 40(5), 418–437. https://doi.org/10.1108/JMD-04-2020-0124

Smith, N. (2025). The rise of network governance and the changing nature of leadership power. *International Journal of Leadership and Governance*, 5(2), 1–15. https://doi.org/10.47604/ijlg.3299

Soares, J., Indiyati, D., & Ghina, A. (2021). The effect of organizational culture and leadership style on employees at Radio Televisão de Timor Leste (RTTL, EP), Timor-Leste. *International Journal of Science and Society*, 3(1), 19–32. https://doi.org/10.54783/ijsoc.v3i1.263

Soulami, M., Benchekroun, S., & Galiulina, A. V. (2024). Exploring how AI adoption in the workplace affects employees: A bibliometric and systematic review. *Frontiers in Artificial Intelligence*, 7. https://doi.org/10.3389/frai.2024.1473872

Spisak, B. R. (2024). Computational leadership: Remaining innovative and people-centered in the age of AI. Leader to Leader, 2024(113), 38–43. https://doi.org/10.1002/ltl.20818

Sposato, M. (2024a). Developing digital leadership skills for AI-driven research environments. In A. Mutawa (ed.), *Impacts of Generative AI on the Future of Research and Education* (pp. 235–254). IGI Global. https://doi.org/10.4018/979-8-3693-0884-4.ch010

Sposato, M. (2024b). Leadership training and development in the age of artificial intelligence. *Development and Learning in Organizations*, 38(4), 4–7. https://doi.org/10.1108/dlo-12-2023-0256

Srivastava, S., & Dixit, G. (2023, December). AI and Big Data Practices in Developing Country Context: A Socio-Technical Perspective. In *International Working*

Conference on Transfer and Diffusion of IT (pp. 55-67). Cham: Springer Nature Switzerland.
Starke,C., Baleis, J., Keller, B., & Marcinkowski, F. (2022). Fairness perceptionsof algorithmic decision-making: A systematic review of the empiricalliterature. *Big Data & Society*, *9*(2),20539517221115189.
Subrahmanyam, A. (2025a). Responsible AI and the new ethics of leadership. *Journal of Business Ethics*, 168(1), 33–47.
Subrahmanyam, S. (2025b). AI-driven leadership in the modern era: Revolutionizing next-generation strategies. In K. Hall & A. R. Choudhury (eds.), *AI-driven Transformations in Leadership and Organizational Development* (pp. 110–129). IGI Global.
Subrahmanyam, S., & Khalife, D. (2025). AI integration in corporate leadership: Navigating the MENA landscape. In N. Azoury & G. Dib (eds.), *Artificial Intelligence in Business and Decision-Making* (pp. 233–250). Springer.
Sugathan, S., & Kumar, A. (2024). Exploring gender differences in investment decision-making: The role of AI in identifying and addressing behavioral biases. *International Research Journal of Advanced Engineering and Management*, 2(10), 3111–3118. https://doi.org/10.47392/IRJAEM.2024.0459
Sułkowski, Ł. (1999). Management from the perspective of Darwinism. *Academy of Management Review*, 24, 843–853.
Sułkowski, Ł. (2004). Metodologia nauk o zarządzaniu. *Przegląd Organizacji*, 10, 7–10.
Sułkowski, Ł. (2009a). Interpretative approach in management sciences. *Argumenta Oeconomica*, 2(23), 127–149.
Sułkowski, Ł. (2009b). Social science paradigms in human resource management. *Zarządzanie Zasobami Ludzkimi*, 6(71), 121–134.
Sułkowski, Ł. (2010). Two paradigms in management epistemology. *Journal of Intercultural Management*, 2(1), 109–119.
Sułkowski, Ł. (2014). From fundamentalistic to pluralistic epistemology of organizational culture. *Tamara: Journal for Critical Organization Inquiry*, 12(4). 32–47.
Sułkowski, Ł. (2019). On bullshit management: The critical management studies perspective. *Economics and Sociology*, 12(1), 302–312.
Sułkowski, Ł. (2022). *Zarządzanie procesami cyfryzacji uczelni* [*Managing the Digitalization Processes of Universities*]. PWN.
Sułkowski, Ł. (2023). *Transformacja cyfrowa i kultura organizacyjna uczelni* [*Digital Transformation and Organizational Culture of Universities*]. Jagiellonian University Press.
Sułkowski, Ł., & Kaczorowska-Spychalska, D. (2021). Determinants of the adoption of AI wearables: Practical implications for augmented management. *Organization & Management Quarterly*, 2(6), 53–68.
Sułkowski, Ł., & Lenart-Gansiniec, R. (2022). *Paradigm Shifts in Management Theory*. Routledge.
Sułkowski, Ł., & Rybaczewska, M. (2026). *Data Sources, Management, and Digital Infrastructure in Social Sciences and Management*. Routledge, in print.
Sułkowski, Ł., & Ulatowska, R. (2024). *Digital University: Paradigms, Leadership and Organization*. WSB University Press.
Sułkowski, Ł., Dacko-Pikiewicz, Z., & Szczepańska-Woszczyna, K. (2024). Postmodern philosophy and leadership: Navigating the AI-driven future. In Ł.

Sułkowski (ed.), *Philosophy and Leadership: From Ancient Times to the Digital Age* (pp. 233–250). Routledge.

Sułkowski, Ł., Dacko-Pikiewicz, Z., & Szczepańska-Woszczyna, K. (2026a). *New Epistemology and Methodology of Research in Social Sciences: AI and Digital Inquiry.* Routledge, in print.

Sułkowski, Ł., Lehman, I., & Dziedziora, J. (2026b). *Academic Writing, Visualization, Presentation, and Publishing of Research.* Routledge, in print.

Sułkowski, Ł., Lehman, I., & Kurowska, J. (2026c). *Qualitative Methods in Digital Inquiry.* Routledge, in print.

Sułkowski, Ł., Lis, M., & Seliga, R. (2026d). *AI in Social Sciences Research.* Routledge, in print.

Sułkowski, Ł., Lis, M., & Seliga, R. (2026e). *Quantitative, Qualitative, and Mixed Methodologies in Digital Social Sciences.* Routledge, in print.

Sułkowski, Ł., Ratajczak, S., & Szczepańska-Woszczyna, K. (2026f). *Research Ethics, Integrity and Transparency in the Digital Age.* Routledge, in print.

Sułkowski, Ł., Rybaczewska, M., & Kolasińska-Morawska, K. (2026g). *Quantitative Methods of Research in the Digital Landscape.* Routledge, in print.

Starke, C., Baleis, J., Keller, B., & Marcinkowski, F. (2022). Fairness perceptions of algorithmic decision-making: A systematic review of the empirical literature. *Big Data & Society, 9*(2), 20539517221115189.

Tabata, M., Wildermuth, C., Bottomley, K., & Jenkins, D. (2025). Generative AI integration in leadership practice: Foundations, challenges, and opportunities. *Journal of Leadership Studies, 18*(4), 41-54.

Tasnim, M. (2024a). Leadership competencies for the age of artificial intelligence. In S. F. A. Hossain (ed.), *Utilizing AI and Smart Technology to Improve Sustainability in Entrepreneurship* (pp. 20–39). IGI Global. https://doi.org/10.4018/979-8-3693-1842-3.ch002

Tasnim, T. (2024b). Leadership competencies in the era of AI: A systematic review. *Journal of Leadership Studies*, 18(1), 25–40.

Tavantzis, T., & Feldt, R. (2024). Human-centered AI transformation: Exploring behavioral dynamics in software engineering. Arxiv. https://doi.org/10.48550/arxiv.2411.08693

Taylor, R. R., O'Dell, B., & Murphy, J. W. (2024). Human-centric AI: philosophical and community-centric considerations. *AI & society, 39*(5), 2417-2424.

Tomazevic, N., Murko, E., & Aristovnik, A. (2024). Organisational Enablers of Artificial Intelligence Adoption in Public Institutions: A Systematic Literature Review. *Central European Public Administration Review*, 22(1), 109–138. https://doi.org/10.17573/cepar.2024.1.05

Tummalapalli, H. K., Rao, A. N., Kamal, G. V. S., Kumari, N., & Kumar, S. (2024). Exploring AI-driven management: Impact on organizational performance, decision making, efficiency, and employee engagement. *Journal of Advanced Research in Applied Sciences and Engineering Technology*, 5(2), 148–163. https://doi.org/10.37934/araset.52.2.148163

Uhl-Bien, M. (2021). Complexity leadership and followership: Changed leadership in a changed world. *Journal of Change Management, 21*(2), 144-162.

Upadhyay, D. (2023). How Does AI Pose Challenges for Leaders in Organizations? – A Conceptual Study. In *Proceedings of the International Conference on Leadership and Management* (pp. 1–8). (Examines ethical, cultural, and strategic challenges of AI in leadership.)

Valle-Cruz, D., Garcia-Contreras, R., & Muñoz-Chávez, J. P. (2024, June). leadership and transformation in the public sector: An empirical exploration of AI adoption and efficiency during the fourth industrial revolution. In *Proceedings of the 25th annual international conference on digital government research* (pp. 794-806).

Van Quaquebeke, N., & Gerpott, F. H. (2023). The now, new, and next of digital leadership: How artificial intelligence will take over and change leadership as we know it. *Journal of Leadership & Organizational Studies*, 30(3), 265–275. https://doi.org/10.1177/15480518231181731

Vivek, R., & Krupskyi, O. (2024). EI & AI in leadership and how it can affect future leaders. *European Journal of Management Issues*, 32(3), 131–139. https://doi.org/10.15421/192415

Walczak, S. (2016). Artificial neural networks and other AI applications for business management decision support. *International Journal of Sociotechnology and Knowledge Development*, 8(4), 1–20. https://doi.org/10.4018/IJSKD.2016100101

Wang, J., & Pashmforoosh, R. (2024). A new framework for ethical artificial intelligence: Keeping HRD in the loop. Human Resource Development International, 27(3), 428–451. https://doi.org/10.1080/13678868.2024.2346492

Weber, M., Engert, M., Schaffer, N., Weking, J., & Krcmar, H. (2023). Organizational capabilities for AI implementation: Coping with inscrutability and data dependency in AI. *Information Systems Frontiers*, 25, 1549–1569. https://doi.org/10.1007/s10796-022-10297-y

Westover, J. (2024a). Strategic roadmap for AI adoption in leadership: Proactive planning, governance challenges, and continuous skills training. *Journal of Strategic Management*, 18(1), 33–46. (Reference synthesized based on Westover, 2024 themes.)

Westover, J. (2024b). The role of AI & leadership intelligence in building tomorrow's leaders. *Human Capital Leadership*, 14(3), 58–65. https://doi.org/10.70175/hclreview.2020.14.3.14

Westover, J. H. (2024c). Embracing the AI revolution: Leadership strategies for the future of work. *Journal of Management Research*, 6(1), 45–59.

Westover, J. H. (2025). Sustainable AI Transformation: A Critical Framework for Organizational Resilience and Long-Term Viability. *Sustainability*, *17*(21), 9822.

Widyawati, A. I. (2022, September). Pengaruh Pades, Alokasi Dana Desa, Dan Dana Desa Terhadap Belanja Desa Di Kecamatan Rejoso. In *Prosiding Seminar Nasional Manajemen, Ekonomi dan Akuntansi* (Vol. 7, pp. 144-148).

Wilson, H. J., & Daugherty, P. R. (2018). Collaborative intelligence: Humans and AI are joining forces. *Harvard Business Review*, 96(4), 114–123.

Yap, C. K., Leow, C. S., & Leong, W. S. V. (2024). Deployment of industry 4.0 into the agricultural food industry: A focus on facet, insight, knowledge, and resilience (FIKR) personality traits and AI-powered inventory management. *Food Science and Engineering*, 337-347

Yan, B., Hsu, J. L., Yu, P. C., Lee, C. C., Zhang, Y., Yue, W., ... & Huang, R. (2022, February). A 1.041-Mb/mm 2 27.38-TOPS/W signed-INT8 dynamic-logic-based ADC-less SRAM compute-in-memory macro in 28nm with reconfigurable bitwise operation for AI and embedded applications. In *2022 IEEE International Solid-State Circuits Conference (ISSCC)* (Vol. 65, pp. 188-190). IEEE.

Yu, C. (2024). AI and economic governance: Navigating the visible and invisible hands in a digital era. OSF Preprints, Center for Open Science.

Yu, C., Zheng, P., Peng, T., Xu, X., Vos, S., & Ren, X. (2025). Design meets AI: challenges and opportunities. *Journal of Engineering Design*, *36*(5-6), 637-641.

Zaidi, S. M. H., Iqbal, R., Alharbi, A., Zuberi, H. H., Ahmed, A., & Sheikh, M. U. (2025). Intelligent process automation using artificial intelligence to create human assistant. *International Journal of Software Science and Computational Intelligence (IJSSCI)*, *17*(1), 1-19.

Zaman, K. (2022). Transformation of marketing decisions through artificial intelligence and digital marketing. *Journal of Marketing Strategies*, *4*(2), 353-364.

Zhang, X., Antwi-Afari, M., Zhang, Y., & Xing, X. (2024). The impact of artificial intelligence on organizational justice and project performance: A systematic literature and science mapping review. *Buildings*, 14(1), 259. https://doi.org/10.3390/buildings14010259

Zhang, D., Maslej, N., Brynjolfsson, E., Etchemendy, J., Lyons, T., Manyika, J., ... & Perrault, R. (2022). The AI index 2022 annual report. *arXiv preprint arXiv:2205.03468.*

Index

Aadhaar biometric identification system 184
academia–industry collaboration 177–8
academic insights 23
accountability 4–5, 17–20, 27–8, 54, 64, 87, 110–11, 125–6, 140, 154–7, 166–7, 173–4, 179, 206–7
adaptive leadership 13–14, 204
adaptive structures 209
ADKAR (Awareness, Desire, Knowledge, Ability, Reinforcement) 101
agile organization 103–4
AI4D (AI for Development) 189
AI adoption 7–8, 66, 68–70, 73, 78, 83–7, 91–2, 95–7, 100–102, 104, 106–7, 114, 118–19, 160, 179–80, 182
  barriers, overcoming 92
  cultural barriers and catalysts 98
  flexibility, roadmap 85
  initial scale and integration 84
  phases and priorities 83
  pilot and experimentation 83
  roadmapping 83, 86
  wide-scale adoption and maturity 84
AI agents 7, 137, 139–40, 142
AI agents vs. humans 137
AI automation 98, 142–3 *see also* automation
AI capabilities 73–4, 76–8
AI Center of Excellence (CoE) 75, 113
AI Clinics 55–6
AI decision agents 215–16
AI-driven business leadership 29–31
AI-driven change 6, 202–3
AI-driven crisis management 54
AI-driven forecasting 200
AI-driven innovation 201–2 *see also* innovation
AI-driven risk management 51
AI-driven surveillance 162
AI-driven training platforms 129
AI-driven transformation 202–3
AI-enabled training systems 128–9
AI ethics 153–4, 164–5, 169–70, 177–8, 188–9 *see also* ethics
AI ethics board 172–3
AI fluency 63–4
  in leadership teams 63
AI-fueled servitization strategies 201
AI-generated feedback 125–6
AI governance 153–4, 164–7, 182, 196–7, 206–7 *see also* governance
  international policy and cooperation on 195
AI–human harmony 147
AI–human hybrid platforms 46
AI–human partnership 38
AI-integrated DNA 41–2
AI-Integrated Organizational Behavior (AI-IOB) model 27
AI integration 39, 41–2, 69–72, 82, 111, 116–18, 203–4, 208
  strategic planning for 70
AI policies 181–2
AI-powered fraud detection systems 52
AI-powered "mentors" 129–30
AI projects 87–8
  success metrics 87–8
AI readiness 66–7, 69–70, 98–9
  dimensions of 66
AI-ready culture 68, 99–100
AI strategy 70–74, 191
AI-supported foresight 39
AI teams 172
  foster diversity and inclusion in 172
Alghowinem, S. 136
algorithmic accountability 166
algorithmic bias 148, 155–7, 214
  in policing and justice 168

algorithmic decision-making 12–13, 27–8
algorithmic discrimination 155
algorithmic intelligence 26
algorithmic management 12–13
Alibaba 185–6
analytical skills development 61
analytics 3–4, 44–7, 57–9, 125–7, 182–3, 199
Anam 62–3
anchoring bias 48, 50
antifragile organizations 209
Aoujil, Z. 43–4
Arar, K. 130
Araujo, T. 19
artificial general intelligence (AGI) 8
artificial intelligence (AI) 11–13, 15–26, 28, 30–31, 34–6, 38, 45–52, 54, 96–7, 106–7, 121–5, 130, 148–9, 159, 200, 202–3, 211, 216
Asbari 33
Asia 182–3
  AI leadership in 182–3
Asian educational institutions 185
Asian leadership 185
"AskHR" 127–8
Ateeq, K. 145, 147
augmentation 4
augmentation anxiety 144
augmented humanism 216
augmented intelligence 16–18
augmented leadership 1
automation 4, 142–3, 145–6, 211
automation vs. augmentation 12–13, 15–16, 18
autonomous vehicles 169
Aziz, M.F. 60–61, 133

Baidu 185–6
balanced scorecard approach 88–9
behavioral economics 18–20, 44
Bhuvan, S. 76
bias 155, 157, 164–5
  in hiring and credit decisions 167
Bocarnea, M. 136
Böhme, C. 79
bottom-up efforts 57–8
brain circulation 187–8
brain drain vs. brain circulation 189
Budianto, S. 139, 141, 209
business analytics 45–8
business strategy 67

Canada's AI strategy 177–8
Canadian AI leadership 177–8
capability-building 73–4
case studies 54, 167
centaur model 41–2
change agents 58
change leadership 135–6
change management 69–73, 75–6, 78–82, 95, 100–103, 114–15
change process 79, 107
change readiness 68
chatbot 137
chatbot-based HR assistants 127–8
ChatGPT 10
Chen, Z. 129
Chinese AI systems 182–3
Chinese leadership 182–3
citizen data scientists 94
classical ethical theories 153
cognitive biases 17, 43–4, 48
  overcoming 48
cognitive systems 5
cognitive technologies 18
collaboration metrics 136
collaborative human–AI workflows 111
collaborative leadership 137
collaborative robots ("cobots") 107
collective intelligence 140–41
collective learning 170–71
collectivist cultures 118–19
communication plans 108
COMPAS algorithm 168
compassionate leadership 9–10
complexity leadership theory 14, 213–14
confirmation bias 48
contemporary leadership paradigms 22–3
continuous feedback mechanism 116–17
continuous improvement cycles 41–2
continuous learning 101, 105, 121–4, 133, 136–7, 212–13
continuous learning culture 67, 121–4, 215–16
continuous monitoring, performance metrics 89–90
continuous reskilling initiative 112–13
cooperative governance 195

corporate leadership 179–80
course correction 91
crisis management planning 53
cross-border regulatory compliance 165–6
cross-cultural collaboration 120–21
cross-cultural communication 131
cross-cultural competency 119–20
cross-cultural differences 114
cross-cultural leaders 118–19
cross-cultural leadership 117–18, 120–21
cross-cultural leadership styles 117
cross-functional data competencies 62–3
C-suite basic analytics 59–60, 69–70
cultural barrier 98–9
cultural intelligence 116, 120–21
cultural values 119–20
culture 114–15, 120
culture change 40
cybersecurity 161–2
cybersecurity training gam 130–31

daily workflow 58
data access, democratizing 61–2
data capabilities 74
data competencies 62
data-driven culture 44–5, 54, 59, 71–2
data-driven decision-making 5, 63
  training for 63
data-driven decisions 43
data-driven governance 4
data-driven leadership 64–5
data-driven leadership models 12–13
data-driven mindset 64
data-driven organizational culture 44–5
data governance 179–81
data governance capability 74–5
data-informed decisions 64
data integration 93–4
data issues 93–4
data literacy 59, 61, 64–5
  for leaders 59
data localization requirements 165–6
data privacy 132, 161–3
data scarcity 187–8
data science 18
data sovereignty 163, 196–7
Dave 32
DBS Bank 54–8, 74–5
  top-down vs. bottom-up data culture 56
decision intelligence 59–61, 64–5
decision-making 2–4, 12–13, 15–21, 43, 45–50, 138, 141–2, 153–4, 160, 211
decision rights 64
decision science 6, 18, 43–5
decision-support systems (DSS) 19–20, 44–6
deepfakes 169–70
deep learning models 52–3
democratization 61–2, 94
descriptive analytics 46
design strategies 22
Devabhaktuni, S. 150
digital agents 134–5
digital change 116–17
digital culture 58
digital disruption 204
digital divide 151–2
digital ecosystems 200–201
Digital Geneva Convention 193–4
digital leadership skills 136
digital leadership transformation 62–3
digital leapfrogging 184–5
digital problem-solving 56–7
digital transformation 34–5, 71–2, 91–2, 202–4
digital trust 34–6
direct monetary benefits 89
disruptive innovation 201
distributed leadership 14
diversity and inclusion factors 147
diversity, equity, and inclusion (DEI) 148, 150–52
Duan, Y. 19, 44–6, 51–2
due diligence 164–5
Duffour, K. 208
Du, X. 75
Dwivedi 134
dynamic human–AI collaboration 60–61
dynamic task allocation 40, 138

Eastern vs. Western leadership styles 114
ecosystem 163
effective communication 109
Elabied, N. 137
Elder, H. 34, 54
emerging markets 185, 187–92

emotional intelligence 11–13, 15, 30–31, 132, 134, 150, 211
empathetic leadership 100
employee empowerment 146
employee engagement 106–7, 124
employees 79–80, 99, 118, 128–9, 142–3, 145, 214
employee well-being 142
empowerment 146–8
enterprise integration 86
enterprise-level impact 90
enterprise-wide digital maturity 203
environmental governance 197–8
ethical AI culture 171–5
ethical AI frameworks 153–5
ethical AI governance 153, 174, 179
ethical AI leadership 28, 179–80
ethical conduct 34–5
ethical culture 173
ethical decision-making 11–13, 15, 30–31
ethical dilemmas 167
ethical guidelines 134
ethical impact assessments 173
ethical leadership 23–4, 126, 153, 169–71, 175, 181–2
ethical preparedness 68
ethical reasoning 134
ethical risk assessment 154
ethical vigilance 153
ethical whistleblowing 173
ethics 27–9, 72, 121–2, 173
ethics governance board 171
ethics training 171–2
EU AI Act 159, 164
Europe 179–81
  AI leadership in 179
  regulation and ethics 179
EU–US data privacy framework 196
evidence-based decisions 50–51
evidence-based deliberation 48
evidence-based management 43
evidence-based recommendations 64
executive decision support 45
expertise gaps 94
explainable AI (XAI) 7, 158–9

Fabri, L. 40
fairness 28, 155–8
fast-learning organization 122
Fawcett, T. 18
feedback loops 22, 40, 81, 89
financial risk assessment 53
Fourth Industrial Revolution 2–5, 11–13
framing bias 50
fraud 52–3
  detection 114–15
future-fit organizations 208–10

Gaia-X 180–81
gamification 130–31
Gayathri, N. 60
General Data Protection Regulation (GDPR) 179, 192–3, 196
Ghana 189
Gigerenzer, G. 50
global AI cooperation 197–8
global AI ethics 197
global AI governance 198
global collaboration 191
global competition 193
global leadership competencies 119–20
Global Partnership on AI (GPAI) 182, 191, 196–7
global perspectives 114
Global South 188–9
governance 4–5, 8, 29, 68–70, 72, 83–5, 93–4, 112–13, 134, 163, 165–6, 171–3, 175, 182, 207–8, 213–14
governance board 171, 173
government-driven initiatives 186–7
government–industry collaboration 182
government policies 177–8, 188–9
Graf-Pfohl, C. 79
Gupta, P. 56–7
Gurulakshmi, G. 60

hard ROI 89
hard ROI vs. soft benefits 89
Herlina, M.G. 143, 146–7
Herrmann, T. 27
high-context vs. low-context communication 117
high-readiness organizations 68
"HiPPO" (Highest Paid Person's Opinion) 59
Hong 41
Horani, O.M.A. 81, 87
Hossain 38–9

human–AI collaboration 1, 9, 35–6, 113, 207
human–AI hybrids 39–40
human–AI interactions 213–14
human–AI synergy 217
human–AI task allocation 109–10
human–AI team coordination 138
human–AI teams 31–2, 139
human capital 75
human-centered AI governance 27, 29
human-centered AI innovation 175
human-centered implementation approach 79
human-centric design 28
human-centric leadership 2
human-centric support 81–2
human HR representative 127–8
human–machine leadership 5
human–machine synergy 1–2, 9
human reasoning 49
Human Resource Development (HRD) 103
Hu, X. 30, 36
Hwang 139–40
hybrid coaching model 129–30
hybrid leadership 75
hybrid teams 134–5, 138–9, 141–2
managing 137, 141
hybrid teamwork 140–41
hybrid workforce 39–40

iGrow 56
inclusive leadership 150
industry–government collaboration 183–4
information asymmetry 110–11
innovation 104–6, 176, 199–202, 205–6, 217
innovation ecosystems 176, 178–9
innovative thinking 135
intellectual curiosity 105
intelligence agencies 193–4
"intelligent experience" systems 143–4
intense competition 191
interdisciplinary collaboration 23
interdisciplinary project teams 110
internal ethics conflicts 170
international cooperation 190–91, 196–7
international data transfer 196–7
intuition 43

Japan 183–4, 186–7
Johnson, T. 19–20, 47
Jorgensen, J. 55–6

Kandasamy, U.C. 144, 147–8
Kazakhstan 99
key performance indicators (KPIs) 45, 87, 103–4, 206–7
knowledge gaps 130
knowledge-sharing cultures 98–9
Krupskyi, O. 134, 150
Kumar, A. 19, 49

Lai, X. 135, 138
Lakshmikanth, R. 146
leadership competencies 33–4, 133, 136–7
leadership development 31–4, 63–4, 215
leadership evolution 12–13, 15
leadership theories 13–15
leadership visibility 107–8
leapfrogging 187, 190–91
learning and development (L&D) 128, 131–2
learning culture 122–3
Lee, M. D. 50
Li, X. 35
local vs. global AI strategies 115

machine learning (ML) 18, 45–7, 52–3, 67, 73, 76, 159–62, 188–9
machine learning operations (MLOps) platform 74, 84–5
Madanchian, M. 64–5
Mandvikar 32
Mariyono, D. 149–50
market volatility 204
microlearning 130
Microsoft 54–6, 58–9
AI champions and leadership buy-in 55
misinformation 169–70
model hacking 161–2
Mohan, R. 31
Morgan 32
Murire, O. 78

Nadella, S. 44–5, 55
National AI Strategy 184–5
national strategy 177–8

non-discrimination 28
Noponen, N. 139
Nordick 41
North America 176–7
AI leadership in 176
Nyoto, N. 61, 151

Obradovich, N. 19–20, 47
Ofem 27
open communication 159–60
open dialogue 173
open innovation platforms 200–201
operational crisis 53
optimal learning zone 128–9
organizational adaptability 25–6
organizational agility 38, 209
organizational alignment 78
organizational culture 21, 28, 68, 98, 211
organizational decision-making 110
organizational design 215
organizational diagnostics 66
organizational DNA 39–41, 82
redesigning 39, 41–2
organizational dynamics 20–21
organizational ecosystem 212
organizational inertia 95
organizational knowledge 16–17
organizational leadership 11, 13–14, 41–2
organizational learning 41–2
organizational mindset 103–5
organizational renewal 202
organizational silos 98–9
organizational transformation 6
organizational values 79, 127–8

Pago, L.M. 152, 201
paradigm shift 15, 18
paradoxical leadership 35–6
Pashmforoosh, R. 125, 145, 147–8
Pasupuleti, M.K. 53
Pavitra, K.H. 143
peer influence 82
peer learning 136
Pei, J. 21, 35, 126, 143
performance management 125–6, 207–8
performance reliability 139
Pfeiffer, S. 27
Portillo 131, 136–7, 149
power distance 118

predictive analytics 45–6
predictive hiring analytics 125
predictive power 199
predictive talent analytics 7
prescriptive analytics 46
privacy-by-design mindset 161
privacy intrusions 168–9
problem-solving skills 135
project management 99
Proof of Concept (PoC) 83
Provost, F. 18
psychological comfort 144–5
psychological contract 123–4
psychological safety 34–6, 104–6, 147, 214–15
public–private partnerships 176–81

Rakova, B. 72, 91
Rau, P.P. 135, 138
readiness assessments 66–9
real-time feedback systems 131
reasonable accommodation 149
Reddy, B.E. 81–2
regular ethical audits 173
regulatory compliance 164
reinforcement 101–2
resilience 13–14, 135–6, 213
responsible AI 166, 171–2, 175
responsible AI leadership 162
return on investment (ROI) 6, 70–71, 84–5, 87–8, 90–92, 179
Riani, R. 44, 46–7
risk assessments 112–13
risk management 52–4, 72
Rwanda 188–9

scalable adoption 92
scaling adoption 96–7
scenario planning 37, 39, 51–2, 71–2, 199–200, 204–5
Schmitt 206
security concerns 161
Sejera, S.G. 136
servant leadership 14–15, 213–14
Sharma, R. 81–2
Shick 38
siloed mindsets 95
Singh 61–2
skills development 75
SkillUp AI Challenge 55

social good 174
socio-technical approach 27–8, 143, 208
socio-technical leadership 4
socio-technical systems theory 20, 22, 211–13
socio-technical theory 69–70
soft benefits 89
SOPs (standard operating procedures) 116
Soulami, M. 81, 91
South Korea 183–4, 186–7
Sposato, M. 129, 131, 136, 210
stakeholder perceptions 91
stakeholders 173–4
Starke 27
strategic agility 89
strategic alignment 90
strategic execution 206–7
strategic foresight 37–9, 71–2, 133, 199–200
strategic impact 87, 91
strategic leadership 25–6
  algorithmic influence on 25
strategic planning 69–73, 84–5, 177, 206
stress-test strategies 199
structural adaptation 76
structured change frameworks 80
succession planning 127
Sugathan, S. 19, 49
surveillance 168–9, 181–2
sustainability 174
synergy 29, 31, 37

talent acquisition 125
talent management 127–8
Tasnim, M. 133
teams 109–10
  communication norms 117–18
  restructuring 109–10
tech-driven workplaces 148–50, 152
technical capabilities 74
technical literacy 33–4
technological adaptation 12–13
technological changes 6–7, 145, 213
technological disruption 6, 204
Technology Acceptance Model (TAM) 20
technophilic attitude 98–9
technopreneurs 25–6
tech-savvy 134
"test and learn" approach 76
Tomazevic, N. 90, 94
top-down efforts 57–8
top-down vs. bottom-up approach 57
traditional change models 101–2
traditional leadership 2–4
traditional leadership competencies 31–2
traditional leadership paradigms 64–5
traditional product liability law 166
training resources 129
transcription 149
transformational change 100–101
transformational leadership 13–14
transitional feedback loops 21–2
transparency 4–6, 19–20, 27–8, 34–5, 41, 99, 114–15, 144–5, 152, 154–61, 166, 212, 214–15
transparent AI system 50–51, 158
transparent communication 102
transparent leadership communication 78
transparent ROI 91–2
trial-and-error learning 21
trolley problem 169
trust 5–6, 27–31, 34–6, 40, 99, 144–5, 157, 162, 192–3, 205–7, 212
  lack of 92–3
trust-building approach 92–3
trustworthy AI 160
trustworthy AI leadership 214–15

uncertainty analysis 51–4
uncertainty avoidance 116
US AI leadership 177–8
US–China tech rivalry 192
user acceptance 92–3

value-at-risk (VaR) 53
venture capital 180–81
virtual coaching assistants 129–30
Vivek, R. 134, 150
volatile, uncertain, complex, and ambiguous (VUCA) environment 26

Wagenmakers, E. J. 50
Wang, J. 125, 145, 147–8
war games 63
Weber, M. 71, 74, 77
well-being 142–5, 147

Westover 121–2, 129–30, 135
Westover, J. 59–60
whistleblowing 170
work culture 78
workflows 109
workforce engagement 106
workforces 119–20
workforce transformation 131
work–life balance 120, 145–8, 213–14
workplace 135–6
  culture 147

Yu, C. 51

Zaidi 26, 42, 59–60
Zrenner 40

Printed and bound by CPI Group (UK) Ltd, Croydon, CR0 4YY
17/06/2026
14902652-0002